MW00939565

Eye On The Prize

Fighting Past Wegener's Granulomatosis

Candace Ross

authorHOUSE®

AuthorHouse™
1663 Liberty Drive, Suite 200
Bloomington, IN 47403
www.authorhouse.com
Phone: 1-800-839-8640

© 2009 Candace Ross. All rights reserved.

No part of this book may be reproduced, stored in a retrieval system, or transmitted by any means without the written permission of the author.

First published by AuthorHouse   3/27/2009

ISBN: 978-1-4389-5481-3 (sc)

Printed in the United States of America
Bloomington, Indiana

This book is printed on acid-free paper.

For all of the other people who suffer from Wegener's granulomatosis…

For the doctor who did not give up on me in 1987, and the one today who treats me

For Kay, my friend who stuck by my side for 29 years…

And lastly, for my parents, sister, brother-in-law, and nephew…

Contents

Preface

Most people with Wegener's granulomatosis, or any major illness for that matter, define their lives in two parts: before the illness and after the illness. But this book is dedicated for those with Wegener's. There are so many books for so many different illnesses. I wanted to be the first to write about this rare, often misunderstood disease.

While slowly writing this book, another person wrote an account about a family member with Wegener's. This is, I believe the first book about the experience of Wegener's, what it is like to live through it, first hand.

For those of us with Wegener's, our defining moments are the time of diagnosis, and the time when we realize that we are not the only one on the planet with this illness. Back when I was diagnosed, in 1987, it was a lonely time for a person with any rare illness, let alone Wegener's granulomatosis. There was no Internet, there were no pamphlets, and most health care professionals were unaware of the illness. The Internet is a place where you can find good information, and also a lot of hearsay. Whether or not you are a trumpeter of its provision of knowledge, or an opponent of some of its sleazier aspects, you must at least see that it has provided some lonely people with supports in various chat rooms and health sites. In 1987, finding information was a bit trickier.

I could not get much information from my doctors, nurses, or social workers then. I think I know why: first of all, there simply was not much information to be had, and secondly, that which did exist was often very ominous. What I mean, is that the only printout I could locate of Wegener's told me that I had a nine month life span, untreated. Too late. I was sick for a couple of years before diagnosis.

In 1988, I was on a search at the local library for more information, and all I found was the address of a national database for rare disorders. I wrote to them, and received a list of a lot of strange, unfamiliar illnesses. There was no listing for Wegener's granulomatosis, but there was a listing for Vasculitis. Well that was my original diagnosis, so I was getting a little exited about this. It's almost like seeing your name in print when you first see your illness in print. To receive a printout, one had to send five dollars, and wait several weeks. I anxiously waited for what I thought would be a large pack of information, maybe even delivered priority!

Several weeks later, I received a standard 4 by 9 envelope. Inside was a copy of a copy of a copy, with dark, difficult to read print, and all of one paragraph about Vasculitis. Additionally, there was another order form to send away for more five-dollar pages. However, there was also something handwritten, in reply to my handwritten inquiry as to whether any information about Wegener's granulomatosis existed.

Someone had written in a margin that there was a support group out of Platte City, Missouri, and they provided me with a contact name: Carolyn Hamptom.[1] I wrote to her that day, and expected another long wait, and another order form. In the letter I must have mentioned how frustrated I was, as I had been ill for a long time with little information. Less than one week later, a large, overstuffed package came from Missouri, along with a letter from Carolyn, dated November 6, 1988. It read, in part, as follows:

> My dearest Candace…I was glad that you found our support group, but so sad, that like so many of us, that you were so sick for so long…that is exactly why I started the support group so that everyone, especially doctors will think WEGENER'S and so many will not suffer so many disfiguring manifestations of the disease before they are diagnosed…I do know what you are saying when you say that people do not take your disease seriously because they have never heard of it…you are young…and there is much hope for you.

That was the first of many encouraging letters I received from this amazing woman. She and I corresponded for years, and her letters were frequent in the beginning, when I was the most isolated. I often do think that it would have been so much easier had the Internet been available, but I also treasure that large folder of letters from Carolyn and others from those early days of the support group.

---

[1] I have changed the names of all real people and hospitals in this book (famous referenced people and books have stayed the same)

In that massive envelope, there was a lot of general information about what one must do to care for the body that is being treated by chemotherapy and immune suppressed. There was actually a pamphlet all about Wegener's, which encouraged copying and distributing to doctors.

I wrote to some of the people Carolyn suggested, and made some new friends. I also realized that as sick as I was, and had been, there were people who had endured even more due to prolonged manifestation of symptoms. The focus was off me, me, me.

It was then, that hope did begin. It would be a long road ahead, as it had been a long road behind me, but I now had some sort of sense of community, even if it was stretched across the globe, and only accessible through the U.S. Mail.

That little grass roots organization grew, and the Wegener's Granulomatosis Support group became the Wegener's Foundation, then the Vasculitis Foundation years later. You can find them on the internet or write to them.

I now see "our name" (Wegener's granulomatosis) in print in books, and every time it happens, I want to shout out in the bookstore, "We made it! Hey! We're in print!"

I have met some doctors, nurses, social workers and other health care workers along the way who were apathetic. But I don't like to remember them. The folks that I like to remember are the ones who sat down, answered my questions, and made me feel like a human being, and gave me answers, before we even knew what the heck "internet" meant. There are many people out there who still do not have that access or who just might be afraid to ask questions.

I am now a health care provider. I provide services for people with mental illness ranging from mild to serious, and I strive to be that person who answers questions, takes time, makes that person feel special, like a human being, not just a number. That is why I was spared my life, and I take it seriously. I am always so happy when someone who does not understand something leaves my office and says, "Now I understand, you helped me see it," or "I think I see some hope now."

When you have an illness, or are someone with an identifiable disability (or even unidentifiable, chronic disability) life is not always about your disability. But it takes a long time to get to that point, if you are ever lucky to get there.

It was not easy to write this book, and it took over eight years to finish. It was difficult to relive some of the chapters. The book itself is not lengthy. I then struggled over whether to finally look for a publisher when it was finished, because I was not sure that I wanted to put the story out there. Then I remembered who I was writing it for: other Wegener's survivors. They had no other first hand story, other than some magazine articles, newsletter articles, or internet blogs.

The book that meant the most to me while I was recovering was a book by Victor Frankl, MD, called *Man's Search For Meaning*. He was a holocaust survivor. While he was in the midst of his unspeakable suffering, he developed a strong will to survive, based on three principles, and these principle are: 1) To create a work or to have work that is meaningful, 2) to encounter someone who makes a difference, and 3) To suffer, and through your suffering to develop an attitude of strength and fortitude. I knew that I had to have a purpose in life, and I decided that instead of feeling sorry for myself, I had to turn the focus on others. I had already encountered people who had made a difference in my life, good and bad, and was certain I would continue to have such encounters, and I knew that with my illness, I would continue to have suffering, so I could choose to feel sorry for myself, or I could just keep on going.

If your life is all doom and gloom, it becomes very exhausting for you and everyone around you. I also have a mission in life, and that is, that I help others for a living. If I become stuck in my own rut, what kind of example am I setting for those that I am trying to guide?

I wanted to write this book really for two reasons: the aforementioned reason to give Wegener's patients their glory, and also, because I want to give some hope to all people, not only Wegener's survivors. I have survived a few other things besides Wegener's, and I want to point out that you can go on. Life is not easy. I hope that if you are choosing to read this book, you may find that we, as humans can survive a lot, and still endure, and come out stronger.

Chapter 1 - Blondes Have More Fun

I was born a skinny, baby, on time, on a Thursday morning, at 8:55 a.m. in the summer of 1967. I like to point that out (that I was born skinny, that is), because, I have struggled with weight all of my life! I also like to point out that I was born with light hair. We don't know how that happened, considering my parents were dark-haired, dark-eyed Italian- Americans. My father was half German-American and I later found out his mother's family was Jewish.

My sister, Lucy, used to tease me mercilessly about how I was either adopted, or hatched under a rock, because I did not look like anyone! Then I began to get the dark hair around age five. I was, by all accounts very active and healthy up until age five. See, blondes do have more fun! Gradually, I went from being an active, 40-pound child to a 90-pound couch potato. The word that the doctors used a lot was "sluggish."

My mom, a stay-at-home-mom until 1975, taught me how to read when I was 4. I was already reading children's books and cereal boxes. She refused to use "baby talk." I would look in the dictionary, and my parents were amazed at my reading ability. I looked up the word "slug" in the dictionary. I was upset to learn that I was some sort of crawling, slimy bug. My father's definition to the doctors was more to the point: "She is blown up like a water balloon." He meant no harm, but I focused on that sentence for years.

My father, a natural artist, would draw a picture, such as a cartoon character, like Popeye, or Fred Flintstone, and leave it on the kitchen table, and it would say "Draw this." I would copy it for him by the time he got home. He did this also so that I would have something to stay occupied all day. I also began to play drums on anything and got a set of drums for my fourth birthday and eventually a harmonica, xylophone, and guitar. Music and art became my life.

I began to see nothing wrong with staying in, reading, listening to and playing music, and drawing all the time. My dad was not happy that I was inside, drawing all day. He wanted to see equal playing outside and inside. He was a very active, fit, powerhouse. He did not lift weights, but looked like he could bench press a house, because he was a freight driver for a local Teamster trucking company. Back before trucking deregulation, drivers unloaded and loaded all their own freight. He was 5 foot, 7 inches, and 160 pounds of solid muscle. He did do push ups every day, and sit ups. He was proud of how he had lost a lot of weight a long time ago, when he had met my mom. He did not want to see me heavy, and unhappy, because he warned me, kids can be cruel.

I was born and spent the first part of my childhood in a little factory town, east of Pittsburgh. I was taken to a few local doctors. Some said that my parents should put me on a diet. One doctor took a good family history from my mother, and suggested that it may be something more complicated than just needing to diet, especially since I did not eat much. There was one other important factor: my mother had recently been diagnosed with hypothyroidism. Her father and paternal aunt also had battled problems with their thyroids. In fact, in July 1967, my maternal grandfather was inpatient hospitalized for his malfunctioning thyroid, in a Pittsburgh hospital, about the same time I was busy trying to be born.

I had a friend, but she was an older lady who lived next door to us on Division Street. Division Street was a working class street, with different races, and we all were very simple, down to earth people.

My older friend's name was "Ginger." She had a little dog named "Poncho," a Chihuahua, who was 19! That was astounding to me! How could that little dog be so much older than me? Ginger used to come out, sit on the picnic bench in the yard of the apartment building and we would talk. She would smoke, and I would suck on a lollipop or a candy cigarette. She had bleached blonde hair. She wore colorful clothing, sometimes leopard skin or animal prints, and gold "mules" or slippers to walk around in. I wanted to look just like that! She would always give me candy and little gifts. She had no children of her own.

Days went by and Ginger did not come out. A neighbor guy and I banged on her door. I do not remember much more, other than police being there and an ambulance. Then after that, the grass grew in the front for years after. My mom always told me "Stay away from there!" I wanted Poncho, but my parents just told me he was "put down." I didn't know what that meant. Where did they put him? How far "down" did he go? We had a metal thing that stuck out of our yard that was a hole. Did they put him "down" there?

Shortly after that, my dad took me for a ride, and we went to see an old German lady who had a farm. She sold my dad a five year old standard dachshund, and that's how we got Heiney, and I have had a crazy love of dachshunds ever since. Heiney, short for Heinrick (I have not changed his name. I don't think he could sue me, and plus, he is dead now) was purchased because my dad told me years later he could not find another chihuahua in that small town.

I also had another problem that developed around that time: migraine headaches. I can remember the first one I had. My family had a big card game every Saturday night. I would sit under the table. I just loved sitting there, listening to my grandfather (mom's dad) as he told raucous jokes, and my uncle would tell even more raucous ones. It was a time of food, fun, the smell of cigarette smoke, laughs, and table pounding. They played with pennies that my mom kept in a big coffee can. Heiney (also a bit overweight) would sit there with me, and sometimes we would even fall asleep. I still like noise—from a radio or television, to get me to sleep.

The monsignor from the church came to play. We just knew him as "Tony" on Saturday nights, and he could smoke, drink, and play cards with the best of them (my grandfather, his friends, my uncles). That was the best time of my life , when everyone was alive and all in the same neighborhood.

But one night, I did not feel well. My head hurt and I was so nauseated, I did not want to eat.

Mom said, "Then you should go lay down for awhile." I woke up puking my guts out. I yelled, and my mom and uncle came in. I told them what happened. They took me to the bathroom, and I had a searing pain in my right temple and eye. My dad came in and said, "What's wrong with her?" After my uncle gave him the rundown, he said, "I guess she got those from me." I was batting a thousand here: my mom's thyroid, and my dad's head.

My mom tells me that she used "an old Italian remedy": a cool cloth soaked in vinegar.

She tells me that it did help the pain. The problem is, my mother used vinegar for everything: to clean windows, to clean the floor, and to put on salads. I think it had a diversionary affect—the smell was so gross that I probably forgot the pain! I hate the smell of vinegar even today!

One of my favorite pastimes as a child remains one of my favorites today: I loved listening to music. I wore out records of my mom's like "Crystal Blue Persuasion", "All Day and All of the Night," "Ruby Tuesday/Let's Spend the Night Together." My dad would sit out in the living room on his night off (a rarity) and listen to *Sinatra at the Sands* or something similar. My sister, Lucy, was a big fan of Motown, and early 1970's soul. Her favorites were "Ball of Confusion, "Freddy's Dead,", and "Betcha By Golly While."

I began to become fascinated by records: who sang them, what label they were on: Motown had several—blue Motown, Purple Tamla, etc. I even knew serial numbers on some of them. I miss records. CD's just are not as fun. I have sold all my records in lean college days based on my knowledge of what is rare and what is not. I appreciate that my family was so diverse in their tastes, because my taste today remains diverse: I like rock, rap, R&B, old country, easy listening, show tunes, just about everything.

My parents knew I loved every Wednesday night so much because it was the *Sonny and Cher Comedy Hour*. It was the only night I was allowed to stay up past 9:00 p.m. My took me to see them live when I was five! I sent them a fan letter (that my mom helped me write) after the concert, and I still have their autographed photo (now on my wall in a frame) that they sent to me. Music has lifted my spirits on many occasions in my life, with all its ups and downs.

I feel very lucky and thankful that my family gave me an appreciation of entertainment: music, and movies—as it has given me a means of escape in troubled, as well as good times.

mom sister me 1972

Candy drawing 1976

Dad 1976

We lived three houses up from a church. Along with the monsignor who was a colorful character, there was also a young priest who sat outside and played guitar all day. He had long hair. He played songs by Simon and Garfunkel, and Crosby, Stills and Nash. The most complicated one that I can remember him singing is "El Condor Pasa" by Simon and Garfunkel. I loved spending time talking to him, and then when he got the motorcycle. Forget it! I was on the back of it. He was cool. He lasted about a year, and the rumors were all over the place. He joined a hippie commune. He was fired. He "ran away" with a woman.

A lot of people have the misconception that a stranger picking up children is a new thing. In 1972, my mom and grandmother and I were at a department store, and my mom turned to help my grandma try on a coat. I was walking around, looking at the dresses, and a man came up to me, wearing a suit. He said, "Hi young lady. Your mom had to take your grandma home because she got sick. She told me to take you home." He then offered his hand to me, and I took it. I was not afraid of him at all. He was wearing a suit. No one in my family ever wore a suit except when they went to wedding, or a special dinner.

He took me out to the parking lot right out the front door. He put me in the back seat of his station wagon, and put his seat belt on me. This also made me think he was important, because no one in my family enforced seat belts.

This was not a law back then, as it is today. Before he could close the door, my mom came running out. I can remember it like it happened an hour ago. She had on a mini dress, white with orange paisley swirls, and her curly black hair was wild. She was yelling, "Where are you taking my girl?" I said, "Mom he told me you took grandma home." She yelled, "Oh no you don't, you sicko." She then swung her purse at him. "Gimme my daughter, you pervert!" What? I never heard that word before? What did that mean? He was strangely calm, "I was just trying…" "Yeah, you sicko, I KNOW what you were trying." I mentioned this to Dad later, and he hit the roof. Today, 30 some years later, he rides her about it, "You can't pass up a sale, can you?"

The neighborhood we lived in was very close knit, as were many neighborhoods in and near Pittsburgh. Ours was made of an ethnic fabric of Italian-Americans, and African-Americans. I knew diversity early on, and did not judge people by skin color. This made it very difficult for me when we did move to an all white neighborhood later in childhood, and I heard people use the "n" word, and other ethnic slurs. I just did not "get it" that people were so narrow-minded about people because they had different colored skin. So what? I saw people in my own family with dark skin.

I liked the old neighborhood. It was one of those types where everyone knew everyone. My father knew the police chief, and he cooked up a scheme one day, as I was giving my parents all kinds of trouble about going to sleep. My dad, who, was pretty high strung, working twelve hour days, liked to come home, watch a little TV after his 8 0'clock dinner, with no interference from a kid. After I was on synthetic thyroid hormone, I was either tired or bouncing off walls: no in between, depending on what my thyroid functioning was. He tried everything, turning out all the lights at 9:00, taking away my record player. I would still be talking through the door as I heard the television. My dad was big on police and medical dramas.

Finally one night, I was lying in bed. My bedroom was in a back alley. I saw a red flashing light. It looked like a police car. Then I heard a bullhorn. "Candy ? Are you in there?" I stood up on my bed and looked out the window. There was a police car! Holy cow! The full uniformed officer was standing out there and talking to me with a bullhorn. "Candy, why are you still awake? If you don't go to bed when your dad says so, you'll be coming with me. Understand?" I just shook my head. He then turned off the red light and drove away. My dad came in and said, "Did you hear that?" I said I did, and this put an end to my obedience problems about going to sleep. My parents had a pretty twisted sense of humor. I recently asked them about this and my dad admitted he didn't know what else to do, so he asked his buddy to play this prank!

One day we took a ride in to the city of Pittsburgh. We were going to find out about the headaches and other problems. My father had taken off work to drive us there, so it must have been serious, I thought. I was now at a giant hospital for children. It took all day to find out what was wrong. I had blood tests, and was asked many questions. A nurse weighed me, and she would be the same nurse to weigh me for years to come. She would always say, "My. We're fat today," or, "Hmm…lost some. But we're still a little chunky." The irony was that she weighed no less than 300 pounds. I used to ask every time I went, "Am I getting a shot today?" I would be told no, and then I would eventually get pricked with the needle. In their minds, they probably thought that they were not lying, because a shot is, after all, different than a blood test. One time I acted out so much that I was cowering in a corner, with a male nurse or orderly threatening to tie me down to get the blood. I know that times have changed in healthcare, thank goodness. But back then, coercion was the name of the game.

I am very thankful that I had a mother and father that never gave up. My mother tells me today that she would plead with doctors in our small town and explain, "But you don't understand. My daughter was reading at four. She is an artist. She play instruments. She is smart. It is not just about gaining weight. Now she seems like she is not as sharp as she was! You are all focused on her weight!" She said the local doctors did not even want to test me for thyroid, and one even told her, "Kids don't have thyroid problems. Keep an eye on your kid. She is sneaking food when you aren't looking."

I waited all day on that first visit to the big hospital with my family in a waiting room, where public television was the only choice of channel. It was one of those televisions that are bracketed to the ceiling, and this was before remotes. I liked the big puppets and their songs about numbers and letters, but I am sure that the adults there, including my own parents, would have liked to shoot an arrow at the giant birds and monsters on the screen. This I gathered, from the groans and eyes rolling to the ceiling of many adults, when they would sigh, "Is this all that's on?"

About six hours after the initial blood tests, my doctor came out with a pleased look on his face. I thought that the happy look must mean that I could go home, and that this, too, shall pass. Wrong. In my years of experience as a patient, I learned to decipher those looks doctors have. That pleased look means, "There is a reason you feel like crap. We have a pill for you!" I was told that my thyroid was "slow." So, in 1972, at age 5, I began taking this little pill. It was synthetic thyroid hormone. It was not bitter, and the doctor told me I could even chew it. I chew it even now, many years later. My weight went down, and my energy increased. The headaches remained, but at that time aspirin and some carbonated anti-nausea drink would help. But, it has been a balancing act since then, keeping that thyroid-stimulating hormone on the level.

Back then, the most emphasis was placed on the weight. The doctors, nurses, and dieticians would bring out that chart that showed the appropriate weight to correspond with one's height. The doctor would tell my family to only "allow" me to drink skim milk, and to eliminate this, and add that. My father taught me to diet because he used to be a fat kid, and he had spent his life restricting himself from eating what he really wanted to. He was short but built, and the young guys in the neighborhood used to call him "Mr. Clean," because that is who he kind of looked like---that character on the bottle Mr. Clean---white T-shirt and all. He taught me how to do sit-ups, push ups, and he told me how he had gone from 250 to 160 by eating one meal a day and cutting "everything in half," or "not eating after seven at night." He told me that there are "two secrets to losing weight: willpower and concentration." He told me that with those two mind-sets, you could do anything. I have remembered those two golden rules in many areas of my life.

My older sister, Lucy, was eight years older than me—a lifetime when you are a kid. She could eat three super-duper hamburgers with fries, wash it down with a shake, and consume a package of cookies, and never gain weight! My father used to tell her, "One of these days, you're gonna wake up, and all that is gonna catch up with you. You'll be 300 pounds." Well, that did not happen. However, later in her life, she also became ill with our inherited thyroid problem; in fact, very ill.

Until the medication for the thyroid helped to stabilize the gland's levels, we would make a trek to Pittsburgh monthly, then eventually, every few months. I realized from then on, when we passed the county line, that it was going to involve sitting in some freezing examining room, in my underwear, getting weighed, getting a blood test, and getting a headache from the stress of the day.

Due to the erratic thyroid, I experienced what it was like to be a fat kid: a fate worse than death, if you have been there. Back in the early seventies, the world was not so politically correct. For example, in the giant catalogs that came out in the fall, children's clothing sizes were separated, but certainly not equal. Girls were "slim," "regular," or "chubby." Boys were "slim," "regular," or "husky." Some years, depending on my thyroid's functioning or malfunctioning, I was sometimes a "regular." Sometimes, I was a "chubby." But I was never a "slim."

If I was in a chubby period, I even heard cracks from teachers. One gym teacher told me I was lazy and needed to get off my "duff." I told her that I had a thyroid problem. She said that I was lying and she didn't want to hear it. This was second grade, 1974. Now they have seminars at most employment settings called "Diversity" training. I am not in the educational field, but I would bet that in educational settings, teachers are taught about respecting differences in their students nowadays.

Other children were of course, also less tolerant of fat kids. I noticed at an early age that the way I was treated depended on that "chubby" or "regular" outfit I was wearing. I played mostly with boys. Girls were very picky. If you were ugly or fat, they just would not want to be seen with you. Boys would accept me as is, if I could play softball or goof off with them. I also was a heck of a softball player. I became a class clown to fit in. I just happened to fit in with the male class clowns. We would wait until the teacher turned his or her back and switch seats, so that when the teacher would turn around, they would see us in a different seat. I think we gave one teacher a nervous breakdown. She ran out, yelling, "I can't take this shit!"

I hated moving because most of our family was in the "old neighborhood." The suburbs seemed so cold and unfriendly. I could care less about a "yard." I stayed in and read a lot of the time anyway.

One saving grace in moving to the suburbs is that I developed a friendship which became what every kid should have growing up—that best friend that you love and play with from the time the sun comes up until the sun goes down. Her name was Denise. Sometimes , we fought like cats and dogs, and made up the very next day, and sometimes the fights/make-ups were even the very same day. But oh, our fight could be vicious. I believe as pre-adolescents, we got along, because we were both "tomboys". We were both tree-climbers, and bike riders and were not afraid to get dirty and scraped up. She also knew how to shoot and kill, courtesy of her father. My father was not a hunter, and I was not interested in learning to shoot animals, so when they did this, I firmly declined.

One of our fights involved us pretending to make up in which we both left boxes of Vanilla wafers stuffed with our dog's turds on the doorstep for each other. We had that kind of sense of humor. But this gal and her family were there in spirit and physically, after I became ill years later, I got a card every single day from the family all the months I was in the hospital and a great cheery yellow vase (that I still have). I think of her often to this day. I have only spoken to her a few times in the past decade, but she is still in my heart as is her family.

When I was in third grade, I began growing out of my regulars again. But I was developing bumps in the front. I had no idea what the heck was going on. One day, after riding my bike with some neighbor boys, I came in to use the bathroom. There was blood all over my underpants. I ran to tell my mother. She said, "Well, you have a cut. Wear this big bandage." My sister was home, and hit the roof. She rarely came to my defense or even acknowledged that I was a human being. But that day, she said, "Oh no! You're not gonna do this again. Tell her." My mom said, "No, she's too young."

My sister yelled back, "If she has it, she isn't too young to know what it is!" My sister ended up explaining to me what the blood was, and even gave me some pamphlets she had stashed away. That was how I learned about sex, and why I had this period thing. She then told me that she also had been eight when she got her period. She had been a little girl in frilly dresses that played with dolls and had tea parties with them (I, on the other hand, played with toy cars, got dirty, and insisted on wearing pants). She ran inside, when she felt like she had peed her pants, but saw blood and got scared. She yelled for my mom. My mom told her, "Well, it's a boo-boo. Put this big bandage in your underpants." My sister said that she was assured that it would "go away" in a few days. She was horrified when it came back several weeks later. Finally, a neighbor lady told her the facts of life.

I joke to my mom nowadays that I am still waiting for her to have "that talk" with me.

I needed a bra at age nine. I had one other friend who got her period early, but not until fifth grade. These pals of mine who were boys were suddenly acting strange around me, and making cracks about boobs. I was no longer welcome in the boy's club, so to speak. Who wanted to play ball, climb trees, and wrestle with some "guy" with a bra on? I got the old snapped bra strap routine more days than not from these boy friends. The girls did not accept me either, except for the other early developer, Gail. She moved away after fifth grade.

I entered sixth grade wearing a real bra, not one of those training bras. I still was a large framed girl. I was 5'2" and weighed about 120. There were some other girls in my grade who were slender but developing. I felt like I fit in nowhere.

I still fought that trip to Pittsburgh every few months, because I felt that the staff treated me in a patronizing way. That nurse still was making her "fat" jokes. So I fought until my parents agreed to take me to a doctor who treated adults, too.

I would go to my grandmother's house on weekends, as often as I could. She was pretty insensitive. She would say, "No man will ever want you if you don't lose this weight now. You'll grow up fat and be all alone."

My grandmother lived across the street from us in the neighborhood I spent my first few years in. I only knew my mother's parents, but never knew anything about my father's. We moved to the suburbs when I was around eight. I never felt we fit in, because it was, as my dad called it, "a white collar neighborhood." He used to say that he was "the only man who carries a lunch box to work, and has to shower after work." My sister told me years later that she felt out of place in that high school, because everyone's father was a lawyer, doctor, engineer, or other professional.

We shopped at discount stores, not department stores. My dad made a decent salary as a truck driver, but he did have some hang-ups about the whole working class versus middle class life. It was my mom's idea, because she wanted to live in a better neighborhood, and to get away from that place where she grew up. My dad used to argue with my mom, and say, "We're living above our means."

I felt more at home in that old neighborhood. It was a small price to pay to be called fat, or to listen to my grandmother talk about my parents "mistake" of trying to move up in the housing development food chain.

But I found strange comfort in some of the things that she taught me. She taught me how to use a teabag two or three times. She taught me how to make the best fried eggs, and cake frosting. She would tell me stories about growing up poor and hand washing clothes, bathing in a big tub once a week in her kitchen, and how some of her ten siblings died. One committed suicide by refusing to give himself his insulin shots. He had dramatically thrown his needles and insulin in the creek one day and said, "That's it. I am done. Now I will die." My grandfather would always tell my grandmother to stop calling me names, or talking about my family the way she did. He was really my best friend.

He would squeeze my hand, and say, "C'mon Suzie. Let's go watch *Sanford and Son*." He called all females "Suzie," and called grandmother, "Mom." She called him "Dad."

Now, I try to focus on those things that Gramma taught me: frugality when I was really poor and on Public Assistance and Disability, as those tips came in so handy. I teach my clients now that we can learn from everyone, and to try to focus on at least one thing we have learned, positive, even from our worst enemies or those who have hurt us.

I became fascinated with some of the neighborhood characters. This was the seventies, and most of the teenagers in the neighborhood were using marijuana, and going to big beer parties. One of my uncle's friends, who was nineteen, passed by the porch that my grandmother and I used to sit on. He had a bouncy walk, with long hair flapping as he walked. He was so cool. The next day I woke up to hear my uncle, also nineteen, crying. That dude who talked with us the night before died of an overdose. My uncle was either there when it happened, or shortly after. I was inspired to draw a big picture of all these characters that I saw. It is a black and white ink drawing. I include it in the photos section. It was drawn one afternoon in 1978 at my grandmother's house. I often would tune out by drawing, reading, eating, or listening to music.

My grandfather was in bed most of the time by summer, 1975. He was now eating baby food. But he would throw up for hours after he attempted to eat. No one would tell me why. I knew he also had a bad thyroid. But I did not throw up like this all the time. He went to the hospital for the last time in July. I only visited him once in the hospital. He really was out of it. I don't think he knew who I was, and that made me angry. I just did not understand. My dad came home from work one Friday night, and said, "Your grandfather looks good tonight. He was talking better than he has in weeks." My dad said that he might be getting better.

The day after my dad saw him, the phone rang. My sister answered it, and I heard her say, "Oh, so he died." I started screaming, "Oh My God! Is Grandpap dead?" My sister said, "No, stupid. Your aunt's cat died." All day I was yelling, "I know he's dead!" All day long, my sister would walk away or lock herself in her room. My dad came home and my sister grabbed him and they went into the room. My dad came out about five minutes later. He said, "Sit down Candy." I was screaming and crying, which is something my dad did not tolerate. He hated crying. I was screaming, "I know he's dead! You're all liars!" He was uncharacteristically calm. He said, "Now listen. Yes, he did die. He was very sick." I remember collapsing with sobs. My dad said, "You go get dressed. We'll go out to see a movie."

Dad took me that night to the theater in our old neighborhood. We saw *Bambi*. When I have told friends about this, they are shocked at the choice of the movie we went to see because there is a death scene. I do not remember that part of the flick at all, and I have not seen the movie since. All I know is that for two hours or so, I forgot that my grandfather was dead. When we walked out into the night air, my dad holding my hand, I remembered. Then I cried all over again.

On the way home that night, I asked my dad if I would ever see Grandpap again. It was then that my dad told me about his parents. His Italian immigrant father, moved to the United States when he was about twenty. He was a married father of two. When he got here, his first wife died at twenty, probably from that big flu that was going around in 1920—many of my grandmother's relatives also died from it, too. His father was a boxer, and later a bartender. He changed his last name when he came here. My dad was the last child born to his father's second marriage to a German-American woman of considerable wealth.

My paternal grandmother's family did not approve of this marriage, as she was college educated, and near thirty. She had gone to nursing school. She never worked, though, because my father told me that she hated the sight of blood and suffering. She met this suave Italian, and married him, and she was not supported emotionally or financially any longer by her family. Dad's father was not formally educated, and could not write in English very well. The two had five children.

My dad told me about a sister he had. She was the fourth child, and about five years old when she died. My dad said he could not comprehend that one day they were eating sausage at the dinner table, and the next day, she was dead. He had asked that same question: "Will I ever see her again?"

He went on to tell me that when he was thirteen, his father ended up in a hospital in Pittsburgh. His dad died there of heart problems. Six months later, his mother died, my father feels, "of a broken heart." She actually had a mystery illness involving poor circulation and chronic lung problems, and died after a long bout with pneumonia. Dad witnessed his parents' deaths in that hospital; he was in the room when each one died. He was essentially an orphan at fourteen. He quit school at that age, and went to work. He had his employer sign the papers to approve his termination from school.

Dad was then so poor that he had two pairs of pants that he washed several times a week. He also was a large boy for his age. I saw a picture of him at that time, and he was already his full height of 5"7". He was not comfortable with his poverty or size at that time. He worked at a gas station, washed and waxed cars for people, and mopped floors at a car dealership.

As a teenager, he later told me, he had a gang of friends. They would race cars, and do what young men did in the 1950's. One night, one of those friends broke from the pack and said that he was going to get his girlfriend so that they could see a movie or something. On the way back from Pittsburgh, my dad and the other guys saw a wreck on the side of the highway. They stopped to see if they could help. It was my dad's friend, in a pool of blood; the friend later died after arrival at the hospital, while Dad was at the bedside. He witnessed his third devastating death in four years.

He also told me once about a favorite radio personality he used to listen to as a boy, before the advent of television. This announcer would tell stories, and sing. My dad read in the paper one day that his favorite announcer died. He tuned in that night, expecting a repeat broadcast or a big tribute show. The new announcer opened the show with, "Well friends, the show must go on," and proceeded to do a whole show with nary a mention of the deceased star. Dad said he could not believe how insensitive this was. But he told me that after living with so many deaths, now he understood.

My dad was trying to tell me that he knew a thing or two about death. It was something that I talked with him about almost every time we were alone, for the next year while I was grieving my grandfather. He was always very calm in describing how life goes on, even if it is not easy.

Another very important lesson that my dad taught me is that to "make it" in this world, you must speak and spell properly. It took him all summer one year to correct me of one mistake I used to make. I would say, "Dad, look at them cars!" He would say, "No, it is look at *those* cars! You don't use the word 'them' unless it is at the end of a sentence!" He would interrupt me frequently to correct me. In fact the entire summer between second and third grades, it seemed like all he did was correct my English! It used to irritate me, but I am so glad he did. We would go to pick my mom up at work, and he would tell me, "Look at that word on the sign. Let's see how many words we can get from it." The word "Tires" could become "rites, " "sit," "rest," etc. He also promptly took me to get a library card when we moved from the old neighborhood, and every two weeks he would take me to get two books to read. He told me that if you read, you will understand a little bit about a lot of the world.

It is true, I think. One of the best skills you can have is communicating properly in different situations. This is something that an eighth grade graduate taught me.

faces 1978. picture I drew at age 11

Chapter 2 - Growing Up all Wrong

I continued to spend weekends with Grandma. We would sit out on the porch and drink a glass of beer, every once in a while. She said, "A glass of beer is better for you than pop." For those of you who are not from Pittsburgh, "pop" is soda. My first taste of beer was at age 5, also from my grandparents. I liked that feeling it gave me, if not the taste.

I got to know all the characters in the neighborhood. It seemed that every teenaged male had dated every teenaged girl at one time or another. My grandmother explained to me that the girls had "reputations." There was a woman across the street that my gramma told me was "a call girl." There was often a sweet smell coming from the house next door. My uncle explained to me that the distinctive smell was marijuana. I got what I considered an education on life by going back to the old neighborhood. Sure, it did not always keep me out of trouble in the long run. But I also was not naïve later in life. I believe, as cliché as this may sound, that we are everywhere that we are supposed to be, for a reason. It, as well as all the good and bad that has happened to me, has prepared me to be a better, nonjudgmental social worker. But here I am again, jumping ahead of myself.

I was intrigued by all this activity. Saturday nights in the old neighborhood were always awash with activity, laughing, loud music, cars going up and down the street, and parties. My parents did not drink, and my dad smoked a cigar at night, but never in the house. Even my sister, who was not the best example of a suburban teenager, did not even smoke, let alone drink or do drugs. But this sort of thing held a lot of interest to me. I would read all about my favorite rock stars, and many openly admitted to using hallucinogens to enhance their writing. I loved rock and roll music, and those singers and musicians were my heroes.

One day, a Saturday afternoon, a teenage girl came to the porch to talk with me. She knew my uncle. She said she could not believe I was only twelve, because I knew so much about the rock stars and songs of the day, which was what we always talked about. She also noted that I "looked 18." I think she also had a big crush on my uncle. She asked if I wanted to come up to her house and listen to some tunes. My grandmother approved, but told me to be back before dinner. We did listen to music, and again, she couldn't believe that I could name all of the guys in Led Zeppelin. She lit up a cigarette. I mentioned that I always wondered what it was like to smoke. She swore me to secrecy, and let me have one, as she taught me the cool way to hold the smoke and how to inhale or avoid inhaling. Later, her brother came home, and he pulled some foil out of his pocket. She said, "Now you aren't gettin' any of this, man. I aint givin' no kid this shit." It was what looked like dried up leaves or twigs, and it had some seeds. It was marijuana. I did not have any, but that would change a few months later.

Back in the suburbs, I was now entering junior high. Quickly, the cliques congregated. I naturally gravitated toward the people who snuck smokes. I went to a "party" in a trailer park one day after school. I then smoked that sweet smelling weed. I never totally enjoyed it. But if it was there, and free, I partook. I also drank if it was available. Soon, pills were added to the mix. I tried some pill called "black beauty" when I was thirteen. I used those every day until I was sixteen. I used them, because they made me disinterested in food. I was thinner than ever, and I wanted to remain that way.

I began to leave school at lunch to go to a friend's house. We would listen to Rolling Stones albums and smoke cigarettes. Lunch was usually some saltines and diet "pop." I got caught leaving through the boiler room door by the principal one day, and he suspended me for three days. No problem. I could stay at home while Mom and Dad worked, and listen to my tunes all day. I was in trouble a lot throughout junior high for smoking or skipping school. The punishment was always suspension. My parents were not harsh on me about this. They just had a lot of things happening. They always were talking about or arguing about money and not being able to afford things. Everything was bought on layaway and credit. I did not understand why they moved. Yes, the old neighborhood was not the greatest, but their house was nice. And there is that old song, about "a house is not a home." I would say this and then they would get more upset, so I would retreat more. I vowed not to put so much stake in things when I got their age so that I was drowning in debt and so unhappy. Another complication is that they were often housing my sister, her spouse, and my new nephew. Since she got married in late 1979, she had moved back with her spouse and baby who was born in 1980, and the cutest, most well behaved baby I have ever seen.

I drank a lot of beer, and even whiskey on weekends with the friends. Out of all of my friends from that time, I remain in contact with three. We live clean lifestyles now. I think we were all able to get away with this drug and alcohol use because we were often unsupervised. Our parents were working a lot, and some of them were too trusting. It is very sad. I am not a parent, but I would want to know everything my kid is doing, and I would talk with my child, and would encourage education first and foremost, especially if I saw potential in that child.

But I look back, and see that parents were often just young, often younger than we are now, and doing the best they could. A lot of times, when clients come to me nowadays, and say "Why me?" I relate that maybe their situation happened because parents were not educated, and did not know better. I tell my clients to look at it from that perspective. From my perspective, I used to wish, as so many of us do, that I could have chosen my own parents. Maybe I would have chosen parents who encouraged my desire to go to school rather than make it clear that there is no money for college, end of story. But there is only so long we can cry, poor pitiful me, now is there? Besides, as I said earlier, we are put in situations and in places for a reason—to shape our very unique characters. Would you or I have been so driven to succeed? Maybe not. I think it would have been easier in many ways if I had parents who were typically middle class, but I would not be the person I am.

I eventually started hanging out with some more drug using type of peers. Some had parents who did not care, some had parents who actually supplied the booze or covered for us, telling our parents that we were at their house when we went out partying. I will spare a lot of the details, because I am not proud of any of this. But I was in some situations that now, when I look back on them, cause me to cringe. There were always twenty-something men available to buy drinks, share their weed, and drive us around. These men, of course were interested in one thing from teenage girls. As an adult, the thought of these sickos turns my stomach. Today, this sort of thing gets a lot more press. Back in the early 1980's, a lot of activity could go, as they say under the radar. Corrupt behavior is not new.

I began to really have a melancholy personality. Even though I was quite thin, I became obsessed with my weight. In addition to the pills I took (purchased or given to me by dealers at school or on Friday nights), I also started taking a few laxatives to rid my body of any food I might have eaten. I starved myself and drank diet drinks, loaded with saccharine back in those days. By the time I was fifteen, I was shoplifting and consuming 60 laxatives a day.

I started writing really dark poetry almost daily. I was inspired by endless hours of listening to the Doors and John Lennon. Here are a few lines (I will not torture you by offering any more):

Drown yourself in your deepest fear
Drive upon the highway of terror
Then come back to this setting
And see which is fairer

Here is another cheerful little one:

Soon comes the arrival of the night's edge
Till then we're suspended from a restless ledge

I have a full journal of these poems, which I was sure that one day I would either sing or sell to a rock group. I even wrote the lyrics to a rock opera. It was called *A Deathly Experience*. I have little musical talent. I have been told I can sing. But, I thought, The Who will take this on the road, and I will be rich. I am struck by a couple of things, as I look at these poems—they were some deep words for a young teenager, and my spelling and vocabulary were fairly impressive at that age.

Some friends and I would sneak out of our windows at night over the summers, and often accept rides with strange young men who looked "cool." If they had weed, were playing cool tunes, and had booze, we would go. I never got involved with any of the older guys. They struck me as creepy. Even then, it seemed inherently wrong that a man would see a teenage girl as sexually attractive.

I made bad decisions because of drugs and company I was keeping. I have no doubt that I would have ended up a petty criminal, or involved with someone who was into petty crimes had I continued on the path I was on. I could tell many stories, but I will tell one. A friend I hung out with regularly, and with whom I smoked weed nearly daily for three years, named Wendy lived about a half mile from an older couple. They had a 1964 Ford Fairlane. Wendy knew how to hotwire the car underneath the steering wheel. My father had unsuccessfully tried to teach me how to drive a standard shift car. I had some of the basic mechanics down, but I stalled it out, and my father had been yelling at me when he was trying to teach me weeks earlier. He was yelling that I would ruin his clutch. However, Wendy did not know how to drive at all yet, let alone a standard. At least I had one lesson under my belt. Luckily the trip to the mall that night was all straight, no hills, and the old couple went to bed at 8:30. The mall was closing at 9:30, and I pushed that clutch in and away we went. This was shameful. We got our bag of weed, and then we needed to leave. Backing out of the parking space was tricky. We had a male friend help me out, and he was appalled at how we got this car. (He later became a state trooper). When we got back, Wendy put the wires underneath the steering wheel (I do not know how she learned this trick—possible from hanging out with the older guys she was dating). I made a very loud, tire squealing, stalling out stop in the people's driveway. No lights came on in their house. Never again did we do something that stupid.

But with my growing dissatisfaction over this lifestyle, and just feeling ennui, and malaise mounting, I began to think that I did not want to continue to live this way. I saw a television movie one night on a teenager going into rehab, and I thought that the story could have been about me, with the exception of the fact that the rehab in the movie looked like a middle class facility, and I would have to totally come clean to my parents. I knew there would be no way they could afford such a place. So the decision to quit kind of was made for me over the next few months.

Eventually, a few very negative events occurred while under the influence. The first inclination that this was not a lifestyle for me came when I was out with a male friend and a female friend one Sunday afternoon, when I was sixteen. It was snowing. We were all underdressed in denim jackets, layered over sweatshirts and rock star image T-shirts. We smoked some pot. They were knocked out, lying on the snow-covered ground, getting "mellow." I, on the other hand had a terrible reaction. I realize my reaction could have been due to the fact that I ate maybe three crackers a day, and drank a couple mugs of coffee a day. First, it felt like the whole world was spinning wildly around me. I actually remember kneeling on the ground trying to hold on so that I would not "fall off" the world. I then lost my sight temporarily and experienced a loud ringing in my ears. My friends were very high, and they even admitted, "This shit's potent." But they did realize that something was wrong.

These two friends had amazing singing voices, and they tried to calm me by singing, because by this time I was in a full-blown panic. We had this one wooded area where we would get high, year round. It was literally miles from any houses. They realized that they had to get me indoors because I was shivering, flushing in the face, and panicking because I was sure I would be blind forever, or die. Eventually my sight returned. They assisted me in walking, singing all the while. They were so calm, and reassuring. The guy, Jim, said, "I think there's this house nearby. My brother hangs out with this couple, and they know of me, so let's just concentrate on getting there."

It was a log cabin. We knocked on the door, and sure enough the lady of the house recognized Jim. She was obviously high, also, and was very suspicious for some reason of my girlfriend and me. Jim told her, "No, man, it's fine. They're cool." I sat on the couch and Jim explained to the couple what was going on. The lady welcomed me then, and brought me some tea. She was 30, but had the worn face of a woman who looked like she'd been out in the sun a lot. She had long, stringy hair. There was a fireplace. Her "old man" was a large, unshaven man, also looking older than his years. They had many bongs (pipes for smoking dope) all over the coffee table. They had some more exotic ones on the mantelpiece, as art, I suppose.

The couple explained that there has been some "bad shit" going around, and rumored to have PCP-or some other drug. My two friends admitted that they experienced some mild hallucinations and felt very worn out from the high, and then proceeded to fire up another bong and get high again.

Weeks later, I smoked some marijuana with someone at school. I went to my tenth grade English class, and felt the room spinning. I became incoherent. A guy I always sat next to in class leaned over and whispered, "Did you get high?" I shook my head yes, and he told me to try to keep it together until break. He then walked me to the nurses' office, and explained that I was sick. The personnel at school had already approached me about their suspicions in the past. The nurse asked me point blank if I was high. I lied. She looked unconvinced, and pointed to a room, and said, "Lie down in there." I proceeded to experience auditory hallucinations, which sounded like an 8-track tape gone awry. For those of you who remember the inferior sound quality of 8-tracks, after a few uses, the 4 tracks began to 'bleed" onto one another, creating a warped sound, in which you could hear up to four songs at one time. I held my ears, and slept it off and went home that day, and that was the last time I ever smoked marijuana. It was April 16, 1983. I used the diet pills, still, but that would also soon come to an end. Later, in my career in mental health, while being trained at a University Anxiety Disorders Center, I learned that people who have a predisposition to anxiety disorders do not experience the mellow feeling of marijuana, but the opposite. They experience a panic, and in worst cases, a paranoia or even a worse form of psychosis. I have had various forms of anxiety, so it all makes sense.

One day the principal came to pull me out of class. He said that he had a witness to my receiving pills in study hall. They questioned the person who had sold them to me, and he had denied it. I had a stash of about fifty of the pills in my purse. On the way to the principal's office, I reached in the purse and discreetly stuck them down my pants, in my underpants. This was easy, because all of my pants were several sizes too big due to the continued weight loss.

The principal searched my purse, but they could not search my body. In that sense I was off the hook. However he insulted not only me, but asked me what my parents did for a living. This was a school of inequity: you either were a child of a professional or from a working class or underclass background. I told him that my father was a truck driver. He said, "I don't need your kind in MY school. This is a good school. We have doctors' sons and daughters here." I felt very ashamed because I knew how hard my dad worked, and I tried to tell this man what good people my parents were, but he just dismissed me and said, "Get out of here. The next time I drag you in here, there will be state troopers present."

I came home from school one day, and my sister who was living there with her three year old and husband, told me I was in "deep shit." My mom and sister took me to my room. Years later, in my training, I learned that this was something called "an intervention."

I doubt that my sister and mom knew that they were staging an intervention, but, nonetheless, my mom put in front of me, my pills, joints, bottles of beer, whiskey, vodka, and said, "This is what I found in your room!" I denied that any of it was mine or that I had any idea where it was from. After much arguing, they gave up, and left me, where I lay down and had a momentary twinge of regret for lying. Lying is something I always prided myself on not doing.

Later my father told me that he knew I had been using and drinking. He did not pass judgment. I had no reason to lie. He said, "I went through a rebellious period. But you can't burn the candle at both ends like this. You have to grow up. You don't need this." A few times after this talk, I did come home staggering drunk. He always would confront me head on, but in a calm manner. He would say, "We had a talk. I am disappointed in you."

I stopped using the pills after the incident with the principal. I was scared about the state police, even if it was just something to threaten me with. I also stopped drinking at age 17. Again, there were defining moments that made me stop.

The first one occurred when, while drunk, at age 16. It was New Year's Eve. I was at a friend's house. Her parents were out all night at a hotel. We saw it as party time. But even at that age, I was getting to the point where I wanted to stop. This was 1983. I did not think that there was a rehab for someone like me. Maybe at the time there was. I had a couple of drinks, but it was before midnight, and I was ready to go to sleep. This house had 3 bedrooms. I put a flannel nightgown on, went out to the living room, and went to sleep, waiting for a bedroom to become unoccupied. By this point in my life, I had been to too many house parties where all people did was get high all night and "hook up".

I am not saying I was an angel, holier than though, or that I was not someone who had my, as my mom would say "wild steak." I had just come to the point where I wanted to change. Innately, I was a homebody. I would rather be home, reading and listening to my music. I also cared about my friends, and now was starting to think that they were destroying themselves. This lifestyle was no longer fun. I felt someone tugging on me. I recognized who it was. It was a local guy who showed up at these parties. He was 26, a separated guy, who also had a son. My one friend had a sort of relationship with him. The man always scared me. He was, I felt too old to be around us, and he was always making comments like, "One of these days, I'm gonna get you." He was tall and large framed. I fought this guy with all my might. I ended up with a ripped nightgown; somehow my contact was ripped from my eye. I was beaten from the struggle. My friend was high and drunk and was told by him that we had a great time, so what she heard were screams, but she assumed I was having a great time. I never reported it. He threatened me and threatened to hurt my family. I never told my parents. I told my mom many years later. I felt filthy, and at fault. I thought "If only I had not had anything to drink." It kept me isolated, and it still keeps me in on New Years' Eve. I have a picture of myself the next day, because my grandmother was at our house. My dad wanted a picture of my mom, my grandmother and myself. You can see how swollen my face is, and I am caked in makeup to hide it. I took so many hot showers in the 24 hours after, that I felt scalded. But I went out to an underage dancing club the next night and tried to dance and be happy, because I was desperately tying to make new "straight" drug-free friends.

I told absolutely no one about this sexual assault. I carried this around for years. I ate a lot, and I think it even contributed to my staying overweight after I got off medications that kept me bloated. Fat acts for some people as a protective shield. I blamed myself. I knew if I told my parents, they would have forbidden me to see my friends, and they would have blamed me. That is just the way it was, not only with me, but also with a lot of us. It was not like it is today, where people could talk quite as openly. This was before wonderful talk shows like *Oprah* (who has been such an inspiration to me) and education on date rape. In fact, the words "acquaintance rape" did not even exist then. So you knew him? And he raped you? Your fault!

In the year after high school, when most of my friends were either at college, or beginning their lives with childbearing or planning their future, I was heavily into writing. It was then that I wrote something about the rape. I still did not talk about it. But this was my testament to what had happened, and I spoke for all of us who had gone through this. I called it "Assault":

> *The sound of sobbing*
> *comes from behind*
> *A shower curtain*
> *in which a battered woman*
> *Crouches*
> *Her life uncertain*
> *She's been there for hours*
> *Not knowing whom to blame*
> *No amount of soap and water*
> *can wash away the shame*
> *Outside she will heal*
> *but the scars remain the same*
> *She wonders if she will*
> *ever regain her pride*
> *Will she be convinced*
> *that it was not her fault?*
> *That she's just another victim*
> *of sexual assault*

The last episode which was my wake up call, or "rock bottom" that abusing alcohol and pills occurred when the young man that I considered my big teenage romance was asked by a friend of mine to drive me home because I could not drive in my inebriation. This young man said that he was not doing any more favors for me. My female friend offered to pay him. All she had was three dollars. At that moment it hit me that I was worth three dollars to be rid of. He lectured me the whole way home about what a wreck I was, drinking myself to death, and how disgusting I was. He dropped me off at the door. He used to tell me that he had a couple of big dreams in life: to have two kids by the time he was twenty and to manage a supermarket just like his dad. I did not want kids, at least this young, and later made a choice not to have them at all, and then the choice was made for me, medically. And I did not want to get married and become a housewife. After I was home from the hospital a couple years later, I heard he was married, had a couple babies already, and was on his way to supermarket management.

My friend, Tracee, who I told this to years later, did not see that she "sold me out." "You were trashed, I couldn't drive you home. It was a way to get you home. I was just trying to get you home safely."

I began to turn my life around as best I could. By this time, I was a senior in high school. I barely scraped by with C's. I even had some D's and F's, but scored rather high on aptitude tests. My last semester at school, I had to really work hard to bring those grades up in order to graduate.

I had a very tough English teacher that year. She talked about her military career often, and ran that class like a drill sergeant. She made us write every day. I would often bring out that old class clown character to get through what I thought was a very stupid exercise. She would have none of this buffoonery. She took me aside after class many times, and said that she wanted to read the journal entries. She said, "Look. You can write. You need to start seeing yourself as someone who is smart. I want you to share this with the class. Quit acting like a clown in here, and be proud of this skill." I did feel silly sharing this, because I still was embarrassed about my "reputation" But I did share the stories, and some of the classmates said, "good job."

This was the first high school teacher who ever saw any potential in me and tried to nurture it, and I have never forgotten her patience. But with my grades, and no savings for education, college was out of the question. I used to bring it up with my parents, and I could see that it would greatly upset them.

That last semester, I was clean and sober. I lost many of my drinking and drugging buddies. Some of them had made comments like, "Who do you think you are? Miss Priss!" I let these comments roll off my back, and did not care. I looked at them now almost sympathetically. I may not have known where my life was headed, but I knew I did not want it to head down the road of looking like I was 50 when I am 25 like those old hippies in that shack I saw that day when I was high.

I even cleaned up my appearance. Before I got clean, I had loose, long, wild, dark hair. I dressed in jean jackets and jeans with T-shirts and boots. With my new clean lifestyle, I began dressing neater, and even had my hair cut and styled (it was still long), and I became a blonde. I made some new friends. I had made a friend who was a male, Dennis. He was just a friend to me, but he seemed to me, so sincere and kind. We would spend hours on the phone. I had no romantic feelings for him. But it was nice to have someone to talk to, trust, and share my feelings with. He was also very smart. But most importantly, I learned to become self-reliant, and to value time alone, to read, to write, and to be with Carrie if I did not have a party to attend or people to see every weekend. Because as I learned many times, sometimes, this is the way you get into trouble.

In my senior year, something else happened. I began having some health problems. I experienced repeated corneal problems. I was seeing an optometrist who then sent me to an ophthalmologist.

Candy 1985 before Wegener's

Chapter 3 – Radio Days

The ophthalmologist, Dr Bernstein, was a very tall, thin man. He was very blunt, as he said, "This looks like it could be an underlying problem. I think it could be systemic." This was late 1984 when this began occurring, my senior year in high school, when I began to take my school seriously, and clean up my act.

When my former friends would see my red eyes, I would get cracks from them like, "Yeah sure..you quit the smoke. Uh huh."   I was told by Dr. Bernstein that I had to apply a salve directly to my eyes, sleep with a patch (my right eye was affected more, and the cornea was almost worn off) and I had to apply several different types of drops. Some of the drops burned severely.

Dr. Bernstein informed me that I had inflamed corneas; the right eye was scarred from the months of damage. (I was unable to wear contacts again until 1997 due to the scarring).

I asked if I could wear contacts when I graduated, and Dr. Bernstein looked at me and said, "I don't care if you are getting married tomorrow. You are not wearing contacts." I graduated high school as a bleached blonde, wearing high heels, with no glasses, no contacts, and sinking into the mud, as it had just rained, and I could not see more than a foot in front of me. My hair was bleached almost as white as my cap and gown, and the clumsiness I had from not being able to see I am sure made me look "real smart." As I sat there waiting for my name to be called, I did think, I wish I had applied myself. I listened to the Principal talking about some of the scholars who were awarded scholarships to universities. Well, that will never happen to me, I thought. After I graduated from high school, I continued to work as a waitress and also entered into radio, which was my original calling in life. I decided that I wanted to be on the radio, where I could use my knowledge about radio. There was a school for aspiring radio announcers in Pittsburgh. I asked my parents if I could go there, since college was out of the question. My first year out of high school, 1985, I applied to this school. I sent for information and decided that I would do all I could to gain entry.

Cost would be an issue. It was $1,500. My parents took out a loan. (I later repaid them many years later, in 1995 after I got out of graduate school) I had no money. I was the worst waitress, so my tips were not great. I got a job at a bar very close to my house, and was told by the bar owner that I did not wear short enough skirts. "Your tips are never going to be big if you don't raise this," he said as he pulled my skirt up one day. I thought he was obnoxious. I told him that he could not make me wear short skirts. He said, "It is my bar, and I can make you do what I want." He put me on the lunch shift, as he told me he would not have me ruining his business at night looking like "Mary Poppin." (sic) One of the waitresses was my age and confided in me that she was having a relationship with him. He was 36 and married. He was often cornering me in the storage area, and touching my butt. "I don't get it. You are attractive, why won't you show what you got?"

I quit that job. I went home and told my parents that I quit, and they were livid. I told them it was because they wanted me to wear short skirts and I did not want to. I then got a job at a supermarket chain. I was put on bagging duties at first as we all were, and then you would get promoted to cashier.

I was good at what I did, but would talk to the customers and often to the cashier. The manager warned me, "No talking to the cashier. Greet the customer, but shut up, and no fraternizing." I got warned about this twice. This is the only time I was ever fired. Now, when I go to the supermarket, I see cashiers and baggers talking to each other, other cashiers, and everybody but the customer. My, how times have changed!

I then applied for another job at a Chinese restaurant. I had worked at one throughout my senior year in high school as a waitress. I learned to love Chinese food. This was a new Chinese restaurant in town. I applied for waitress, and told them I would do whatever else they wanted me to do. I had quit the last restaurant as the owner treated the staff so poorly. He at first rewarded all staff with one free meal per shift worked. He then arbitrarily changed that rule to "You pay me half price for your meal" Finally; he told us one day, "Now, you pay full price for all meals when you work." Needless to say, this restaurant is long out of business.

The new restaurant I applied for had nicer owners. I started working there in Fall of 1985 when I started the Broadcasting school. Broadcasting school was done on site and through correspondence. You had on site instructors, who were local radio personalities, and then you sent in your air checks and fake news. There was a studio there, and Hollywood announcers would grade you.

It may have been a scam. A lot of these diploma type schools indeed promised the world to people. They promised job placement, and touted that some of their graduates were now working on the air at some of the biggest radio and television stations all over the country. I wanted to work on talk radio. My heroes at the time were Larry King, whom I listened to often all night; a guy named Joe Donovan out of Louisville, Kentucky (he spun some rare oldies overnight) whom I could pick up on the a.m. dial after midnight clearer than I could some local stations; and a New York personality named Howard Stern.

I loved music, but I was more interested in maybe breaking into the talk radio market. I submitted my fake air checks, and the local radio announcer/instructors said I was doing great, and encouraged me to apply to local radio stations. I applied for my F.C.C. license (Federal Communications Commission) and received it in November, 1985. I spent all my waking hours that I was not working making tapes and applying to radio stations all over Western Pennsylvania.

In late 1985, I walked into a small radio station in McKeesport, on drizzly Monday morning. The receptionist at the front desk stopped me, and asked "Can I help you?" I said, "Yes, I want a job here." She told me to have a seat, and shortly afterward a man came out with a cigarette in hand. The whole place reeked of cigarette smoke. He came out and had a smirk, and shook my hand. "So you want to break into radio? My name is Rick Gritt."

It may not have been a big radio station, and I had been in other radio stations before, but none of the ones I had ever gone to had ever had the on air personality come out to greet me, and shake my hand before. I had filled out an application at one in a county south of Pittsburgh with paneling on the walls, and I had done a tape audition and never heard back from them. This was such small time radio, that there was a carton hanging on the wall of a man shoveling elephant crap. Another man says in the cartoon "Why do you stay in this job when you complain all the time?" The man shoveling says "What??? And quit show biz!?" Someone had written on the cartoon "This is all of us!!"

Rick said, "C'mon back to the office." I followed him and we passed the studio on the right. Another announcer was talking on the air, and the light above the studio was red. This was a country station, not my favorite format, but whatever, I would work at a Polka station, I thought.

Rick said, "So why does a nice young girl like you want to work in this shady business?" I told him that I love radio, I sleep with a radio. I love all kinds of music, I told him who my favorite announcers were locally, and I told him that I already had my FCC license. He listened to me, and was impressed with my knowledge, and said, "You are sick, but I like your ambition."

I then told him I was going to the Broadcasting School. He said, "Oh, God, no." I asked, "What? Why do you say that?" He shook his head and took a big drag on his filter less smoke, and said, "Well, it is my opinion that they are not really invested in making you a good announcer. They took your money, right? If they were good they would have cleaned up your diction." I said, "What do you mean?"

He said, "Well for instance, you said that you go to school down' air. This is such typical Pittsburghese. It is lazy dialect. You mean to say 'down there. That is very poor grammar. It is as bad as saying 'yinz" (a lot of people from Pittsburgh will say this as a plural for you-uns but they pronounce it as yinz. I believe "youns" originated actually in the Appalachian regions, but Pittsburghers are known for this word).

Rick told me, "I like you. You have gumption. But you are not going on the air with your lazy dialect. Can you type?" I could not, but I told him I could and I would. He told me, "I will tell you what. You call that broadcasting school and tell them I will accept you as an intern, and then we will pay you minimum wage if you work out after three months. Get the paperwork you need to fill out, and you will be my news writer. I can't write all my news, and announce it. I will teach you better than those crack announcers they have 'down air n'at at that so called school. You ready to see how radio really works?"

I said I was! He said, "Learn to type, and be here next Monday at 5:00 a.m. sharp. Clean up that dialect. Action verbs like going have a 'g' at the end. The word 'and' has a 'd' at the end, it is not pronounced 'an.' I want you to e-nun-ci-ate!" I went home and told my parents about this, and they were not understanding of the concept of internship and unpaid, but I explained that after three months, if I did well, I would be paid.

I then explained that I needed a typewriter. My father, who knew just about everyone in the Pittsburgh area, thanks to being a freight driver, said, "Ok. I know a guy who sells everything. I know where you can get a good one for $50. He took me that day and got a German, 1950 manual typewriter from a man who sold all kinds of business machines out of his garage, in the Trafford area, near Murrysville, Pennsylvania. For the next week, I typed everything. I took all of my old poetry, record album covers, magazine articles, and just copied them. Some nights, I stayed up until 5:00 a.m.

I was what you might call a "hunt and peck" typist, but I did it. I still am that way. I never took a class. But I can type pretty quickly, now, all these years later. Seven days later, I was up at 3:30 a.m. and on the road at 4:00. I got to the radio station, and Rick gave me all of the area newspapers, and said, "Now this is what we do. You take the top stories. You also listen to the competitors. You call the local police. And you paraphrase what you see, Facts only. You do not ever, ever put your personal spin on any of this. You might be for capital punishment, but you never let that leak into your writing of the news. You might be too young to remember *Dragnet*, but Jack Webb would say, 'Just the facts, ma'am'. That is what you do."

Pretty soon, I had to also write sports. I knew nothing about sports, other than boxing, because that was my father's favorite sport, and I also grew up in the era of the Steelers Iron Curtain, and in fact, met several of those players, and have the autographs to prove it. The training camp was 15 miles or so away from me while growing up. After the third Superbowl win, I lost interest. Rocky Bleier and Jack Lambert were my favorites, and I met Rocky, a true American hero, a couple times.

The big Pittsburgh team now, was the Penguins. I was assigned the task of speaking to team members to get what was called a "soundbite." This is when I would either call one of them and ask a question, or wait for them to call us, as they called all the stations, and they talked about last night's game, and I would use a quote under one minute for the sports section of the news. This would be an example of a sound bite: "Yeah, last night we slammed that puck into the net, and gave it all we got." I regularly had to listen to these guys, many of whom had thick French-Canadian accents, and try to capture one 60 second or less quote from them.

Since I was not a star struck fan, it did not faze me that I was talking to any of these players. I spoke regularly to one player who was the same age as I, named Mario. He had a very thick accent when he first started playing. After a year in our city, he was speaking very well. I was more concerned with getting the quotes, and then the arduous task of editing the tape. We hand to manually edit the reel to reel tapes.

I did this with a straight edge razor, and then used the razor blade to cut the audio tape, and then used the razor to cut the scotch tape to tape the underside of the audio tape to "splice" it. This was obviously back in the old days before digital. We had to do some creative things. This definitely was a better education than the broadcasting school was providing for me.

I finally got to do some on air announcing of my own news stories about three months into my time at this radio station, after Rick decided that my diction was sufficiently cleaned up. I now am very careful not to say "Down 'air," unless I am being sarcastic 'n 'at. There are very humorous books devoted to "Pittsburghese," and I hope that I am not ever guilty of speaking in that manner any longer.

I was relegated to the 5:00 a.m. and 5:30 a.m. newscasts, and a local police officer who sat across from our radio station would wave at me while I was on the air, so I knew for certain that I had one listener.

There was a female announcer who worked the afternoon shift who became a mentor, and also in a personal way. She taught me a lot about the business, and also shared with me that she was a practicing Buddhist. I went with her to a few meetings, and although, I was not interested in any organized religion, I took some of the concepts of this faith and philosophy, and it has served me, even to this day. The basic chant that is used to ground you, and keep you focused, is integral in keeping you focused on what makes the universe hum. That ability to focus is also is a key element in one of the therapies that I use in practice today—it proposes that everything is connected in one way or another.

I also picked up another job at a convenience store right near the radio station. This was short lived. Initially when I was hired, I was hired under the agreement that I would work second shift, as I worked at the radio station from to 5 a.m. to 1 p.m. I often stayed over to edit tapes, so I planned to go across the street to the convenience store after work. Shortly into my stint there, I was informed my shift would be 11:00 p.m. to 7:00 a.m. I lasted a week. I saw quite a few characters: drug dealers, prostitutes, shoplifters. The store manager said, "I want you to guard that cash register with your life." I decided that I would rather guard my life in more interesting ways.

After I became a paid staff, even though it was only minimum wage, a new station manager came on board. The on air jocks did not like him. He snapped his fingers at me once. I told my father about this, and my father was appalled, as he said that no employer should ever snap his fingers: "You are not a dog." This manager changed the rules daily. The manager started making cracks at me, such as, "In the future, I am only going to look at hiring people with college educations."

The next step came when Rick came to me and leveled with me, and said, "Here is the number for the station manager at WIDK[2]. It is five miles away, if you go out here and make a right at our light. I asked what this was all about, and he said, "Look, this station manager is being an ass. He is hiring some interns from Point Park College. He wants people from his alma mater. He is really big on only wanting college graduates. We tried to go to bat for you. We really did. I am going to call Jim Jackson and give him the heads up. In the meantime, you send him an air check, and resume."

Resume? How do I make up a resume? I waited until Kathy, the afternoon drive deejay, came in and asked her about resumes. She pulled one out of her tote bag. "Here. Take this as a guide," she said. "I always carry several with me." I asked her why, and she said, "You never know when you are going to be let go, or, when you might meet someone

---

[2] Not this station's real call letter's nor any known station's call letters

who will want your resume. Always have one on hand." I learned an important lesson early in life: never get too comfortable.

I was not happy about this at all. I am sure if this change had not been forced on me, however, I might have remained there indefinitely, like the cartoon character, sweeping up the elephant crap. So I went home, and, using Kathy's resume as a reference, I created a resume for myself. I then sent it in to WIDK, and within a week, I herd from Jim Jackson, the general manager. He called me in for an interview.

I went to the radio station dressed in a typical 1980's suit: it was day-glow yellow, with large shoulder pads. Yes, my hair was also "big" and long, and by now was sort of back to brown. I had dyed it brown several months earlier, but was not aware that just dying bleached hair brown could cause it to turn green (due to lack of pigment). So I had to re-dye it red, and then dye that dark brown. So it was now a faded brown, and my real dark brown hair was growing in. It was also very frizzy. This was way before straighteners existed for the general public.

I was directed to sit in the waiting room. The waiting room had a view of the studio, which was more spacious that the last radio station where I had worked. This was still not the "big time" by any means, but I was still excited to be getting an opportunity to be in this field. In was 18, and trying to break into the field I wanted to work in.

The show that was on the air was an interesting one, as it was obscure oldies. The jock on the air had a tight polyester suit, and no shirt, and gold chains. He had a female with him whose job was to sit on his lap and giggle, and fawn over him. I sat and watched this spectacle, and then a distinguished gentleman, with grey hair came out and said, "Candace, Jim Jackson, nice to meet you!" He ushered me into his office and told me that he was impressed with my resume and air check and that he also spoke with Rick. I was not confident at all back in those days, and my confidence had taken a beating having just come from a place where it was stressed that someone with a college education was highly favored over me.

I could not believe that anyone frankly would want me. I also felt that way about myself personally, but that is because I was starting to feel tired, and sick. I was just not feeling good. If I had any medical knowledge, it would have even seemed like depression. I accepted the job offer and worked at this radio station as a "board operator" on weekends. It was a dawn to dusk station, meaning that FCC regulated it to be on air from sunup to sundown. Naturally this changed with the seasons, the longer the days were, the longer we were on the air.

I was at times the only one in the studio on the weekends. It was a very creepy place. It was located in a very old shopping mall with attached parking garage, and subsidized apartments were above. Once while doing my top of the hour station break announcement (e.g. "This is WIDK, it is 2:00 p.m., the temperature is 31 degrees"), I heard a chainsaw in the apartment above me. I was the board operator, announcer, secretary, janitor, plumber (we had clogs a lot).It was one of those "what..and leave showbiz?" situations for sure. I also was in charge of editing commercials while the pre-taped broadcasts were on the air. I used the good, old straight edge razor technique I had learned.

I did not love the job, but I was skilled at keeping the station on the air, and making sure it got off the air at night, which was important when you have the dawn to dusk rule. I continued to send out air check tapes and my resume to every station in the area, and remained hopeful, and stayed there for a year

In the fall of 1986, 1 began to lose my voice a lot, which is not a desirable thing to have happen when you have radio aspirations. I also had terrible aching joints, and seemed as if I had a cold that I could not shake. I had smoked cigarettes all through my teen-age years, maybe about 15 a day. I quit smoking thinking that my "cold" would eventually go away.

I began to notice while working my restaurant job, that I hurt severely at the end of a shift, as I worked at night, for the dinner crowd. I had what felt like arthritis. The arthritis started in the hands, and the lower back, and then the shoulders. When I woke up in the mornings, my bones ached terribly. I started telling myself that this was a normal part of getting "older." I also started noticing pain in the thoracic region of my back, and a deep, hacking cough, which had not abated even after I gave up cigarettes.

My secret was that since I had become "drug free," I had also stopped taking my thyroid pill. I wanted to be completely drug free. I did not want to put any drugs in my body. I had read some articles about how the thyroid could be healed naturally. That does not apply to someone like me who was born with hypothyroidism. I was off my synthetic thyroid hormone for about a year. I took no medication, other than an aspirin or maybe cold medicine for the increasing cold like symptoms that seemed to be occurring more frequently.

My family members, particularly my mother, and sister, two people who never minced words, began to confront me and flat out say that I looked like hell. My skin color was getting, as my mother referred to it, "sallow." They insisted that I see a doctor. I did not want to go to our family doctor. I frankly did not like our family doctor. He did not have a nice bedside manner, and he was a doctor, much like in my childhood, who focused greatly on weight.

I was 5 foot 4 as a young woman. I struggled all through my teenage years with weight, and forced myself to stay slim. At 130 pounds, he would tell me that I was too heavy. Now, after a year of not taking my thyroid pill, I was up to 150 pounds. This was not a doctor that I wanted to see, especially now, when I knew something was wrong. I avoided as much as I could. I understand denial very much, as this was a severe case. I just kept hoping that my severe "flu" would go away. It would not for a very long time.

Chapter 4 - It's Just Pneumonia

The first time I sought medical help for my "flu" symptoms was in November 1986. This was for my recurrent bouts of laryngitis and the aforementioned hacking cough. With my radio aspirations, this was affecting my dreams of moving toward independence. There was also joint pain, but I did not bother to tell the Emergency Room doctor that. In the small town where I lived, there were three hospitals, and I chose to go to one of the closest. I was prescribed a codeine based cough syrup and an antibiotic. I was off work for a couple days, and coughed a lot. I had a fever.

It was at this time that I consciously began to isolate people, because I sounded bad, and I was tired of hiding my appearance. I did not like friends just dropping in, because putting on makeup was a big deal. Many of my friends were in college (some were close by in branch campuses, and some would come home on breaks), but if they would stop by unannounced, I would tell my mom, "Tell them I am at work." I had open sores that had to have a lot of preparation. I went to great pains to cover them. I did not mention this to the doctor at the E.R., either.

This antibiotic and cough syrup chased away the symptoms for a few weeks, but the symptoms came back, and weight loss continued. I also neglected to tell anyone—my family, or the E.R. doctor whom I saw; that the last time I took thyroid pill (my dose at the time should have been .125 mcg per day) was late 1985.

In late December, 1986, it felt like I pulled a shoulder muscle, and I could not lift my left shoulder. I saw a doctor in the E.R. He X-Rayed it, and said that it looked like arthritis. I also told him about the cough, and he said it was bronchitis. I got some cough syrup with codeine. He told me it would also help with the shoulder pain.

In January 1987, my mom, being hypothyroid since 1967, and also being very blunt, said, "What's wrong with you? You've let yourself go. Are you taking your thyroid pill?" This was the woman who raised me not to tell a lie. But I was pretty good at omission of truth. "Why?" I asked. "Because you look like shit, Candy. Look at you. My God. Your skin is a mess. You plaster on pancake makeup. Your hair has been dyed, okay, it's dried out from being every color of the rainbow, but even so, it used to have a shine. It looks like witches hair. You're bloated, even though you've lost weight. You can't fool me. And you're walking around here as slow as molasses." This is the only time we were direct--when insults were involved, and man, did this insult me! I could deny it. But she was right. "Okay. I will call Dr. Gotti," I said, "But I don't like him."

He was chosen as our family doctor because my family knew his father. My parents admitted, "He's not like his father. His father is nice." But we still went. Doctors were Gods. And in our small towns, if you did not have an education, you didn't question people who did.

I called Dr. Gotti, and he called back late in the day, and was very rude to me. I explained what was going on: the joint pain, the hoarseness, and the skin problems. He was curt, abrupt. I told him I did not have any thyroid pill refills. He told me he could not phone in a refill unless he physically saw me. He then added, "I should charge you for this phone visit."

His earliest appointment was early February 1987. My father took me. My weight was down. I think I did weigh 135. But he did comment about my weight being "up." I was coughing constantly, and had to stand for about 20 minutes in a scalding hot shower due to the pain that all of the increasing joints in my body were suffering.

Dr Gotti mentioned that he was prescribing me the thyroid pill in a higher dose, being that my weight was "up," and since I was coughing, and had swollen joints. "By the end of the month, you should feel like yourself again." He then asked, "Did you learn your lesson?" I said, "Yes?" between coughs. My father was asked if he had any questions. Even though my mom and dad usually did not ask questions, my dad asked, "Do you really think this is just thyroid? I mean, she has been coughing, I mean literally barking like a dog for months." The doctor just laughed reassuringly, "Yes, she just needs to know that you can't stop taking thyroid pills. Once you're on it, you're on it for good. Okay? Now go home. Get some rest."

By the end of February, I was no better. I was worse. I was still, as my dad put it, "barking." I was now coughing up pink tissue. I had missed so much work from both jobs, that I called both bosses, and told them that I would like to take a leave, because I had a "flu" that was taking inordinately long to get rid of. Both bosses were very nice, and asked if there was anything they could do. My radio station boss sent flowers, perfume, and many notes of encouragement. I still have the little card that came with the flowers somewhere. My restaurant boss also told me anytime I would like to come back, to let him know.

I now was in bed all the time. This became somewhat accepted by the family. The door to my bedroom was closed. I was retaining urine, and I was glad about this (not knowing that this was a sign of my kidneys failing), because getting out of bed was torture. I dreaded having to walk the three feet across the hall to the bathroom. I could barely walk. My joints were swollen. I sweated horribly. My mom brought a tray in daily, and banged it on a table—she was just very angry that I was not getting better. It held pills (thyroid pill, antibiotics, cough syrup, water, and some toast with margarine to soak it all up). I was turning into a bag of bones. My dad, who was working different shifts with a trucking company, would bring home a burger and fries, or other meal. They were trying to take care of me, and must have been utterly horrified.

My dad would knock on the door. Timidly he would say, "If you don't get up and walk, I am afraid you are going to get so weak, you won't anymore."

My mom turned angry. She knew something was very wrong. I think she was very angry because this doctor was also someone she trusted, and he told her "give it time," every time she called him. She now tells me that was the response she got every time she would call, and she would say, "Does it take this long for thyroid pills to start working? And this coughing does not seem like thyroid!" But her anger was sometimes displaced at me.

On March 1, my mom demanded that my father take me to the emergency room of the hospital that Dr. Gotti was affiliated. She even packed a bag. She said, "I do not want her back here. He has to see how sick she is." This began a curious period of being referred to by my parents while I was present as "she" and not even being consulted anymore. No more "what do you want?" I was now relegated again to child status, or as a person who had no rights or could no longer make decisions. My mom was angry and in action mode. I did not want to go to the hospital. "I am not going to the hospital." Her answer, "I don't give a shit. You are not staying here like this anymore." Again, I am not angry. Remember, we did the best we could.

This was a Sunday evening when my dad took me in to the emergency room (this was before HMO's when we used the E.R. as our doctor's office) and it was a skeleton crew. They X-rayed the lungs and saw that I had some sort of lower lobe infiltrate. The doctor on duty contacted Dr. Gotti and aid that Dr. Gotti wanted to talk to me and to my father. We both got on the phone. Dr. Gotti sternly said, "Candy, why didn't you take the medicine I gave you?" My dad said, "She has been taking the medicine since February 1st everyday!" he said, "Excuse me. I am talking to your daughter." I said, "I am taking the thyroid pill." He said, "No. No. NO! Not the thyroid pill! I mean the pills for your lungs. This is why you're not better. Well I guess it doesn't matter now. You have pneumonia now." My dad and I just looked at each other. Luckily, my dad had been there when the doctor had prescribed the pill a whole month earlier. I told him that there were no pills for my lungs. He insisted that there were. The doctor in the E.R. just shook his head, and wrote out something with the name "Tussin" and "L.A." at the end. Dr. Gotti said that I should go home with the pill and I should be "all better after taking this pill." They also did still send me home with more codeine syrup and more antibiotics.

We were not thinking about lawsuits back then. There were not commercials that had lawyers pointing fingers at the television promising to get money for you, and telling you all about your medical malpractice rights. Plus, as I said, if you were not formally educated, you just did not think of questioning people who were.

When we came back home, my mom hit the roof. She swore, and felt that my father and I did not assert ourselves. I was so tired, and worn out, I just had to lie down, My father explained, in vain, what happened over the phone, with the doctor. I was so worn out from the trip to the hospital. I just wanted to lie down. My book at the time was an autobiography by Tina Turner. This woman, who had a dream, lived through illnesses, abuse, poverty, racism, and came out proud and fierce, inspired me. I needed to keep my mind occupied with brain fuel like that at a time like this.

I began to self-blame. I had not had a cigarette in about six weeks, but I took my pack out of my purse (I was always a one or two cigarette a day person) and immediately threw it in the garbage can. I caused this, I thought. Then I began to think about that attack back when I was a teenager. Maybe this is really AIDS. It was still a disease that was misunderstood, and I knew that the perpetrator had a drug history, which involved needles. I pushed that thought out of my head. I read a little of my book. It was seven at night. I slept for twelve hours.

My mom was so angry. She would bring my tray in, and now was not speaking to me. The tray had tea, water pitcher, all the pills (thyroid, aspirin, antibiotics, the lung pills) and some toast. I had my day planned out so that I could limit my trips to the bathroom. It was about four feet away, but those four feet were agonizing. My joints were swollen to at least three times their size. I had a system. I would roll out of bed, and crawl to the bathroom. I would use the other bathroom in my parents' bedroom to take my hot shower, because I could stand in the hot shower. I began to realize that I was losing hair by the clumps. No one saw me do this. No one was home during the day. My dad got angry a week later, and came in and said, "This is pneumonia. If youkeep laying here, you'll never get better, now you have to get up."

My dad had lost a job of twenty-five years about three years earlier, so he was now working for a trucking company that had him working many strange hours and days. His days off now were Sundays and Wednesdays. He was home Wednesday when he came in and said that I needed to get up and get in the bathtub. He insisted that baths were good for the steam factor and good to soak. I did my systematic roll and crawl. He was appalled.

I wondered how on earth people survived pneumonia if it was this horrible. I asked if he could help me in the bathtub. He said absolutely not. I had avoided the bathtub for months, and did showers, because I knew I did not have the strength to raise myself in and out of the tub. The bathroom had a large, full-length mirror. My parents' shower had no such thing. I took my clothes off, and that is when I saw the most shocking thing. I have never seen my body that thin and emaciated, even when I was consciously depriving myself of food as a younger teen. My muscle tone had completely wasted. My skin was completely gray. My weight was probably about 105. I counted every rib. Bones stuck out everywhere. Backbones, shoulder blades, hipbones, open sores. I looked like one of the figures that were on the special I had seen on PBS about the Holocaust. I felt like I was going to throw up.

I wished my dad could help; he called in and asked if I was ok. I told him, "I feel so weak, Dad." He said, "Pneumonia is like that. You're going to feel weak." I had the water so hot that steam was rising from the top. I got down on the floor and pulled myself over the tub, one limb at a time. It hurt, especially as my bones were sticking out. But the heat of the water did feel good.

After I was clean, I put my right arm outside of the tub, then my left arm, then hung my torso out then pulled my hips out then threw my legs out, so that I could literally fall out onto the floor. My dad heard the thud. "Are you alright in there?" Inside I was screaming." "Yes. I am fine." Again, I looked at my body. I had no breasts. I had blisters and sores all over my faces, all along my hairline, on my back, chest, legs, and tailbone. My teeth were also wiggling in my gums. My hair was falling out. I realized I was probably dying. This was not pneumonia. Pneumonia is something that you hear about pretty regularly. People do not look like this with pneumonia, I told myself.

This experience of taking a bath really took all of my energy away. I went back to my room, wearing one of my wraparound robes (raising my arms to put on T-shirts hurt) and I turned on my little 12" black and white television. It only got two channels, but I liked that TV. I watched (or more accurately, listened to) *The Honeymooners*, a new talk show named *Oprah*, old episodes of *Bewitched*, *I Dream of Jeannie*, and old cartoons.

By the end of that horrific week, I was absolutely no better, despite this new pill that was supposed to chase away the pneumonia. For the weekend, there was a friend of the family in town, visiting. Barry was a childhood friend of my father. He was the local neighborhood boy who really made something of himself, according to my dad. He also lost his parents at a young age, just like my dad. But he chose to go to college. He went to the school of mortuary science, and developed a very successful practice in the suburbs of Detroit. Once when I was a teenager, we had visited him. It always kind of freaked my parents out, but it fascinated me what this guy did for a living.

Barry was now divorced, and I could hear him, his new girlfriend, and my parents out in the living room. He knocked on the door. He came in and said, "Your parents tell me you have a bad case of pneumonia? No way kid. You look like something else is going on here." He asked what else was going on. I tried to hide my face, which was covered with open wounds. I buried my head in the pillow, and told him, "You know, joints are hurting, tired, it's like the flu." He said, "I don't want to be the next guy you visit. I told them you need a second opinion. Don't mess with these hospitals around here. Get to Pittsburgh, ok? Take it easy kid. You'll be fine. You're too young to give up." He then said I was welcome to join them for dinner. I remember telling him I would take a rain check, knowing full well two things: that I would royally piss my parents off if I accepted, and that it would be an impossibility to get up, find anything to wear (I had not worn shoes in weeks as I wore slippers to the E.R., and make this face look presentable). I did appreciate his kindness.

He turned the light off and the room was blue from my little black and white flickering television. The door opened again. My mom said curtly (she was still angry), "We're going out. We'll be back later." Back to blue light. After I heard the diesel engine of Barry's Mercedes pull out of the drive, I decided to get out of bed, and take a shower, hoping the hot water would help. I also was determined that I needed to be active and stop lying in this bed. It had already been close to six weeks since I had been here.

I went to my parents' shower. I made the water scalding hot and stepped in. When I bent my head back, I noticed that the arthritis must have been in my neck now. All the discs in my neck hurt, and this was new. It hurt to move my head back to the upright position. Clumps of hair continued to fall out each time I showered. Visions of that movie *The Fly* continued to haunt me, as I was bleeding from all the sores, all over my hairline (which would cause my hair to become clumpy and matted) and neck, back, chest, and face. My legs also had these sores. I did accomplish getting clean, which was very important to me. I could not stand if I was not clean, even if it drained me of all energy. All through my illness and recovery, this remained sometimes the only goal I might accomplish during the day.

I wrapped myself in a flannel nightgown; about two sizes too large now, shivered, and went back to bed. It was about 9:00 p.m. About three hours later, I awoke to my parents' and Barry's voices. I started to drift off again, when I saw red lights flashing outside my bedroom window. This is either the police, or ambulance I thought. Adrenalin kicked in, and suddenly, all the pain in my body was gone. Ok, who called the frigging ambulance? Was it Barry? He has some medical training and he knows what is wrong, so he did it. How can I escape? Maybe I can climb out the window? I got up. Hey! I can sit up straight! No pain! I looked out. Shit, it is an Emergency rescue Ambulance. I am going to run. I heard two male voices and a female voice. They will catch me. I got back under the covers. I will pretend I am dead. I was shaking. I will resist. I am nineteen, and an adult. No one can make me go to the hospital. What is the worst that can happen? My mom will throw my ass out. Big deal. She is already treating me like shit. I will go on welfare and live in the projects. I don't care.

I heard the voices, "Take it easy. You're gonna be OK." Then it registered. They were not here for me. Then who was it? My door opened, the crack of light shone through my pitch-black room. My mom's curt voice said, "We're going to the hospital. Barry had a heart attack." The door closed, taking the crack of light with it." I heard the engine of the EMS vehicle, sounding like a semi, and the diesel Mercedes, and they were all gone. I turned on my television to get a sense of what time it might be. Jan Hooks and Phil Hartman were on, so it was after midnight.

I still had a surge of adrenalin and my heart was pumping. I got up, walked around. I smelled cigarettes. Barry and his girlfriend smoked. I had been coughing up blood and bits of pink tissue all week. I did a disgusting thing. I smoked a butt that had hardly been touched. It had been many weeks since I enjoyed a cigarette. There was a dent in the wall, and it occurred to me—this must be where Barry fell. There were a lot of dishes, and I filled the sink with scalding, soapy water. I did the dishes. I stayed up, with my eyes wide open all night. I had this sudden fear that I might die if I fell asleep. The magnitude of how sick I was finally hit me.

My parents arrived home at 4:00 a.m. They saw that my light was on, so my mom came in. She was talking to me, instead of yelling or speaking in her curt, angry tones. She said, "Barry had a heart attack after dinner." I asked if he fell in the living room. She said, "Yes." She thanked me for doing the dishes. She said they were sitting there after dinner, talking, and he got up to get a glass of water, and fell against the wall. His girlfriend said, "Call 911!" Mom also said, "Barry thinks we need to get you to a different hospital but I think Dr. Gotti needs to see how sick you are, and he knows you best. So tomorrow, or later today, I am having Dad take you back to the hospital here since you're not any better."

I wasn't arguing. I was not better. I wanted to get back to work. I had dreams. I did not know how to assert myself about doctors, or medical problems. I figured if this medicine I was on did not work, then another round would work. My dad and I made yet another trip to the hospital's E.R. about 4:00 that afternoon. My dad did most of the talking. He explained that we were here one week ago and that I had not gotten any better. I was again sent to have a chest X-ray, and sent to wait behind a curtain.

I was met with a different doctor. He was pleasant, and said, "You have a really bad case of pneumonia, kid. What I'm going to do is give you a narcotic, which will quiet the cough plus take care of the joint pain, and a heavy-duty antibiotic. Give it another week, and you'll be as good as new." I believed him, and did not think to question him or any other doctor.

I hobbled out to the waiting room, as all my joints were now hurting and swollen. My dad said, "What room are you in?" I told him what happened. He drove me home without one word. When we got home, and my mom looked at me, she screamed, "What in the hell is she doing back here?" I just went back to my room. I felt like a hot potato that was being passed around. I had no control over this. I was telling the doctors exactly what was going on at this point, and was being told that this was "pneumonia." I continued to think that pneumonia must be the most horrible disease on the planet.

My mom came in, opened up the suitcase that she had packed, and threw all the clothes that she packed. She was angry that I was not admitted, but why was she angry with me? I got up to use the bathroom, and heard my mom talking on the phone with my sister. "She's getting paid back for all the drugs and her diets. Oh I know it's a miracle it didn't happen sooner. Well, if she wants to stay here and die, she's crazy. I'll put her in a home. I can't take care of her." I lay there that night, wondering if everyone who had "bad pasts" such as mine—and really, mine was not so bad, ended up getting big "paybacks" (as my mom had said) , with illness, like mine. Although, I had not been an angel, in recent years, I had turned my life around. I did not drink, I last smoked marijuana in 1983 (this is still true) and I wanted to work, and move on with my life.

My father and I were the only people home the next day, as my mom was at a Tupperware party. I stayed in my room, as I knew to stay "out of the way." I was seen as a leper. One of my aunts had even called and suggested I may have leprosy. My father was in charge of guarding Barry's Mercedes and possessions. This made him nervous, as his watch and car, were worth close to what our house's worth was.

The beginning of the new week, two days after the last E.R. visit, my mom came in, and said, "I called Dr. Gotti, and told him about that dumb E.R. doctor. He thinks he was wrong. You're being admitted at 4:30 today. Your dad is at work, so be ready when he gets home. Get a shower and put on clean pajamas."

She left the house at 9:00 a.m. This gave me over seven hours to get ready. It was March 9, 1987. I was very sick by this time. Despite having been on oral antibiotics and narcotics for weeks, little had helped. I now had a bed rest and pillows propped up in my bed because I could no longer lie flat, or I would choke on fluid that was somehow coming out of my lungs. Also I had to support my neck when I slept, because the arthritis in my neck was causing pain all the way down my spine. My feet were swollen to about three times their normal size, and had turned purple. When I fell asleep, it was almost as if I became unconscious. I would take would what feel like little catnaps, and wake up three hours later.

I heard Oscar and Felix arguing on my television, then fell asleep, then I heard the new talk show hostess named Oprah talking, woke up

56

a little longer, and I still could not wake up. I would wake up for a few minutes, and then doze for hours. My father was home at three, and was alarmed, "Why aren't you ready?" I told him I was trying, and he was annoyed. "Go get in the shower and get different clothes on. Put on pajamas, c'mon!"

I went into their bathroom where the shower is, and tried to lift my arms, but they were so stiff from the arthritis. I asked if he could help. He said, "No, you have to do that yourself. I am not helping you dress." It took me about ten minutes to get the pajama top off." He did slip some clothes in that would be easier to put on, without me raising my arms, as I told him through the door what was taking me so long. I was able to wear his pajamas (huge) and a wrap around robe.

I could not put on any shoes. My feet looked like purple balloons. I showed them to my dad. He did not show any shock. He said, "Well, We will have to put two pairs of my work socks on you." My father was incredibly calm in these life and death situations, probably because of what he had to go through as a young man, losing his parents and fending for himself. I think he realized the magnitude of how sick and in pain I really was, when he saw the condition of my feet.

Now the real challenge began, which was walking down the stairs to get out to the car. My father was at the bottom waiting. I tried to bend my legs, but could not. I finally grabbed on to the banister, hoisted my body down, sat down, and bounced down, very gingerly, one step at a time. "What are you doing" my dad asked. I told him that I could not walk. He finally picked me up and now just carried me out to the car. He said nothing the whole way to the hospital. His face looked extremely worried.

When we got to the registration department, there were some cheerful, older ladies. They asked if I wanted my admission date published in the local papers. I said that I absolutely did not. I was a direct admission, and on the first floor. It was a dark room, and there were four people in my room. This was my first inpatient admission. It was culture shock. My dad sat with me in the room for a while. Finally he spoke. "See, you should have had this taken care of earlier. It got out of hand." I did not argue back. Over the next several days, this would be the consensus, as it was still thought that my diagnosis was "pneumonia."

Chapter 5 - You Did This To Yourself

The first night, I was given tests for tuberculosis, and had my blood drawn ten times, once from the wrist. I asked what the blood work was, and I was always told, whenever I had any test, "Ask Dr. Gotti." I was in Small Town Hospital four and a half days, and saw Dr. Gotti twice, for about 10 minutes.

The second day I was there, I was told I was being sent down for " a test." The words "Ultrasound" were on the door. When I got there, the woman said, "Did you drink the water?" I said, "I had some water this morning." She picked up a phone, and said, "I have 1B here and she hasn't had any water, what the hell is this? We have a schedule here. Now we'll have to be backed up because of this shit." She then got off the phone, and said, "You have to drink two quarts of water. Here!" I asked what this was for. Her answer was, "Ask Dr. Gotti." I said, "I just want to know what all the water is for," She exclaimed with a large sigh, "To extend your bladder, ok? Then we take pictures of it."

I drank it, although it was ice cold, and very uncomfortable. She kept saying, "C'mon, you need to hurry. I am already backed up because of this." As I was drinking, she was looking through my chart, and saying, "Jesus Christ. Holy Shit." I said, "What?" And she said, "Oh. I can't say nothin' about your chart. You have to ask your doctor." She then saw my demographics and saw what my mother's name was and mentioned that she grew up with my aunt, and continued to say, "Jesus Christ, what a shame to be this sick."

An hour later, I was taken to a department called CT scan. A woman came to me and handed me a big cup, about 16 ounces, of a chalky liquid, and told me that I need to drink it. I asked her why. "Ask

Dr. Gotti." By this time, I had to urinate. I was left out in the hallway to wait to be wheeled back to my room. I saw a person in the hall, and tried to get their attention, because I thought they might be able to help me to the restroom. I said, "Excuse me?" The person kept walking. Three more people did the same thing. I had to wait until noon when I was wheeled back to my room, and then a nurse's aid helped me into the restroom. It was then that I noticed that I was urinating a dark brown colored fluid.

That was my first full day in the hospital. I was not permitted to eat until dinner due to all the tests, and I still had no answers to any of my questions about what all the tests were, and all I was told was "You have pneumonia," or "Ask Dr. Gotti." Every time I would dose off, I would be woken up to have more blood drawn. I learned to stop asking what it was for. My cough was getting much worse, and it was producing mucous, blood, and visible tissue. My feet were round on the tops and bottoms (something, I later learned is called "edema"). On the 3:00 to 11:00 shift, a male nurse's aid, came in and loudly clapped his hands, just as I was about to finally take a much-needed rest. "C'mon, get up. You can't sleep. Dr. Gotti said you have to move, you are being lazy! This is only pneumonia. I want to see you do three laps around this ward." I said, "I can't walk. Look at my feet." He said, "You have pneumonia. You are able to walk; I don't see anything on your chart about your feet. Let me look."

He looked at them and said, "Oh my God. Let me tell a nurse." A nurse came in and looked at them. She said, "Honey, did you tell Dr. Gotti about this?" I told her how when I saw him in February, I explained the joint pains, and also how it hurt to be on my feet at work, and that they would swell, and how I again explained them when I spoke to him on the phone in the E.R. on March 1st, and how I explained them every time I went to the E.R. She started asking me questions about urinary problems, some of them related to dark urine. I told her that I did notice today it was very dark and that when I was at home, I sometimes did not go all day. Maybe she was on to something? She said she was going to "note all this in the chart for Dr. Gotti," who still had not been in to see me.

Later that evening, maybe around 6:00 p.m. after typical hospital food, (liver, peas, cake) my father visited. My mom did not. She still was angry. The anger was about my waiting to see a doctor, still and that I "brought this on myself." Dr. Gotti also finally came in. He was very curt, rude. He said, Candace, Your father can stay or leave. I asked that he leave. Dr. Gotti looked at my feet first. "How long have they been like this?" I told him for about two weeks." He asked why no one told him. I told him that I did tell the E.R. doctor on Sunday. He looked royally pissed. He listened to my lungs. He tapped on them, then had me breathe deep, then breathe shallow. He looked at my face, chest, and back. The open wounds were all over. He asked how long the wounds had been there. I told him they had begun in the fall but in the past six weeks they had stopped healing. He asked if he could see the rest of my skin. There was one behind my right ear that was very bad, that would eventually eat away at my earlobe. It continually drained and my hair was matted with dried blood. He could barely hide his shock.

He said, "This could have been avoided by one simple thyroid pill. You know that?" He then said, "I am going to ask you some social history questions, because there may be other things going on here. Do you drink? I told him that I do not. He asked if I ever did. I was honest and told him yes, "How much?" I told him that from ages 13 to 17, I was a regular weekend drinker, and even on weeknights, sometimes, I drank to get drunk. I quit on my own, never had withdrawal, shakes, DT's. He asked about drugs, and I was honest. I told him I smoked marijuana from ages 13 to 16, last smoked in 1983. He asked about other drugs, and I told him about the "speed" (which was likely caffeine or Dexedrine pills) that went around that I used for weight loss and that I last used also around 1983. I had no intravenous drug use.

He got to sexual history, and I froze up. The truth is, I had a fear about AIDS in my mind because of that rape back on New Year's Eve, 1983. Every time my mom or sister, or this doctor said, "You did this to yourself," I thought that this was my fault. If only I had not been at the wrong place at the wrong time that night. He looked at me. He may have been rude and condescending, but he said, "Candace, did someone ever force himself on you?" I said, "Do I have to answer these questions?" He said, "I have to know everything. We need to make a diagnosis." I stopped talking. He then said, "I am ordering more tests, including HIV." With that, he walked out. I got no more answers.

My dad came back in, and asked if I was all right, and asked what the doctor said. I just said, "More tests." The nurses came in and helped me to get to the bathroom, and I was now requiring full assistance walking, as I was now on an I.V. antibiotic. I asked if I could take a shower, and I was denied this, as there was no shower in the room, but was offered a sponge bath, and asked to take off these flannel pajamas I had worn from home. The nurse commented that I was wearing underwear. "All dressed up and nowhere to go?" she said. I told her I have always worn underwear to bed. She said, "No, that is not necessary. You have to let it breath down there. She helped me with one deft move, into a hospital gown, another as a robe, with great skill over the I.V. pole, after a sponge bath, that made me feel halfway clean again, and then helped me get some of the tangles from my hair. I was able to lie down and my father had a look of pure sympathy. He said, "Just try to relax. I'll be back tomorrow."

In the middle of that night, I became very hot. A nurse coming to check my vitals said, "Good lord, you are burning up. We are going to have to take your temperature every hour. On the last shift, it was 100. Now it is 102. This is not good." By the time the *Tonight Show* was signing off, which angered one of the nurses that I still was watching ("Turn this off!"), which I then promptly turned back on, my temperature had gone to 106. I now was being packed with ice bags. All night ice bags were placed around my body in bed. I did not understand squat about medicine or the body processes back then. Of course, what was occurring was that I had some sort of infection in my body.

The next morning, the temperature was going down. It was back to 102, one of the nurses informed me. By now, each person that entered my room donned yellow Hazmat looking attire: gloves, a clear mask, goggles, surgical booties, and special scrubs. I was wheeled down to OB/GYN. The doctor was a female, and she was very unfriendly. She said, "I understand I am testing you for AIDS . I said, "I have been sick, and have not shaven in a month. I am Italian." She sarcastically said, "You were born in Italy?" I said, "My ethnicity is Italian," She said, "What about AIDS? Are you with a lot of people?" Her nurse looked at me disapprovingly. I said, "No I am not." She said, "I see you have been pregnant." I told her I have not been. She said, "Your uterus is in the condition that it has either been pregnant or traumatized."

Then she looked at my face. "What is wrong with your face? What happened to it? You look like you might have been a pretty girl at once. Shame." Then she told the nurse, "OK, take her back to her room."

I was put out in the hall in a wheelchair again. It felt as if I had been raped again, but this time, my body, emotions, and character were being raped. It felt to me that judgment was being passed on me. I could tell the professionals what had happened to me. But the miscommunication, I felt had started with Dr. Gotti, and was between my mom, Dr Gotti, and I also felt that what I told Dr Gotti might get back to my mom. I may have been nineteen, but I felt as if I had no adult rights. This was back in the days before HIPAA (Health Information Portability and Accountability Act), so I felt as if I had to be choosy in telling Dr. Gotti things, because she was the one who called him at home, she was the one who told me that I brought this on myself, and the doctor told me this every time he saw me as well.

Later in the afternoon, a team of doctors came in, one identified himself as a pulmonary (or lung) doctor and the other said he was an infection specialist. I was asked a number of strange questions, such as have I recently eaten shellfish, and I said , "I can barely afford fish filet!" I learned at this early junction that having a sense of humor was going to be absolutely necessary, though some professionals saw me as amusing, and some saw me as simply a smartass. I was also asked if I had any exotic birds. Well, my mom had a parakeet. (I got her a half price bird at a local pet store, and the bugger lived for about nineteen years! He/she was half-price because no one at the store knew how old it was!) Had I traveled to any exotic locale? Uh, yeah, the South Side of Pittsburgh. Ok. They determined I did not have any sort of tropical disease. I was just a typical working class kid who occasionally got lucky with the leftovers served at the Chinese restaurant.

Then this team had their nurse explain in this very empathic tone, as she sat down, that they were going to do a procedure right now that would be very painful. It would involve a long needle to drain the pulmonary fluid. It was called a thoracentesis. I found out from the obtainment of old medical records that it was an "exudative character" that revealed "pleural effusion with 70% eosinophils. (In normal blood, eosinophils amount to about 0 to 3 percent of the white blood cells)," This did hurt, having the fluid which was described in the records as being very thick, but it was not as anxiety producing as the CT scan and Ultrasound, because these professionals explained everything to me. I was given a local anesthetic to numb the area, and told to sit up in bed, while the needle went in the right side of my back, very slowly. It felt like pressure, more than pain. The layman's term that they used was "needle biopsy." After this, I went to sleep. No longer was I being told, "get up, it's just pneumonia."

The next morning, began as every morning, with a visit to radiology for a chest X-ray and more blood collection. This would be my routine for the next couple months, and sometimes the blood collections (the phlebotomists themselves referred to themselves as "vampires" although I never did) would occur as often as four times a day, because a specialist might come in, and order more blood. This day, March 12, 1987, a nurse came in, and sat down. She was one of the nicest ones that I recall from this hospital. She was young, maybe 30, her hair was blond, pulled back into a bun, and she had kind, blue eyes. She held my hand. She said, "Today, an oncologist is going to come in and give you a bone marrow biopsy." I asked, "What's an oncologist?" She said, "That's a cancer doctor. He suspects that you have leukemia. This is going to hurt you like probably nothing else you have ever felt. I am going to let you hold my hand or squeeze my arm if you have to, okay?"

I waited, and she came back, and so did a small, Asian man. He said, "Candace! I am Dr. Lim. I am here to give you a biopsy. It is called a bone marrow biopsy. We are doing this test because we think that you might have leukemia, and that it might be very advanced. This is going to hurt like hell. I'm not going to lie. I need you to sign a consent form. With any invasive test like this there's small chance you can die. But I have not had any deaths, okay?" He was a bundle of energy for a cancer doctor. I signed the consent. I did not bother to thoroughly read it. I just wanted this to be over with. I was instructed to lie on my right side. The nurse reminded me, "Now I want you to hold my hand, squeeze my arm." "First I am going to give you a big shot that numbs the area, like at dentist's office ok? I am also going to give you something to relax you, " said the doctor.

My left butt cheek felt like it blew up to three times it size, imagine Novocain in your ass (it is actually lidocaine). The two talked to each other for about ten minutes and flipped through my chart, and used a lot of medical terms that I did not understand, as they were discussing it. They asked me, as they patted and pressed on my butt if it was numb. Finally it seemed pretty numb. He said, "Ok. We are going to do it. Now it is going to feel like a lot of pressure. It is going to hurt going in, and then it is going to feel like someone is sitting on you who is very large." And that is exactly like it felt. The needle was not a standard needle you see when getting blood, but it looked, to my 19-year-old eyes, as I put in my journal, "like a big metal tube." It then felt like a large animal was sitting on my hip and was not letting up. The pain was so severe, it brought tears to my eyes. I did hold the nurses' hand, and she was very compassionate. I looked up at her. For the first time, I felt like I was not being judged, as I had felt ever since I came to that hospital. So far, the nurses had seemed to be blaming me. (I later learned in Sociology class, years later, this phenomenon was called "blame the victim"—something that occurs when people do not know how to respond to a rape or trauma victim. So they blame the victim by saying that she asked for it by wearing tight clothes. Or maybe the AIDS victim deserved to get AIDS because his homosexuality is, after all, a sin)

I remember this nurse to this day. She had kind, blue eyes. She had true compassion and empathy in her eyes. Her hair was bleached blonde. She was pale. She wore a white dress and hose, and shoes. I felt like she did not blame me for any of this. I finally reached out for some of the compassion that was finally being offered that day. She told me something that day that I would hear many times to come. She said, "You are so brave." I had no reply, because I did not feel brave at all. I was doing what was necessary.

I felt very weak, and undeserving of that praise. What was so brave about going through this? I was of the belief that I had caused this condition that I was in. Hadn't I been told this by my doctor, and my mother, and by my sister? I believed them. I believed that if the rape caused AIDS, then it was my fault that I was drinking, and I was in that house that evening. I put myself in that position. I did deserve this. This is not brave. Maybe I have cancer. Maybe I deserve to die, I thought. I became resigned to this fact that I was going to die. It now became a possibility for me. It was no longer a "what if?"

After the procedure was over, I drifted off to sleep, and some nurses came in and were checking my vitals. It was already shift change. I heard one say, "Whatever this is, it's gone untreated too long. She probably will die." I opened my eyes. I asked, "Am I going to die?" The nurse who said it looked surprised that I had heard this and looked at the other, and said, "We all are going to die. It is unfair that some people die sooner." They then left the room.

I drifted back to sleep, and mercifully I was let to sleep until dinner. My mom came to visit at dinner. She was crying. A priest came in. He was very dramatic looking because he had black hair, and a heavy "five o'clock shadow." I was in a Catholic hospital. He came in and had the water shaker and was praying in Latin. He did not stay long. He then said (in English) that he had come to give me the last rites of "our Lord Jesus Christ." He put his hand on my forehead and said that if I am taken, all my sins are forgiven. I started crying.

My mom had some magazines for me and sat with me. Later, my father came, as did my sister, her husband, and her son. I loved her son dearly. This boy, when I look back, got me through so much, and I consider him such a lifesaver when I look back. When I think of what this must have done to see me this way at such a young age, I shudder. I have told him now that he is an adult how much he helped me, and he says, "Hey. Glad I could be there."

My mother's mother, my grandmother, also was brought to visit. She had never been tactful with words, and this occasion was no different. She said, "I came to see you because you're probably going to die and I figured this is it. I better make my peace with you." My father was quite angry. He walked out with her, and I do not know what he said, but she came back in. She was still rather crude, asking about my face, feet, and horrific appearance. My father's sister, Mary, was also there, but she was very respectful, and said, "That's okay honey. You are going to be ok." My sister had a look of horror." My poor nephew just tried to focus on the television. He was only 6.

Everyone else went home but my mom and dad. They told me to pray, and read to keep my mind off things. My mom also told me that the next morning, Dr. Gotti wanted a meeting to make an announcement. My father voiced his displeasure, "You know, she has been here three days, and how many times has this guy been here? Has he answered any questions? This poor girl can't walk. She is in pain. Her feet are blown up like balloons. This is unfair. I want some answers. If we don't get them, I want her somewhere where they will answer us. I am at work tomorrow but if I have to take off, I will! You speak up, Yvonne! I don't want her here like this another week . You use some of that mouth in public."

I remember that evening *Family Ties*, the very popular 1980's show had a special episode where Michael J. Fox's character was grieving a loss, was crying his heart out, and trying to find meaning in his life and. I watched the television, and thought, Buddy, I know how you feel. I went to restroom after this television show; after my dad helped my I.V. pole and I over to the bathroom, and per the order of the staff, had to leave it open a crack, because I was a fall risk. The doctor who performed the biopsy earlier, Dr. Lim opened the door, while I was sitting on the toilet, and said, "Great news! You do not have leukemia!" Then he left. I thought that this is not great news because we still do not know what is wrong.

After the hour long *Family Ties*, the announcement was made that visiting hours were over. My parents left, and the nurses came in and told me that Dr Gotti was coming in with "an announcement" the next day. When I asked what the announcement was, I got the standard, "You'll have to ask Dr. Gotti." After the bone marrow biopsy, I noticed I was treated differently from the staff. More came in just to see how I was. And some looked at me with disgust. Before I would just be check once per shift, and the nurse's aid would tell me to get up because of it being "just pneumonia." Somehow, they seemed to know that this was something more serious. I was beginning to feel somewhat paranoid.

I was seriously fearful that I had AIDS. This was 1987. That very week on the news, I saw a prediction that "By 1990, half of the nation's hospital beds are going to be filled with the latest epidemic, AIDS." Because of the looks of disgust I got from some of the nurses, I felt that perhaps I was being judged. Of course, I had not told the whole story of the rape, so who knows what they thought? Maybe I was viewed as being a slut.

Friday the 13th was the day that Dr. Gotti came in to make his announcement. My mom was told to be there in the morning after 9:00. No nurses came in. My mom and I just sat and waited. We watched television. We talked about the latest gossip magazines. While we waited, two other specialists came in. The first identified himself as a rheumatologist. I cannot remember his name. He said that he felt that whatever may be going on has to do with an arthritic process, and that this is hopeful, because there is medicine that can treat it. He brought along a small, yellow pill that morning. He said that it was an "anti-inflammatory" and it would help my joint pain. He also said he was writing an order so that I could have it even if I don't stay. Don't stay? Was I going home? He then said it, too. "Oh, I am sorry, you're going to have to wait to ask Dr. Gotti." The drug is something that is still prescribed but rarely. I did not expect anything from it, but in an hour, I felt as if I were the Tin Man from *The Wizard Of Oz*, literally, like someone had taken an oilcan to me. I was wiggling my fingers, toes, bending my elbows, and moving, my shoulders.

I told my mom, "I have to go to the bathroom, and I think I am going to walk." She said, "Ooh, Are you sure?" I got up, and as weak as I felt, I did it, one step at a time, slowly, holding on to everything in my path. That yellow pill was a miracle! I felt some small sense of hope.

Another specialist came to see me, a dermatologist. He looked at my face and hairline, and ear. He did not have much to say. He said that he was going to prescribe something, and when I get out of the hospital, he wanted me to see him, that he could treat me. About a year later, when I was feeling very upset about the damaging scarring, he said, when I saw him for a follow up visit, "I am so sorry that you have this scarring. Didn't the cream help at all?" I asked, "What cream?" He explained that he had written an order for Dr Gotti to make sure that a special cream be prescribed to follow me to the larger hospital. "The cream is designed to help prevent scarring. Look, I have the order right here. I am sorry." By this time I had stopped seeing Dr. Gotti. Again, suing did not cross my mind or my family's mind.

Finally, at 11:30 a.m. Dr. Gotti came in, and looked very angry. He said. "We have the results of all the tests, and we are dealing with a mystery here. I think it's all a result of your stubbornness, Candace. I hope you learned a lesson not taking your thyroid pill. Do you know how much damage that can cause? It could cause dementia! You could even have dementia! This is far too advanced for us to treat here, so we must send you to St. Mary's in Pittsburgh. There is an excellent rheumatologist there named Dr. McCollom. If he can't help you, no one can."

My mom was stunned, and said, "Can I drive her?" He said, "No, she is too unstable. Do you want it on you if she dies in your car? Do you know how to resuscitate her? She let this go too far. I mean, this is critical. We have already arranged an emergency transport and it is waiting outside for noon." My mom asked if insurance would cover it. He said most insurances do when "a person is this sick and compromised. Any more questions?" I asked, "Do you know how long I will be there?" He said, "I'll be frank. You are looking at months. You are lucky if you ever get out or even live. And this was your doing. Ok. The ambulance is parked out by the E.R.". I never did like him, which is why I stopped seeing him, and now he was completely judging me, and before he walked out, he said that when I got out of St Mary's hospital I could follow up with him when I returned home. Then he turned on his heel and walked out. I thought, Fat chance. I turned to my mom, and said, "Mom, do you see why I never liked him?" She shook her head, yes.

Chapter 6 - Bed 11-18

At 12:00 p.m. paramedics arrived in my room, with a stretcher. There were three workers: two females, and a male. They were all very close to my age, and were extremely gentle with and attentive to me. They asked if I could walk at all. Since taking that pill about two hours ago, I said that I thought I could. The male said, "We were told you were non-ambulatory." I was learning a whole new language. Ambulatory was not a part of my lexicon three days ago.

I got out of bed, but was weaker than I thought, and my knees buckled. "Whoa, girl," said one of the females, and caught me under my right armpit, and the other got me under the other pit. The male was skillfully lowering the stretcher down. He said, "Now what I will need you to do, is swing one leg up on this stretcher, and carefully get the other one up here, too. We are going to strap you down. Not because you're bad, but we don't want you to fall, ok? This is a rough riding ambulance you are in, and this is not the most comfortable stretcher. Are you cold?" I shook my head yes. They wrapped me from head to toe in several white sheets and blankets, and fashioned a hood over my head with a blanket. The stretcher was jacked up to their level of comfort so that they could push me down the hall. Before we left, my mom asked if she could ride with me. They said that there should not be a problem with this.

My mom had already gone outside and spoken with my sister and nephew who were waiting in my mom's car. She asked Lucy if Lucy would be able to follow us behind the ambulance. This was unusual, as neither Lucy nor I were ever "allowed" to drive my parents' cars. But I guess this counted as a special occasion. I was wheeled past the nurses' station, and none of them said a thing to me. I was very happy to leave this hospital. I literally felt like a leper, from my spotted skin, to the way I was treated by some staff.

I was taken outside, and the ambulance was parked outside the emergency department. The stretcher once again was half lowered, and the collapsible back legs were wheeled in the vehicles rear, and I was positioned so that I was facing the back. There were machines and monitors. I was hooked up to an ECG immediately. I knew what this was, because I had one of these done in the hospital. It involves little suction cups placed on your chest and arms to monitor your heart rate. I still had my ever-present I.V. pole of antibiotics. My mom was looking as if she would break down. I was calm. All I knew was that my butt hurt. I had no padding left, and the stretcher felt like it was made from wood. Pittsburgh was 30 miles away.

It was dark in the ambulance as the back door closed, because the only window in the back came from the back window. One female drove, and a male and female sat in the back with me. Now that we were on our way and all situated, they started talking to each other. They were all talking about their plans for the evening, and about which restaurant served the best shrimp (this was Lenten season and many observed Fish/seafood on Friday in the Pittsburgh area). They asked if I minded the radio. I remember hearing the remake of "Lean On Me," which at the time I did not like at the time (much preferred Bill Wither's version from when I was little in the 1970's). The workers were all singing and laughing. I remember thinking, do they realize how lucky they are to have the choice to go to a restaurant tonight, and to laugh and sing, and not be hooked up to anything?

I had forgotten that my sister was behind us until we were on the Pennsylvania Turnpike. Then I saw her, and waved out the back window. She did not wave back. She just had a strange stare on her face. Her son was busy playing with one of his toys. Later, she revealed to me, that she looked up and saw a figure, clad in a white hood, yellow (I was jaundiced) looking tiny, and did not realize at first that it was me. When she did realize this, she said she almost vomited. Then she remembered she was in our mom's squeaky-clean car, and decided just to focus on the road ahead. She also told her son, Tom, "Don't look in the ambulance, OK?"

This was reality time for everyone. But it was a reality I had known for months. I had just carefully, and now, when I look back on it, selfishly, or maybe more accurately, ignorantly, hidden it. Just as denial is part of the disease of addiction, it was at work, here, too. I was ashamed of my deteriorating skin, and afraid of my joint pain, and tired of the scolding of the doctor that was my only choice as someone who lived under my parents' roof and relied on their insurance. So I hid my symptoms. I guess I thought it would go away, or that I would rather die or fade away than face others or that doctor.

When we finally made it to St. Mary's Hospital, the atmosphere was much different. We were in the city now. I did not have to go through emergency. I was wheeled straight up to the 11th floor, nurse's station. The paramedics left my paperwork, and wished me luck. Everything seemed much more organized. People seemed to know what they were doing. I saw people working there of all colors, and the nurse's station was wide open, not closed off like at Small Town Hospital. A nurses' aid came up to me and smiled. "Hi Candace?" She took the "hood" off, and I felt embarrassed because she would now see my face, and she said, "Come on honey, we will take you to Room 18."

When I got to my room, I looked out the window, and saw a magnificent view of the South Side of Pittsburgh. There was no view at all in my last hospital, and it was so dark. Soon a nurse came in, and told my mother and sister that it was going to be a long afternoon and evening ahead, and that although they are welcome to stay, they would not get to spend much time with me. My sister, mom, and nephew chose to leave, as this had been a long week. They would all be spending many days traveling the 60 mile round trip in the weeks to come.

Two women entered my room. One was in her twenties, and one was maybe late thirties. The one in the late thirties said, "I am Dr. Ramone, and this is Dr. Spallone. I am the chief resident and Dr. Spallone is an intern on your case. We are here to get a history and physical." I nicely explained to them that I had a physical at the other hospital, thank you. Dr. Ramone, who had waist length, red hair, said, "We did not get a very thorough chart from that hospital, and frankly, this is a bizarre case. So we are starting off fresh here." I would hear myself described as "bizarre" many times over the next month and a half, and for now,

I took it in stride, because I just wanted people who knew what they were doing to find what was wrong.

This physical took two hours. Dr. Spallone was very pleasant, smiled, and did state to me that she is "not much older than" I was, and how she "really related" to me for some reason. They were very thorough. Dr. Ramone never cracked a smile, was not friendly, and they had me squeeze their fingers, push them (I had to do this every time I saw my rheumatologist over the next several years) pull their arms apart, walk a straight line, touch my toes, etc. I was informed that I was failing the most simple strength tests.

Dr. Ramone said, "I am getting rid of this I.V. It is not working. You have been on antibiotics since what, two weeks ago, at least?" I was thrilled to be rid of the cumbersome thing. But it was replaced with a catheter. This sucked! I also was informed that I was not producing my own saliva or tears any more. Dr. Ramone said that she was going to order "fake tears" for me, to be administered twice a day that I would have to squeeze in my eyes. I was so weak; that it was difficult squeezing the bottle to get the eye drops in my eyes.

The two doctors asked me if I had any questions. I asked whom this doctor is that I was told I would see. I was sent to this hospital to see a doctor named Dr. McCollom. They said that he is my "primary" and that he is in charge of all of them. "What kind of doctor is he?" I asked. They told me that he is a rheumatologist. Again, this was like learning Spanish. "What does that mean?" They told me "He is a doctor that treats arthritis and other diseases like that." I still was very confused as to how my arthritis might be connected to my thyroid, and now my kidneys. I also asked, "Did I do this to myself?" Both doctors said, almost in unison, "No, it's doubtful." Dr Ramone said, "Why do you ask that?"

I told Dr. Ramone that the doctor at the last hospital told me that from not taking my thyroid pill, I probably caused a lot of damage. I also told her, "I have not been an angel." She said, "What do you mean?" I said, "When I was a teenager, I drank. I did some marijuana. I starved myself to stay thin, and even used diet pills. I even smoked off and on since I was 12 or 13." The younger doctor (Dr Spallone) said, "See I knew I could relate to you. Do you know how many of us in college drank, took diet pills? Didn't eat to stay thin? C'mom. If everyone got as sick as you that did what most normal young people do, the hospitals would be full. I want you to stop blaming yourself. You are a sick young woman. That doctor was wrong to lay that on you. Yes, you were wrong to not take your thyroid pill. I want you to know that you can't ever do that again, okay? But as far as you 'doing this' to yourself? Huh uh. You did no more to yourself than most young American women."

Dr. Ramone told me that she was ordering a "nerve test" for me to take early next morning. I asked if it hurt. She said, "I never order a patient a test that I don't take myself. This did not hurt me. Of course I am healthy and I have meat on my bones. You don't. So it might hurt you. Plus you have a problem with strength and that is why we are ordering it. They will wake you up very early tomorrow and take you down for it. Have a good night."

I lay in bed and turned on my right side, and looked out, and saw the clock that lit up "Strohs"—it was a clock, advertising the beer--- on and off, all night long at that time. The reflection on the water looked so beautiful. I turned on the piped in music, which was the urban R&B station, and I felt like I was in good hands. I felt like I would get out of this hospital alive, whereas in the last place, I honestly had a fear that I would die there.

The next morning, as promised, after being woken for the usual blood work (this would be the same every day, as was the case in the last hospital) I was put in a wheelchair, and wheeled down to the testing room by a "patient escort." I later learned that the test I had was called an "electromyelogram" or nerve conduction studies. I was asked to lie face down on an examination table. In the state that I was in, it was painful. And as the resident doctor told me, it was because I had so little weight, and strength. I remember having little needles placed in my legs. Each jolt of the conduction was very painful.

The tests always seemed to drain me of any little energy I had. After it was performed, I was wheeled back to my room, and lay back down. I began to doze off. A man came in and woke me, by touching my hand. He had white hair, and looked to be about 55. He had a very youthful voice. "Hello. I'm Dr. McCollom." He asked if I was able to sit up. I said I was able. He helped me to adjust my bed in the upright position. Then he requested the strangest thing I have ever had a doctor ask me (that I have not worked with) in my life: "I want you to punch me real hard."

I said, "Excuse me?" He said, "Yeah, go 'head punch me."

"I..I can't"

"Punch me. Give it your best shot. Kick me, then."

When he saw I was not going to do this, he said, "I want to see how strong you are."

He then held out his hands, and scrunched his fingers together, and said, "Ok, then squeeze my fingers as hard as you can." I did comply with this request." Then he held his arms straight out and he asked me to try to pull them down. He said, "I have an idea about what you have, and I think I can help you." He had no idea but in my mind, he became God to me at that moment. He never failed me, either. Before he left the room, he smiled, kindly and squeezed my toes, and said, "Cheer up Gus." He would call me that for the next ten years, and I never knew why.

I asked him, "Am I going to die?" He looked at me and said, "I'm not going to let you." I have told this story to others, and some have said, "What an ego." But I cannot say that about this man, because he never gave up on me. Over the course of this hospitalization, other doctors did—or they would give me the option to give up or let go (even the female doctors from the first night did—Ramone and Spallone) . Some talked with me about hospice care when a diagnosis would not come easily. Believe me, I was ready. He was not hearing it. This nice, older man, with the kind smile, who, at times had a steel look in his eyes, refused to let me say, "I give up." Over the years, I said it to him. Many times, and in many ways.

Flash forward, about a year and a half later, when I was in his office and I told him I was going to "f----- kill myself" if he did not take me off all the medication "right now." His response. "Go ahead." Today, years later, as a mental health professional, I would think twice...ok, I would not say anything like this to a patient, if I wanted to keep my job, and my license. This doctor knew me, and knew himself. He looked at me with those steel eyes, and said. "You will not. And you know I know what I am doing here. Have I lied to you yet? I am doing my best to get you off these medications, slowly and steadily. We have to do this right, so you don't have a massive heart attack, and so you can go off them for good, and so you can go live your life. And you are not going to kill yourself. You have too much curiosity about what's out there."

He was right. But he was a calm force in what had to be an infuriating battle.

Because in mid-March, 1987, this doctor had to know he was in a race against time. I was dying. My kidneys were failing. I was diagnosed with a kidney disease called glomerulonephritis. I now urinated dark, bloody liquid. My lungs were filling with a thick fluid. My white blood count was high (48,000) and my hemoglobin (6.6) and hematocrit (19) were very low. My platelets were also very high (over 1 million, 132 thousand). I am printing these numbers in the event that someone who is in the medical/nursing profession is reading, just so that they have an interest. I realize that to the lay public they are just numbers!

I was not on any medications at this time, other than eye drops, my good old thyroid pill, and some acetaminophen, because the doctors had absolutely no idea what this was. I was still being ruled out for infectious processes, and so forth. I still had daily blood tests, and now daily chest X-rays, as I now understand, because there was a growing right lung "infiltrate" or hole in my right lung. They were simply monitoring the size of this hole.

This also was a Catholic hospital, and I would get nightly visits from a priest, and would be sprinkled with holy water. I was not religious, but I did say a prayer to God every night, and it was there that I made a vow to God: "If I get out of here alive, I am going to use this experience to help others somehow."

I was seen daily by what felt like a parade of residents, interns, nurses, and nurses aids. Often it would be a resident who would walk in, describe my "case" and it would be described as "bizarre." Like I said, I took it in stride, as I tried to understand that they were trying to do a job, and these were students. I counted nineteen people in my room once, and when I had my face held, and a medical spotlight shone on it to show my scarring to show how much damage the mystery illness had done to illustrate to all the residents, this did start to feel like I was a piece of meat at times. I was literally a subject.

After one of the visits from residents and interns, I was asked if I would consent to be photographed for a medical journal because of my severe arthritis. It was explained that my consent would help others, and my identity would be obscured. I did consent. Shortly afterward, someone came in with a large camera, tripod, and the big overhead lights were turned on, and my knees and feet were photographed after many consents were signed. I have since seen some of the pictures in medical books of severe Vasculitis and Wegener's, and remembered how that felt being photographed.

I would say that I lost my perspective about being called "bizarre" about a week into my stay at the St. Mary's when I was at my daily trip down to radiology. The trip itself involved being woken up at about seven a.m. With the rheumatoid arthritis in every joint, this was extremely difficult. Thankfully, the staff at this hospital was very understanding, and kind, and would grant me the time needed. I still was a bit traumatized from the first hospital, where I was told, "Get up! It is just pneumonia!" I did require assistance from at least one staff member. I now had a bedside commode. I was also required to "collect" the urine into a little "hat" because I was still not "outputting" what I was "inputting" because of the kidney failure. (I was required to drink a lot, eat gelatin, pudding, etc., basically as much liquid as I could, to keep those kidneys active and try to prevent any more damage.) After my bedside toileting, I had a sponge bath or, if there was time, I begged to have someone spot me while I went into the shower. The warm water felt good and I loved being clean.

This was back in the days when there were enough staff members to have one on one time with patients. What occurs in hospitals now is terrible. I have recently visited a friend of my mother's and next to her was a frail elderly woman. The woman's daughter rang the nurse's call bell. Fifteen minutes later, a nurses' aid came in and said, "Did you need something?" The daughter told the aid that her mom had to urinate, and the aid told her that she could take her mom to the bathroom while she was visiting to "avoid an accident." This is awful. We need to do something about the short staffing that occurs in our hospitals and in healthcare!

After I was clean I would be put in a wheelchair and left at the nurses' station and would wait for a patient escort to go to radiology, and wait up to an hour. I finally would go down to radiology, be parked outside the door of X-Ray, and would wait there. This would be another wait, sometimes up to an hour. I was then brought into the X-Ray reception area, near the X-Ray station, kind of like the nurses' station. This went on daily, weekdays, weekends. I finally broke down, and I just started crying.

I had patiently waited and escaped into myself now for a couple of months, but for some reason, that day, I just could stay a "number" any longer, and be known as "bed 11-18."

Chapter 7 - Comfort Measures

The reason I may have "lost it" after trying for so long to detach and act like just another number, because after being in a hospital for so long, you tend to be treated, as if you are "just a number. " It may also have had to do with the fact that my parents had brought in a picture of me. They gave it to Dr McCollom to show him how I looked before I got sick. It was one of the proofs of my senior pictures that I rejected. I thought it was ugly two years ago. I would have killed to look that "ugly" now. Now the picture was taped to my chart, on the inside flap. The escort who had wheeled me down opened up the chart, and said, "Who's this picture of?" I thought, "Great…"

I said, "That is me." The escort, who was gum chewing, said, "Oh my God! You let yourself go!" I said calmly, "No. I am sick." She said, "Oh. No. That's not what I meant. I mean you look better as a blonde."

I now wanted that picture out of the frigging chart. I feared that every escort would say something to me. I sat there in that wheelchair, and thought about how again, I caused this, and how my life is over, how I am ugly, and how life as I knew it is over. I cannot even walk by myself. I don't have any freedom. I can't even take a piss by myself without it being measured. And I just cried. Before I knew it someone was behind me, with arms around me. It was the lady who worked behind the desk at X-Ray.

I looked up. She said, "What is the matter? Why are you here? What are you getting the X-ray for?" I was now out of control. "That's just it. They don't know. No one knows what it is. I am not a human being anymore. I am no longer a person. I never will be again." She said, "Don't ever say that. You are a human being. You are important." She sat there with me and held my hand until it was my turn to get my X-ray. She was always kind to me throughout the rest of my stay, and was genuinely happy when I began to improve toward the end of my stay, and when I showed her that I was able to walk again. I never forgot her.

After the daily X-Ray, I would wait for a patient escort to wheel me back upstairs to the nurses' station, where I would sit (another half hour) and then a nurse or aid would wheel me back to my room. This was my daily morning routine before my diagnosis, and by the time blood work and X-ray was completed, it was lunchtime, and I was in pain, and absolutely exhausted.

Other tests that were ordered were several more biopsies: one was a biopsy of tissue from inside my lower lip (a saliva gland) to see why I was not producing saliva. This involved a numbing agent, and was done at bedside, so I did not leave the room. A French doctor performed this. ("Now we shall sew ze lip back") He was very pleasant. He explained throughout the process what he was doing, and his nurse was also nice. The result of this, made me feel as if I had been to the dentist and had a massive shot of Novocain, and I drooled for almost a year later. The numbness took about three years to completely go away.

I had a similar biopsy of one of the lesions of my skin on my left calf. It also was numbed with the same local anesthetic, and they took a sizable piece of flesh out with what looked like one of those scoopers that you use on watermelon. I have a scooped out little piece of skin as a reminder on my left calf.

About a week into my stay, the parade of residents came in with looks on their faces of purpose. One said, "Let me see your fingers." I held out my hands. A resident said, "Just like I thought. See those lines!" I asked, "What?" I was not addressed. They talked amongst themselves. I hated when they did that. I was the specimen, and specimens do not talk, I thought to myself.

That same day, a female doctor came in and said, "My name is Dr. Fells. I am a nephrologist." I asked what that meant. She seemed rushed, and said, "I'm a kidney doctor. Look. Your skin, the lines underneath your fingers. We think it all has to do with your kidneys. I need you to do something. I need you to get this ratty hair off your face. You are wearing it down, and we need to monitor your skin's progress. Either you wear it up, or I come in with scissors, got it?"

She walked out. A nurse who I liked who usually worked 3:00 to 11:00, named Nina came in. She said, "You met the dictator, huh?" We'll get this hair brushed nice, and we'll pull it up. Don't worry. She can't cut it. She's a bitch, but you didn't hear it from me, tutz." Nina was my source of hospital gossip. She was twenty-one, just two years older than I. She was, to me, "cool." She let me know that Dr Ramone, the doctor with the red hair, used to be a nurse at this hospital. Dr Ramone, Nina told me, hated being disrespected by doctors, and used to say, "I'm as smart as any of them." Nine went on, "Damn if she didn't go to med school, but the problem is, she treats all us nurses like crap now!"

The kidney doctor mentioned lines under my fingernails. I did not even notice this. Now I looked. And there sure were lines, as if someone had taken a black ink pen, and drawn lines under all of my fingernails. They were drawn vertically, pointing downward. I asked Nina about the lines. She said, "I can't tell you what that means, but they are thinking it has to do with your kidneys and blood vessels." I said, "But what about the arthritis?" She told me, "You got me. They think somehow that's all connected too. You are as they say, a bizarre case, tutz."

I said, "I fricking hate when they call me that, man." She said, "We'll tell them. It's ok." She told me that she liked nursing, the money was great for someone her age, but she could not see doing it forever. She told me how she already had a down payment on a house. I started thinking that maybe I would like to be a nurse if I ever get well again. There was also a male nurse, who was twenty-one, and he worked three to eleven when Nina did not. His name was Rich. He knew I was very down on myself about my looks. He would sit with me, and he told me, "You are beautiful. I can tell you were probably quite a looker, and you are gonna get fixed up and be a looker again! And they are going to find what is wrong. Don't despair." Rich also told me that he wanted to get out of nursing and into administration. When you take up residence at the hospital, and you are young, and the staff are young, I think that the staff feel very close to you and you learn a lot about them.

I was beginning to have trouble eating solid foods at all, because the combination of the lip biopsy, coupled with a new development made it almost impossible. The lesions on my skin now were developing inside my mouth. I now was placed on a liquid diet, as I was losing up to two pounds a day. My weight was near 100 pounds. I began to throw the milkshakes away, because in my mind, I started to think, "I am inactive, what do I need these calories for?"

Eventually, the lines that developed under my left ring finger would turn necrotic, and that tip of my finger would fall off. A couple of other fingers, notably my right thumb, began to follow suit. (My diagnosis came before all the fingertips had a chance to rot away and this is what saved them and all of my skin from necrotizing)

Now Dr. McCollom and the other doctors started to talk about IV feeding. I became angry and told them that I did not care anymore. I did not want to eat. I didn't want to live. I was becoming jaundiced again. I was in pain. Without a diagnosis, they had to proceed with caution in terms of pain medication. I now became hostile. I told a doctor, "If you force feed me, I will rip the tubes out. You can't force me. I refuse any more treatment."

Dr. McCollom said that he was "close" to an answer. He and a team of residents and interns were in my room late one afternoon when my father was visiting. My father was still working strange shifts, and was tired, and I am sure, irritable, scared, and angry, as evidenced by the following outburst. Here is what he said: "You are close? You're close to an answer? My daughter has been suffering for months. You're just taking your time. Meanwhile she is in excruciating pain, you can see it, and she can't even get in a position over there where she is comfortable. For months it has gotten worse. Veterinarians are smarter than you guys! A dog goes into a vet, can't talk, and they figure out what's wrong faster than you can. This is like something out of a horror movie. Look at her."

I could have taken the last comment the wrong way, but this was a frustrated father. I felt awful for him. Dr. McCollom had utter compassion on his face. One of the young residents was angry and said, "Mister, you have an attitude problem." Dr. McCollom cut the young one off, and said, "No, he is right to vent. He wants to see an answer. Today, I am prescribing something for her that will reduce some of this inflammation, and may take some of this pain away. It is a steroid. We are going to start it on I.V." I thought, "Great! another I.V."

My dad said, "Thank God. I can't stand to see my daughter like this. Do you know that I saw both my mother and father die in this very hospital? I don't want to lose my daughter here, too." Dr. McCollom said, "Not if I have anything to do with it." The parade of doctors all walked out. The angry young doctor never came back to see me.

That evening, my new I.V. was hooked up, and Nina said, "This will burn," and it did. The next morning, I had a new destination after X-Ray. Physical Therapy? What the heck? Physical therapy was a shock to all of my young senses. I was sent there because I had essentially been in bed for two months, and my muscles had atrophied so greatly that walking across the room without assistance was impossible. I saw paraplegics, car accident victims, and people with "cages" around their heads. I saw octogenarians who yelled, "I wanna go back to my room." I saw senior citizens who wet their pants. I was sent to "PT" daily after X-Ray until I left the hospital, and in those initial days, I hated it, because I was so weak and in such pain. I also did not understand the purpose, or have a goal. Eventually, I established small goals: to walk with two feet without assistance. My biggest goal (not to be reached for a month or more) was to walk up a couple of steps with assistance).

But in the first days of PT, I was still in great pain. I had no diagnosis, I still was not eating, and now I was having nightmares. The nightmares were so complicated that I was beginning to scream and jump out of bed at night, ripping out my I.V. The nightmares involved blood, guns, murder, and cannibalism. I was having dreams in which I was being cannibalized alive, and another horrible dream in which my beloved grandfather's dead body was cannibalized at his funeral. I would dream I was being shot almost every night. On the news every night, there were stories of shootings in the city, and there was also a horrible story in Philadephia at the time about a serial killer keeping victims in his home. All of these factors along with my own experience must have worked on my mind. When I had a dream, I would somehow get the adrenaline in my body and jump out of bed, all the while, in the process, rip out whatever tubes or apparatus was attached to me.

I also was now urinating solid dark fluid, as I was, as the doctors called it "spilling blood." Seeing this during the day, must have affected me at night. Also just the experience of this illness and being in this situation was a trauma. When I would jump out of bed, I would hurt my body even more, bruising myself, injuring, my already hurting joints.

I had asked my parents not to allow anyone to see me this way (only immediate family). So I was isolated. I began to go out in the hall in my sleep and scream at the top of my lungs. One night, my own screaming woke me up. I was in the hospital hallway screaming, "Where is everybody. Help me!" A male nurse came to me. He said, "C'mon. Back to bed. If you do this again, we will have to use restraints." I said, "Again? What do you mean again" He informed me I had been doing this every night for a week or so. But for the time being, they put up the rails on the sides of the bed. I felt like I was in a crib.

Dr. McCollom told me, "I don't like doing this, but we're going to send in the psychiatrist. He might be able to help you with this Gus." My only knowledge of psychiatry had been the story of Frances Farmer. I had read her autobiography, and seen the movie based on her life. I also knew that a distant relative of my father was in a state hospital. I never met the relative, but my dad told me how, when he was a teenager, after his parents died, and he was looking for family connections, he had visited her in the 1950's, and how awful it had been, in the open wards where she was warehoused. Many years later, as a social worker, I would meet my relative.

I was convinced that I would be headed to the state hospital now, just like that relative. A small man, Dr. Sidhwa, came in to see me later that day. He said, "Hello Ms. Candace. I am the psychiatrist. I understand you are having bad nightmares. Can you tell me about them?" I admit I was feeling very paranoid about talking to this man. I said, "Are you going to send me to the state hospital?" He said, "No. Absolutely not." He asked why I would ask such a question. I told him that my father told me about an aunt of his who ended up in a state hospital back in the 1950's after she read the bible and interpreted it too literally. That story always scared me, and my father's advice to me always had been to not read the bible and try to literally interpret it. His aunt ended up staying in the state hospital until 1995.

I looked at the doctor a long time, searching his eyes, wondering if he was lying to me. But he smiled and said, "It's alright." I do not know why, but I trusted him. He listened to me, as I told him about all the gory images that I was seeing every night, and would give me an "I see," every so often. He asked me about previous problems, and I told him that I had a painful breakup as a teenager, and wished I could be in college, "like a normal person." He said that he would be back to see me, and that he would give me something to help me sleep. I still suffered these horrible "night terrors" for a few more weeks, but this kind doctor came in daily to check. He even would say, "No charge, okay, just wanted to see how you're doing."

The residents, particularly, one young male resident, whom I liked and respected, was very serious with me one day about the subject of death. He insisted that I called him "Joel," but I could not, and still do not address doctors, even docs that I work with, by their first names. He was Dr. Green. He always wore scrubs and always had a Popsicle. He explained, "The liquid from the Popsicle keeps me awake. If you ever have to stay awake, cold liquid helps. I work sometimes 36 hour days." He sat down, and said, "Have you thought about what you will do if we can't find a diagnosis?" I said, "But Dr. McCollom said he will and I am not going to die." He was very gentle, and said, "I know he is a great doctor. He is working very hard on your case. But this is a really complicated case, Candace. And you have been sick a long time. The truth is we have a lot of doctors working around the clock. And you are in kidney failure. Are you willing to wait for a transplant? I know the pain you are in. I know the pain you have been in. There are options."

I frankly did not know what he was talking about. I believe that the months of pain took something from my brain, and I also was a naïve nineteen year old. I never worked in the medical field. I said, "What are you saying Dr. Green?" He told me, "Candace, we can start you on a regimen of pain relievers today. We can put you on comfort care only. You can stop the physical therapy, and stop all the tests. This is your choice. You have a choice. We can make you comfortable and take your pain away as best as we can." I said, "Yes" immediately.

I was ready to die. I wanted this "comfort" that this kind doctor promised me. I had tired of the parade of doctors, and of being called "bizarre." I felt as if my identity and my ability to feel like a human being was gone, and I did not ever really believe it could ever come back. I appreciated the concerns and efforts of my caretakers. But did I really believe when they told me that I could get out and live among the "normal?" No, I did not. To me, that life, if I ever truly had it, was long gone. My urine was being measured, I was still relying on people to help me walk, and I was being trained to walk two steps in physical therapy. I had been in two hospitals in a month. What began as thyroid, and pneumonia, now was out of control. Despite Dr. McCollom's promise that he would not let me die, I was willing to go. I also was going to be physically scarred the rest of my life if I did live. I was in pain, terrible pain. I was lucky to sleep for twenty minutes at a time before the searing pain in my skin, joints, mouth ulcers, side pain (from the lungs and other organs) woke me up. I was glad I had a choice.

I was at peace with this decision. Dr. McCollom came in my room that same morning, nearly at lunch, looking so concerned that he was almost angry. He had a partner with him, also in a white coat. I saw the badge, and it read "Dr. Joaquino." "You didn't agree to any hospice care, did you?" I asked him what that meant. He said, "Comfort care." I said, "Yes." He asked if I signed any papers, and I indicated that I did not, but that a social worker had come in to talk with me right after Dr. Green left.

He said, "I'm not letting you do it." Now I was angry and I spoke and talked back to him for the first time. "Tough shit! I am sick of waiting around. I am not some lab rat for all of you to come in here and poke and prod and call bizarre. I'm sick of this shit. Dr. Green said he can make me comfortable. I want comfort. And I want to be treated like a human being, not some lab rat, goddamn it." Dr Joaquino said, "Young lady you have a foul mouth." I said, "I didn't ask you!"

Dr McCollom, always the diplomat with me, said, "That's ok Gus. We will make you comfortable. I will order some pain meds for you, but I am not letting you go on hospice. I have a consult in with pulmonology because I want to go in your lungs. I want to biopsy that lung." I said, "You want to what? What does biopsy mean?" He said, "I need for us to cut that lung open and get that tissue in a lab. We don't know at this point now if it is or isn't cancer. I have to rule this out, and when I do that, I will have my diagnosis."

I said, "Screw this. I am not having a fricking operation." Dr. Joaquino said, "Maybe you want to listen to this patient talk like this, but I don't." He left the room. Dr. McCollom chuckled, and said, "Excuse my partner. He is a little bit of a prude. When he covers for me, you'll have to be a little less, uh, colorful." I did not give a crap about that other doctor, frankly.

"I am not having a damned operation!"

"Gus, this is the only way. You already have a hole the size of a baseball in there. That has to hurt. What we are going to do is going to hurt, I guarantee, but that hole is going to keep growing, and you are going to die, and all the 'comfort measures' in the world aren't going to make that pain go away. If you don't sign the consent for this, I will sign for you. That's how strongly I feel about this."

"No you won't. Won't you, like, lose your doctor's license or something?"

"I feel this strongly."

"I am not signing it."

"It is 11:30. I am giving you until 1:00 today to sign the damned thing. I already called your parents. You're going to die without it. I ordered two bags of blood. You have to sign the consent for that, too. I told you I would save your life. This is what's going to save it. Your choice. You wanna be stubborn?" His ruddy Irish face was as red as a beet. He walked out.

I was unflinching and determined. I had enough. My parents walked in, looking like they had seen a ghost. "Dr. McCollom called, and told us he wants you to have an operation," My dad said, suddenly looking and sounding twenty years older. "He told us it would save your life. You have to do this." I was adamant that I was not going through anymore invasive tests or procedures. "I am done being a lab rat, Dad."

Dr. Ramone also came in, and had a very stern look. She was holding the consents. "I want you to sign these," she said. I explained I did not want any more assaults to my body, and I did not want a stranger's blood. My dad and I had the same blood type. Why couldn't I have his? She explained that there is a complex filtering process, especially with the HIV and Hepatitis scares now, and that the blood I am expected to get is "clean."

I was not backing down. I asked her what would be involved in the operation. As usual, she spoke to me very plainly, clearly, did not mince words. "I am not going to lie to you. They are going to roll you on your side. Then they will make a large incision, and spread your ribs open. Then they are going to cut out a large piece of tissue from your lungs. They then will run that tissue under a microscope to see if it is cancer or what else it could be. Hopefully, they can make a diagnosis. Dr. McCollom is pretty sure he knows what it is. But before we can do that, you have to have a blood transfusion, because you are very low on blood." She left the consents on my bedside table. "Please read these, Candace. Time is running out. We need to book the O.R. for 5:00 a.m. tomorrow."

Dr. McCollom came back at 12:45. Now I had my parents, and an angry doctor all trying to convince me. My mom was now crying. Dr. McCollom said, "What are you going to do, Gus? I guarantee you. You will die in less than a week without the blood. You are like an empty gas tank. You have a giant hole in your lung and a spot. And if I can't have that surgeon find out what this spot is, it also will kill you." I trusted this man. I looked in his eyes. He stared into mine. I looked at the consents. He took them off the nightstand. He handed them to me, pulled a pen out of his lab coat, and I hurriedly scratched my name on all of them.

"One thing, " I said.

He said, "What's that?" I said, "If I could croak down on that operating table tomorrow, I wanna know where is the best Pizza joint around here. I want Pizza for my Last Supper." He cracked a smile. He said, "Goombahs, right down the block. I'll get Nina to get you the number when she comes in on 3."

I had not had an appetite in days, but I figured, Hell, I might as well eat. When Nina came in she said, "Good girl. I know you don't want to have this surgery, but honey, they are so close to having the answer. Here's the number of that Pizza place." She was also an Italian-American girl. I laughed and said, "What the hell kind of name is Goombahs?" She laughed and said it is great stuff. My mom and dad were ravenous. I took one bite, and the sauce burned my mouth and all the ulcers in my mouth. I tried to just eat the crust, but it was very difficult, so I abandoned it. But it was good to have the small taste of pizza. My parents, looking very worried, were encouraged by staff to go home. They would bring cards from people, but now were very understanding of the fact that I wanted no outside visitors. All of the neighbors who lived on our block were worried sick, my parents told me, and my friend, Dennis was calling every day wondering how I was.

He had asked if he could come down to see me with my parents, but I told them that he would be too shocked by my appearance. Staff also respected this request.

After dinner, a staff member came in to hang my first unit of blood. I did not know, but blood was almost black. I asked about it, and the nurse explained to me how venous blood was dark, and when it hits the air it then turns red. I was finding out more about the body and hospital procedures than I ever thought possible in this experience. I could see that both of my parents were rather squeamish over all this. I told them to leave, as it was nearing 8:30 p.m. and they looked completely drained.

At about 10:00 p.m., I started to doze off, when I heard the click-clack of boots entering my room. I looked up and thought I saw…Burt Reynolds? Sure enough, this guy, a dead-ringer for the star, was dressed in jeans, a western shirt and cowboy boots. "Hi. I'm Dr. Bonzetti. I'm the surgeon who will be taking care of you tomorrow." I thought I was hallucinating. He asked me to sit up in my bed, and he had me breathe in deeply, then shallowly, and said, "Yeah, we've got a lot of congestion here. You've been sick a long time, huh?" I told him that I had. He said, "Don't you worry. I'm going to take good care of you, kid." He walked out, and I thought I was in a dream. I felt less frightened because the surgeon was so sure of himself, I thought, how could anything go wrong?

Nina came in after and said, "Hubba, hubba, Damn, girl. Is he hot, or what! Do you feel better knowing that is the dude operating on you or what?" I said, "I guess so. But I mean who does the operating nurse look like, Phyllis Diller, do they have all of Hollywood Squares down there or what?" She busted out laughing. "You're killin' me!"

I took my sleeping pill that Dr. Sidhwa, the psychiatrist had prescribed for me. I also received something to begin to relax me in my IV, perhaps Valium. Surgery was now about seven hours away. I slept fitfully all night, as pain was constant, and now worry was like an elephant resting on my chest. But I also had hope. This operation was a promise of a diagnosis. However, a priest came and did administer last rites to me that evening. He asked me if I am ready to go and join God. I said that I was. Throughout the night, I was transfused with more units of blood.

At 4:30 a.m. Bernadette, my overnight nurse gently woke me, and said, ""Candace, I am going to get you prepared for surgery. I know you like to be clean. So do you want to try a sponge bath?" I did, and I also learned that you have to have something else prior to a surgery of this magnitude: an enema. I was also given more Valium in my I.V. My poor parents were back, looking very frightened. I was not frightened at all. I was no longer fearful of death. Death was certainly a possibility. This had been explained to me, and I was not afraid. If this operation did not meet its purpose: a diagnosis, I wished to go back to my plan: comfort measures.

By 4:50, Bernadette and some aids were taking the corners of the sheets and transferring me to a gurney. My mom was there, crying. Bernadette, my mom, and dad all wished me "Good luck," as a patient escort wheeled me to surgery. The "O.R." area was a brightly lit area in the bowels of the hospital. For ridiculously early hours of the day, people were wide-awake and chattering. I had no glasses on, and with my prescription of of –7.00, you can imagine what a blur it is. But I saw mostly green scrubbed people. Some had colorful hats or shirts. One person came right up to my face and identified herself as a nurse who would be taking care of me. She began putting more liquid into my I.V. She explained that it was even more Valium. She said that I would become very sleepy soon. I already felt, frankly, the same way I used to feel when I used to smoke marijuana. The nurse explained the operation to me. "What we are going to do is roll you on your side, make a large incision, spread open your ribs, take out some tissue, and they will need to send that to a lab. It is called a biopsy. What we are doing is called a thoracotomy. Now we are going to give you something call Sodium Pentathol."

I now saw Dr. Bonzetti looking at me. "Well good morning. What do you think now?" I said, "I think you look like Burt Reynolds." He laughed and said, "Except for two things. I'm younger and I'm better." He then turned on a very bright light, and I remember nothing else, as everything then went very dark.

Chapter 8 - Never Give Up

I heard screaming. I opened my eyes, and it felt like they were coated in a thick film of Vaseline, and a lens covered with gauze. The screaming was loud and piercing, and sounded like the person was right next to me. It took me several minutes to realize that the screaming was coming from me. Someone was patting my arm. "What's wrong, what's wrong?" I was now hyperventilating.

"I can't see and I've been shot." (This was the theme of one of my recurring nightmares that Dr. Sidhwa had seen me about-- that I was the victim of a drive by shooting. And now the pain on my lower right quadrant had me convinced that this was a reality). The person, a female, assured me that I had not been shot. She explained as she placed a lukewarm, wet washcloth over my eyes, "The Vaseline is in your eyes to keep them from drying out. And you have not been shot. You had surgery, remember. You are heavily medicated. I know you are confused. This place where you are right now is called post-op."

I heard other people also screaming, moaning, crying, and a lot of machine noises. As I became oriented to where I was, two X-Ray technicians came over and sat me up. I let out a guttural, room shattering, Ella Fitzgerald, glass-breaking screech. "NOOOOOOO."

They said, "Yes! We have to get a post-op chest X ray, don't worry, it won't take long." I had just been cut wide open, and I was not yet aware of what the other apparatus was, but I was also hooked to a chest tube and respirator. They sat me up long enough to get the images, as they slid the boards behind me. I now had to hold my breath and go through the process of an X-Ray. Torture, it was. The technicians apologized. They laid me back down as gently as possible. It was then that I asked what the tubes were, and a nurse explained, "They had to put you on a respirator, honey."

"Is that what this is that is tugging at my side?"

"Yes."

It also sounded like an old-fashioned coffee percolator. I asked for my glasses, I looked down, and what was being drained into it was black, bloody, mucous, and thick. I asked, "What is this?" The nurse explained that it was the months of congestion that was built up in that right lung. I asked what they found in the lung. She said that there were tumors, but they did not appear to be cancerous, and one large "infiltrate" or hole. A large piece of my lung was gone, but that since I am young, I had a chance of healing.

I looked around. Some patients were naked. Some were bald. I knew I had gone into surgery around 5:30. I asked what time it was. It was now 12:30, I was told. I also was told that I yelled and cursed ferociously before they woke me up. I apologized for this. The nurse laughed and said, "That's ok, honey." I now was acutely aware of the machine, my new appendage, and the pumping of the fluid, and its tugging feeling.

I remained in post-op, for a couple hours, still very groggy, and eventually was wheeled back up to my room. I was on a gurney. I was wrapped from head to toe, and very cold, and several staff took a cornet of sheet and the apparatus. I objected: "No! It's going to hurt!" Rich, the 3 to 11 nurse, patted my arm and said, " It's ok to yell, and I know it is going to hurt. You are cut pretty bad, and you have this machine attached to you. Yell, punch me, do what ever it takes."

I moaned and groaned but did not yell as they transferred m back to my bed. My social worker, Kathy, came in. She was very kind to me. "How are you? What a day. We have all been so worried about you! " I told her, "I hurt so bad. I don't like this thing next to me," pointing at the respirator. She had a sympathetic look. A nurse was trying to feed me green gelatin, and telling me, "Candace, it is really important that you get liquids in your body."

Later in the evening, as my parents were sitting there by my side, ever-present, I heard coffee being made. I woke from my nap. I said, "Oh that's good. Can someone get me a cup when that coffee is done." My mom said, "Candy, that is not coffee. That's your, you know. The thing." I was so disoriented from the narcotic drip, that I could not get it through my head that the sound of the percolating coffee was the respirator.

As I dozed again, my mom noticed that I was reaching my arms up and talking saying, "I'm coming, and I will be there." I was laughing and having a one-sided conversation with a person. My mom tried to interact with me, but was getting nowhere. Eventually, staff told my parents it was best for them to go home, as I was too heavily sedated, and I was not going to wake up and have much of a decent conversation the rest of the evening. On overnight, I had a dream. I saw my great grandmother (maternal) who was a Sicilian immigrant. She died in 1973, when I was 6. She spoke very little English. But she was reaching out for me. I had my arms outstretched. What I did understand was, "Come get white spaghetti. C'mon spaghetti bianco"

I did, and every time I would try to hold her hands, they felt oily, and I would lose my grip. I kept trying. Grandma Josephine had on all white to match her white hair. Her skin was brown, as I remembered it. She had eyes so brown, that they looked like black olives. A tunnel of white clouds surrounded her. It felt like a vacuum force pushing me both toward her and away from her. Bernadette was my overnight nurse, and she was turning me every hour to avoid having me choke on my own lung fluid. I woke up from this dream and Bernadette was sitting there calmly, stroking my hair. She asked me, "Where'd you go?" I said, "I just tried to go see my gramma." She asked if my gramma was dead. I said, "Yes." She said, "You almost went, honey." I asked what she meant. She said that my heartbeat had stopped for several minutes, and that my blood pressure was 50/30.

I later learned that after this episode, I had been transferred to Intensive care.

As I was hospitalized, my sister, her husband, and son had moved back in with my parents again. So there was a lot of chaos at home. My room was being moved to the corner of the house, and Lucy was moving (as well as her spouse and son into mine. I was getting the corner room fixed into a room for my eventual return home. Lucy was angry, as she had moved back about three times before since her marriage seven years earlier. Each move back resulted in a stay at out house lasting about six months or so, until they could save money for an apartment. Lucy was 27, her spouse 25, and her son was 6.

Lucy also was not able to visit because she became literally ill in hospitals. My mom convinced her to see me after the surgery. Lucy came in with my mom the day after the operation, and had a tough persona. She brought her son. He was amazing. He looked completely nonplussed over any of this. His mom, on the other hand, could not hide a thing. However, she heard the "coffee machine." She walked in and said, "Oh, thank God. You have a coffee maker in here, and before I could warn her, she walked around the right side of my bed. Too late. She was looking right at it. My mom, said, "Lucy! I was going to tell you. I know how sensitive you are. Don't go to that side of the room." Lucy, who is olive skinned, turned white. Her son got a chuckle. He asked what it was. I said, "I don't understand a lot of it, but from what I know, it's taking the bad stuff out of my lungs." He said, "Oh, OK." He then showed me his collection of "Garbage Pail Kids" cards and forgot about it. My humor was about the level of a small boy's, so I always could relate to him, and enjoyed his company greatly.

My mom brought me more greeting cards that some family and friends had sent, and asked again if I was sure if I did not want her to bring anyone in, and I said I was positive. "Mom, I don't want anyone to see me this way. And you can tell them that. I have pride. I have been very careful to hide this." She explained that people are wondering. I told her to tell them. She said, "I want them to see how you are suffering." I argued that it is not necessary for people to see me suffer. I wanted to suffer alone and with the staff that are helping me day to day. I told her to thank the people for the cards, and I even called a few of the folks who were really diligent, like our neighbors who lived across the street. They were like family to us.

A cousin who lived in the city of Pittsburgh was also very concerned. I heard heels walking in my room one day while my mom was there. My mom looked at me and said, "Angie is here." I said, "No, I can't have her see me like this." My mom jumped up and stopped Angie before she could see me behind my drawn curtain. My mom came back and told me she had explained to Angie that I was bedridden for the most part and had many sores, and that I did not want to be seen by anyone outside the immediate family. Mom said Angie understood this. She later became a great supporter of mine in tough times. But I wanted to be sure to preserve my dignity. I idolized her, as she was a strong, independent, single woman, and this is what I aspired to be.

The sores had ended up in a delicate place that occurs for many patients who are in bed for a long time, and in my case, I had been in bed for a couple of months. The sore was right on the coccyx, or tailbone. This type of sore is technically called a decubitus. Mine was right at the base of my very bony tailbone. I was no longer allowed to lie on my back once this was discovered. I had to lie on my sides, which was somewhat of a problem after the surgery, that is, lying on the right side with an appendage sticking out of my right side. I also had to start my day, as part of my morning routine by baring my butt, and having a gauze pad with ointment affixed to the bedsore. Luckily I, and many of the younger nurses had a sense of humor. They would wake me early, and expose my ass, and allow me to go back to sleep, with just my butt sticking out of the covers. I still have a deep scar from where this decubitus was, as it was a Stage 3. This means that the flesh was damaged clear through to the muscle.

The vasculitic ulcers on the rest of my body and face were also ravaging the rest of my skin. I had them all throughout my hairline, and as a result, I had matted, bloody hair, which washing became a delicate debacle. My hair has natural curl, so cannot be combed once it has dried naturally. The nephrologist had the issue with threatening to cut it every time she came in to see me, because it just looked unruly if it was not pulled back. A particularly bad ulcer was one behind my right earlobe. This one literally ate away the right earlobe and the tissue around my neck. My mother used to blame me for having pierced my own ear, (having double pierced ears were becoming in style back in the 1980's) and I had pierced my left lobe. Again, I had to listen to the "It's your fault" chorus. The right earlobe seeped constantly, and the same dressing that I had to endure on the tailbone was applied to the ear while I was in the hospital. I woke up with a bloody pillow until this problem was corrected in late 1988.

I still have the scars all along my hair line, back, chest, face (despite numerous facial surgeries much later). The decubitis scar is still on my tailbone. These things are constant reminders of the fact that my body was completely broken down that spring of 1987.

A small comedy of errors occurred the day after surgery. Someone had forgotten to cancel my standing appointment with physical therapy. So I was woken up, helped out of bed, in great pain, the escort went to the great trouble of attaching the respirator to the wheelchair, with it percolating away, and wheeled me down to PT. I got there, and the head Physical Therapist came over to me with a look of shock on her face. "What are you doing here?" I told her that I was here for physical therapy, of course. She said, "But you have a respirator." I wanted to say, "No shit," but I didn't. She called up to the 11th floor and sternly said, "I have room 11-18 here on a respirator! Who is responsible for taking this poor person out of bed and sending her down to PT?" She then came over and said, "I am so sorry. We will send you up. You can't do this. But we can have someone come to your bedside to exercise your legs while you are on this. Would you like that?" I said "sure" to that. I wanted to get my strength back.

I began to set my mind at this point on small goals. Getting my strength back in order to walk again was one, of course. Now the other small goal was to have this appendage removed: the chest tubes and respirator. I had it for five days. It was inserted on a Wednesday, and removed on a Sunday. It was during these five days, although I do not remember this part, that I was moved to Intensive Care. It is not clear exactly when from the medical records.. But I found out years later, when I was doing my social work internship at the hospital, and worked with Dr. Joel Green (the doctor who talked with me about hospice).

He was giving some of the social work interns a lecture about hospice and how it is a humane choice. He looked at me several times. After the talk, he approached me. He said, "I know you, but from where?" By this time, seven years later, I had become healthier, obviously. I was in the Master's program, and working in the hospital where I had once been a patient. I honestly did not remember Dr. Green. I said, "I was a patient here." He asked if it was on "this floor." I told him it had indeed been the 11th floor. He said, "What illness did you have?" I told him. He said, "My God. You were so sick. You were on a respirator, and we had to move you down to ICU." I told him I did not remember the ICU. He said, "You wouldn't. You weren't responding." He looked like he was seeing a ghost. He shook my hand vigorously. He said it was not everyday, in fact it was "never" that he gets to see a former patient in this capacity. It made my hair stand on end.

I next remember a Friday afternoon, and Dr. McCollom telling me, "I want to get this chest tube and machine out of you, Gus. But getting that out hurts like hell, so we will give you a shot of morphine for them to pull it out." I asked why, and he explained that the skin grows around the area where the tube has been inserted, in the lower right flank. "And when you pull it out, it pulls that skin, and it hurts." The weekend was pretty uneventful, other than I was pretty worried about the chest tube. I noticed I was getting an appetite back, and the nurses told me it was the steroid medicine that was responsible, and that it was also responsible for making my joints feel better. The reviews were mixed on this drug: one thumb up, one thumb down. It makes you fat, but takes your pain and inflammation away.

The nightmares were returning, and now, since the operation, I was having the bloody dreams again. I dreamed that I was being operated on without anesthesia. I had regular nightmares, where I was seeing all my friends and trying to tell them what had happened to me and they were either running from me in horror, or walking away, saying, "Who cares?" I had a dream where I witnessed my own operation, and another again where I was witnessing cannibalism. Dr. Sidhwa returned. He was sympathetic, and explained that some people have a bad reaction to anesthesia, and it can even bring about a psychosis. This word scared me. "So I am crazy?" He said, "No, no. The powerful medications in the anesthesia last in the body a long time. And, you are also on a powerful steroid that is causing your body changes. This could also be causing the nightmares and your hypervigilance." Another fancy word, which he explained, meant that I was super aware of my surroundings, and yes, not trusting.

He prescribed a small dose of an antispsychotic before bed. It knocked me clear out into the next day, for sure. The chest tube removal felt like a tugging, a very strong pulling motion, thanks to the shot of morphine. There was little pain. And then I had a sense of freedom, and thanked God that I did not have to live with a foreign apparatus the rest of my life. I wondered how those poor people who had to live with things like this did it.

Sunday, after the chest tube was removed. I was able to get up, and when I carefully held on to things, like my bed, and the rails on the wall, slowly go to the bathroom myself, thanks to the strength training exercises. I was up and around, and decided to use the handrails in the hallway, and walk around the hospital, with a goal of three laps per day. I did it that day. I paid for it with sore legs the next day. But this was my ticket out of the hospital, I reasoned. I also began to do the leg lifts and bed exercises that the physical therapist had taught me. I was determined to get out, and not be an invalid.

That evening, a roommate came in. She was a young woman named Chontelle. I was in the middle of an exercise. She and I struck up a conversation. She and I were exactly the same age: nineteen. She asked why I was here. I told her my whole story, and she said, "Damn girl. That's incredible. You look like you are trying to get better. You go." She told me she was in because of a blood clot in her lung and also because she was hoping to get her tubes tied, although she was not sure they'd do it because they are a Catholic hospital. We both felt this was outrageous, because we felt it was freedom of choice. She told me she had five kids already, and enough is enough. She lived right up the street. The hospital was in one of the poorest neighborhoods in the city. She was a cool roommate. You get good ones and bad ones.

The first roommate had been there a long time before my arrival. She had a stroke right in front of me and died. I rang the call bell, and they asked what I wanted, and I told them, that my neighbor had convulsed and I think she's dead. A bunch of people came in, ripped off her clothes, and tried to resuscitate her, but it was too late. The second one complained nonstop about the food, and the "wench nurses." She also smoked on the sly, but denied it when her doctors would ask about it. In early 1987, smoking was still permitted in hospitals. It was making my infected lungs hack, but every time I would mention it to the nurses, the roommate would deny that she smoked. Since other individuals smoked on the unit (there was a smoke-filled staff lounge, it was hard to prove).

My favorite was Gerri. She was about 55. She had short, styled hair, and wore silky nightshirts and high-heeled mule slippers. She paced the halls a lot. She had suffered a stroke in the past, lost both breasts to cancer, had a complete hysterectomy due to cancer, and now was in the hospital due to her brittle diabetes. She never once complained, and had a great sense of humor. She talked about her past maladies in a matter of fact manner. She said this was the hospital she trusted. She told me, "Never give up, because you can beat anything." When she was discharged from the hospital she gave me a rosebud vase. Half a year later, when I was back in the hospital for a relapse of my illness, there was Gerri, walking the halls. I came across her obituary in 1988 when I was in Dr. McCollom's office. I was so upset to see her there, because I thought she would beat it all. I still, to this day, keep a nice golden rose in her rosebud vase as a reminder of Gerri, and not to give up.

The day after I had the tubes, respirator and morphine drip removed, I got up, and took a full shower, and it felt so good. I was walking with much better ease. But I did fall on the way out of the shower. I underestimated my strength. But I insisted, despite the concern of the nurses, that I wanted to get rid of the portable toilets and sponge baths. I wanted to try to return to some form of normalcy in my daily care needs. I felt like an elderly invalid with everything being right at my bedside. It was a Monday, and I was sent back to my normal routine of chest X-Ray, and Physical Therapy, too.

At PT, I was raring to go. I wanted to be given more goals, more tasks, and I wanted to walk up steps. The therapist told me that this was a lofty goal, but with some weeks of practice, we could achieve it, but first, walking was important. I also spent the evenings after dinner, holding on to the handrails, walking the hallways. I still had to hold on to something or someone. But the point was, I was walking.

It was this time, right after the respirator was removed, and the introduction of a little device called a Tri-Flo, in which I had to inhale and bring up three little plastic balls all the way to the top (at first I could only bring one, then eventually, two, etc) that the night terrors returned. Every shift, when my vitals were being checked, I had to demonstrate my lung capacity to the nurse, and show how deeply I could inhale, and bring up the balls to the top. I was doing this, apparently in my sleep, and my roommate, commented, "Damn girl, you were blowing that thing all night and saying about how you could get the balls up." One night I had a dream that a team of white-coated residents were standing around me saying "Show us you can do it or you'll have another operation."

I was having this nightmare every night. My roommate, who was confined to her bed, because of a serious blood clot in her lung, was patient, but she was losing sleep. She had a sense of humor, but she told me every morning how loud I was yelling, and how I was swearing. One male nurse really got the brunt of it when he would come in, and I would tell him to "F--- Off" or something like that if he would try to interrupt one of these little night terrors. During the night terrors, my language became filthy, and I became aggressive. I also was doing the climbing out of bed, screaming in the hall routine again.

Dr Sidhwa paid me another visit, and increased the sleeping pill and antispsychotic, and explained that the operation and the steroids were likely causing these reactions. I continued to have these night terrors for months, although less frequently, even after I returned home, and even began to silently walk in my sleep, and wake up in strange places. The strangest place I woke was curled up on our cold garage floor, curled in a ball. I have no memory of walking downstairs, or why I did that. I was curled over the drain in the garage.

I was now, if not "used to" the hospital, certainly institutionalized. I became accustomed to the noises. I was used to the other patient's screams in the night, the moans of "help me," the blips and beeps of other respirators and IV's all night, and because the hospital was in the inner city, I was used to the sirens outside all night. The hospital had a paging system, and I was also used to hearing, "Dr. Johnson, Line 13," and that sort of thing. There was never silence. I don't think that has ever left me, as I can't sleep in silence. I have to have a radio, or a television on. I slept very soundly when I lived in an unsafe neighborhood (after barricading myself) in the inner city while in grad school because of all the sirens and city noises and some small amount of light from the street lights. The experience changed my life forever.

After my chest tube had been removed, what was holding the suture together in my back, where the surgeon, had to enter the lung, was beginning to bother me. They were large staples. They, in fact resembled large box staples. They were pulling, and itchy by about day five. Dr. Bonzetti came in, and had the big, tall presence again of Burt Reynolds. "Hi there. How's it going?"

I said, "I am doing better, except it really bothers me now where you cut me." He had a look of abject offense on his face. "Miss, I did not *cut* you." He sat down. "What I do is art. When this heals, it is going to be smooth, and it will be a piece of art. You will be proud to show it." I thought to myself sure, I will pose for *Playboy* with this piece of art on my back.

"So when will the staples be able to come out?" I asked. He looked at them, and estimated that they would be able to come out in another three days or so, explaining that they were holding together a large suture. He explained that just when people who have arthritis, feel like they can "predict" when it rain, I also will be able to do so with this site. He was right. At times, when it is damp outside, I ache in this area, as I do in all of my surgery sites.

One afternoon, around lunch, after my young roommate had been discharged, I got another elderly woman. From the moment she was wheeled in, she took a look at me, and muttered "Oh God." She closed the curtains. My self-consciousness about my face, and the ravages of the illness, naturally had me thinking that she was frightened or put-off by my appearance. But no! She was on the phone the rest of the afternoon from the minute she got there, telling everyone she knew, "They put me in here with a goddamned teenager. Yes! Can you believe this? I am outraged! I am complaining, you bet your bottom dollar I am . I have been contributing to this damned hospital for forty years. And this?" She stopped her litany when they delivered dinner.

After dinner, when my parents came in, they said hello to her, and she was pleasant to them, but closed the curtains again, but in hushed tones, got on the phone again, and started the ranting and raving. She had a guest and bitched the same tune. My dad overheard it. He said, "What is that all about?" I said, "Oh you know me. I have been partying down over here." She overheard me, and said, "Honey I don't mean you. I just, you know, how some teenagers are." Yeah, okay sweetie. Funny, I did not even think of myself as a "teenager."

Chapter 9 - What Is The Name of This Long Road?

That evening, I was reading a big pile of tabloids my aunt had sent me. The big news at the time was another Elizabeth Taylor medical drama (I related to her as I read about it) and Joan Collins' husband spilling the beans on their intimate details. I could relate to the lack of privacy thing, too.

I put my headphone radio on, not loudly, mind you, so as not to upset my cellmate. The good news is that I was now walking to the bathroom myself. No more disgusting bedside toilet. I had a collection "hat" on the toilet all the time. It still felt like an invasion of privacy to me, even though it had been explained to me that my "input" and "output" had to be monitored because of my fragile kidney functioning. I heard the words "Bun and creatnine" daily, but I did not understand one whit of what it meant. But I would grumble to myself every time I had to empty the contents of the "hat" into a big pitcher. In fact I believe my exact phrase was, "Can't a person even whiz with privacy around here?" Of course, the answer to that was a resounding "No!"

I saw a mouse make its way out from the radiator in my room. I hit the call bell. A nurse I had never seen before entered my room. I told her about the mouse. She apologized and told me that there was construction going on in the street, and whispered, "Good, maybe he'll be a quieter roommate for her," then pointed to the curtain.

The nurse identified herself as a "house supervisor." She sat down on a chair, and said, "Candace. I am so sorry about this. But we are trying to move you. I know it's late, but she is not letting up." She pointed to the drawn curtain where the woman was still kvetching about how loud these "young ones" can be. Funny, she was the only one making noise. The supervisor leaned in, and said, "This is the only way to shut her up. Would you mind if we sent you down the hall. You would be by yourself. Is that okay with you?" I answered with a sarcastic, "Nooo! I would hate that." She winked and said, "Okay, we'll get an aide in here to pack your stuff."

They just released the brakes on my hospital bed, and wheeled me down the hall. The first thing I saw when they wheeled me in the dark room was the view of the lit up Southside. "Holy crap! This is a private room, you'd better call my parents, and I don't think they can afford this!" The nurse said, "Don't worry—we are billing it as a semi-private because it was the only way we could move you—there are no more female beds left in the house."

I called my parents, and told them about it, and my mom chuckled and said she had already heard about it. She said that one of the nurses already called her and told her about my miserable room mate, and how the hospital felt that I deserved a suite after listening to that all evening. I looked out on the river and fell asleep watching the twinkling lights.

By this time, I was granted my request to sleep in. No more lights on at 6:00. A phlebotomist might still come in early in the morning, but I would pull the covers over my head, stick my arm out and practically sleep through it. I knew they took blood daily, so I did not even bother to ask the purpose any longer.

I was also able to get up and walk to the bathroom myself, and even to shower in that cool marble bathroom. I still had the occasional fall—usually every other day, and usually around shower time, and this would happen even after I got home. But I learned to crawl my way to the toilet, hoist myself up by my arms and get up, and hold on to something and keep on going.

I began to watch soap operas. I would watch *The Young and the Restless* followed by the brand new *Bold and the Beautiful* , and also the *Days of Our Lives*. The big problem is that the shows were on at the same time. I mastered the art of remote control operation to pull this off. When one had a commercial, I would immediately switch to the other. Like I said, this was a wild time of partying.

I was beginning to be told that a discharge would be soon. Nothing was ever definite, because it seemed that a test result would always hold this up. My kidneys (that "bun" stuff) were usually the hold up. I was now able to walk the halls and look out the windows, and occasionally, I would hang out and talk with the nurses, depending on who was working. There were some young nurses, not much older than I was, who would let me drink coffee and just sit there. This made me feel a bit more human again. When I got too bleary-eyed, one of them would usually authoritatively state that I had to go to bed, or McCollom would have their heads in the morning.

I still had a daily chest X-ray, in addition to the daily blood tests. I had finally reached my goal, one day of climbing up the steps in PT. After I reached that goal, I was discharged from attending daily PT, as long as I promised to walk around on the unit by myself. That climbing of the steps was akin to climbing a mountain! My days were filled with reading, listening to music, watching television, walking (but still holding on to that handrail). I was sleeping less during the day now, and I was frankly getting bored, and wishing I was back in my own room, among my book and music collection.

Kathy, the social worker stopped in to see me every couple of days. She often would see me while my family was there, but she caught me while they were not. My family's questions to her often centered around "How much is this all going to cost?" She answered them by telling them that insurance was going to cover the hospitalization. She also was aware of what I had told the psychiatrist, about how I had a strong desire to go to college. This is what she came to talk to me about one day while no one from my family was in my room.

I had envied my few friends who had decided to go on to college after high school. I had so desired to do the same, but my parents had told me repeatedly throughout high school that this was not possible because they had no money for this.

They had this dream for me to apply for a job as a turnpike toll taker. I always balked at this idea. I also pushed the idea of college out of my head. My dad referred to anyone with a college education or who did not work in a labor job as "a suit." No one in our family was a suit. People were what they made monetarily in my family. And it was also assumed that if you had a college education, you made "big bucks."

After the string of jobs, and the stint at broadcasting school I did prior to getting sick, my social worker had interacted enough with my family and I to know about my unhappiness, and how it predated my physical illness. One time when my family was not in the hospital room visiting me, she came in and sat down with me, and asked me, "If you could get out of this hospital and go back to work or even go back to school, what would do?" When I told her the barrier of no money, she stopped me, "What if I told you that there might be money?" I couldn't believe what I was hearing.

She went on to tell me that when people have disabling illnesses that prevent them from returning from their previous lines of work, sometimes there is state funding to train them. While in the hospital, she said, I could be introduced to the representative from this program, Work Rehab Program (we'll call it WRAP for short).

About a week later, I was having a very bad day. I was still suffering from decubitus ulcers on the coccyx (tailbone). They were in Stage 3. Stage 3 ulcers involve loss of skin from pressure on the area, (and think about how much pressure is on that tailbone when bedridden for a long time). These are more commonly known as "bedsores", and they occur more commonly in chronic populations, or in those who have been institutionalized for a long time. They are more challenging for the elderly, as the skin is not as elastic and breaks more easily.

In stages 1 and 2, your skin is compromised, in Stage 3; it is essentially a crater. Stage 4 is very bad as it is close to the bone itself. You can imagine the infections you are susceptible to. It is a difficult area to heal, as it is a moist area that does not get exposed to sunlight, unless you are healthy, and wearing low cut bikinis in a warm climate somewhere. Pittsburgh in the winter, well, I was not meeting criteria. So my tailbone area was a mess.

They were doing a treatment every morning on me called wet-to-dry dressings. Staffing was short. For days at a time, the staff shortage problem was slowing down the already slow process of the healing, because I would be woken up and have to go through this process of "wet to dry" dressing." The problem is, with short staff, by the time the next shift would get in to change the dressing on my tailbone, I would have very dry pieces of thick cheesecloth rags dried to my tailbone/coccyx. The removal would take skin with it. This was over twenty years ago, and I was 19. I shudder to think of what some frail elderly people with their paper like thin skin have to go through in perpetually understaffed nursing homes of today, where short staffing is often a rule, not the exception.

I was woken up as per usual one morning while it was still dark, by overnight staff, and had a saline squirted on my tailbone area, and some wet dressings placed there (I still have a huge, pitted, dime sized scar as a reminder of this giant decubiti). The wet dressings were placed there, and I was covered everywhere but my hind-end, which hung out . I would roll on my side, and go back to sleep. Usually about 8:30 or 9:00, someone would come in and take it off about the time breakfast arrived with morning meds.

I still was only permitting immediate family to see me, and my sister was very squeamish about seeing me this way, so it was mostly my mom, dad, and even my nephew, who at age 6, who was a very strong kid, and we saw as "a little old man in boys clothing". My mom was pretty taken aback on mornings when she would stop in before work and see me sleeping there with my full butt exposed and no one around.

Enter my introduction to WRAP, the office of Work Rehab of Pennsylvania. I heard a voice one ungodly sunny morning (I was very negative then, and a bright sunny day just meant a day when other people were living normal lives and I was stuck in this hospital for another day). "…hello Candace. Candace!"

I was lying on my left side and had to turn around, looking over my shoulder to see who this person was. He was not wearing a lab code, so I assumed he was probably not a doctor. . He told me his name was John from the Pittsburgh office of WRAP. I said , "Excuse me but I am uncovered, could I have a minute?" He told me, "I don't care, I have seen it all before. I have a lot of people to see today. I just came to give you some brochures. I understand from talking to Kathy Blum (the social worker) you might want to go back to work or school.

I was still lying there exposed, and felt very uncomfortable, as the way nursing staff had me positioned made it difficult to cover myself. Again I said, "Listen, my butt is hanging out, can I cover myself. He said, this time, "I don't care. Just take a look at this information, my numbers on it. You don't live in the city and you live out of county, so if you are interested, call our office, we'll set you up with a worker." He then was gone.

Later I told Kathy Blum about this and she scrunched her face up, and said, "Well, listen, you got the information and you won't deal with him based on where you live." She then said, "And I am going to make sure I talk to the staff about doing a better job of covering you! There is no reason you should be hanging out like that while they do those dressings.

Dr. McCollom came in one day and asked if I could agree to see him twice a week if I was sent home. I agreed. He told me that I would be facing "a long road back" to health. I asked him always if I would ever be "normal" again. He would always ask me, "What's normal?" I would tell him that I wanted to look normal, drive, work, live by myself, and be able to support myself. He would say, "I think so." That was the great thing about him. He never told me about miracles happening. He would say, "I think" or "I don't know," rather that pretend to be the reigning expert. (My point here is that some doctors did have an arrogance and unwavering presentation) I even asked him if he ever had an operation or health problems. Some doctors, I learned at this young age, would say, "This isn't about me" in a way to show their boundaries. He said, "Yep. Many. But you'll get through this."

I asked Dr. McCollom what this illness is, what caused all this? What was this "long road?" He told me it was something called "Wegener's granulomatosis, a form of Vasculitis." I had to have him repeat it, and he repeated it slowly, a couple of times. He explained that our blood vessels are all through our bodies. What happened with me is that I had an inflammation of the blood vessels, Vasculitis. But my vasculitis was even more specialized, involving joints, kidneys, skin, and lungs, and the immune system. It was a complete system breakdown called Wegener's granulomatosis. He explained that the "skin eruptions" were the "granulomas." The granulomas occurred inside (the tumor formations in the lungs that then turned into the big infiltrate, or hole), and the kidney disease (the glomerulonephritis), as well as on the outside. The outside, the skin disease, was the last stage. I was, as he put it "lucky." I would wrestle with that label of "lucky" for years. Was I really lucky? I finally understood what it meant. Is this what it means to survive? Is this good?

I asked if there was a pamphlet, or any information on this illness, because I liked to read. He sadly shook his head. He told me there is not much information about it, and further told me, "What there is, is not very good, or frankly easy to read. Just ask me questions. I will answer them as best I can for you, Gus. Okay?" he shook my hand. "See you later this week."

I remember the nurse coming in and going over the discharge information with me. A patient escort wheeled me out to the car. I did need some help getting in to the back seat of my parent's car. We stopped for lunch on the way home. I asked my dad as he passed the handicapped parking space if I was handicapped? He said, "No. You are not disabled don't think of yourself that way."

I did look and walk different, though. I was blown up from the steroids. My hair was thin. I became very aware of my odd appearance now that I was "out in public." I was a freak. I got home and went to my room. My family had moved my bed and things to the corner room, where there was a cable hook-up. My sister, her husband, and son were living there. It was a crowded and tense environment.

Now the real challenges were about to begin.

Chapter 10 - Life On Hold

When we got home, I went straight to my newly converted room, which was now in the corner of the house. This had been my room as a child. My parents were very thoughtful to make this my room, because there was a cable hookup in this room. My sister was not happy about this, but my mom felt that I should have it since I was still very ill, and would be spending a lot of time convalescing. I turned on the television and went straight to the MTV channel. "With or Without You" was playing. The song had a spiritual, almost hymnal quality to it. Whenever I hear it now, I associate it with that bleak time, yet it also gave me a feeling of hope. I now had a name for what I suffered from. I will sometimes hear other songs from that summer of 1987, and remember how simple my dreams had been: all I wanted was to wear normal clothes, not look disabled or disfigured, to drive again. On days when I would really dream big, I would imagine myself getting up everyday, getting dressed, going to a job that could afford me to support myself, and to have my own place. But throughout the dreams, I also knew the reality and the dire predictions that had been given to me by some of the doctors, for example: one predicted dialysis, one predicted a kidney transplant, and one predicted that I would never have a "normal gait" again. Another predicted oxygen dependence. Did I really want this life? I had no idea what lay ahead of me, and on the days when I did think about it too much, I could drive myself into an anxious frenzy.

The house itself seemed very small. I had been in the hospital for a couple of months, so the hallways were tiny compared to the huge hospital corridors. I tried my best to stick to a routine, as they had told me in the hospital. But it was a very tense environment, with so many people living there. We all shared one shower. I was still falling in the shower, and I yelled for help once, and my sister made it clear that she would not help, because she would "get sick" if she had to see "that scar" from the operation. So I was on my own, and just was very careful when I went into the shower, holding on to the soap holder, and getting in and out as soon as I could. Because my sister was so angry to be back home, and sat in the kitchen a lot, I just stayed in my room a lot.

Her son, my nephew, would come in, and we would watch television together, and listen to music. He was so smart, and I could have pretty decent conversations about television and music with him. There was a lot of adult fighting going on, and when this happened, he would come in and we would hang out. I got the sense that my parents saw me as an emotional child. So we were the "kids" in the house. I did not mind keeping him company. But I truly worried about him. He had been moved back and forth so much already. I loved this kid so much, and wanted him to be happy. His presence in my life at that time was like a ray of sunshine. I hate to admit this, but I taught him how to make the fart noises under the armpits, and all the other goofy things you are not supposed to teach kids, partially just to annoy my sister. But we needed comic relief in the family so much then!

A few weeks after coming home, my dad asked if I wanted to go to the mall with him. I still had some money left from well-wishers who had sent me cards, so I figured I could get a book. He ran into a young truck driver coworker. Usually when my dad introduced me to someone male, I would hear, "Hey is she legal?" or "You married?" This time the guy looked quickly at me, would not accept the hand I extended to shake, and talked to my dad as if I was not there. This was a very unsettling experience to me. I began to resolve not to go in public anymore except to see my doctor.

I agreed to let some friends see me. I had two friends who said they did not care what I looked like, and they acted the same around me. Their names were Carrie and Joanna. Joanna would ask if she could take me to eat, and one time I was getting dressed, and went to put on makeup. I was so bloated from the medication, and also the large amount of candy I was eating, that I soon was close to 200 pounds. This was a 100 pound gain in a two month period. I had stretch marks everywhere, on my upper arms, legs, breasts, stomach, buttocks, and thighs. I was on such high doses of corticosteroids that I developed some secondary conditions known as "moon face" and "buffalo hump". These are exactly what you think they may be. Your body deposits fat on your cheeks and upper back. That I could deal with, because I was assured it would reverse when the meds were discontinued.

But the hideous scars on my face were only made more garish looking by makeup. I took a towel and roughly wiped all the makeup off. By the time Joanna arrived, my mom told her what was going on with me. Joanna came in my room and sat down. She said that she did not want to pretend that she understood what I was going through, but that she was very worried about my refusal to leave my room let alone the house. She said that she would take us through drive through, but she refused to allow us to order in. "The whole idea is to get you OUT of this house. This is no good!" I agreed, and much of that time in the car was silence. But that silent understanding and respect she showed me meant more than words at that time.

I finally agreed to let my friend Dennis see me. I had been home from the hospital about two weeks when my mom said, "Why don't you call Dennis? He was so worried about you when you were in the hospital" I told her that I really did not think it was a good idea. But I did it. It was a very bad mistake, and I wish I had gone with my gut on this one. He and I had been friends during high school, and after I graduated, we hung out together quite a lot. He apparently had more feelings for me. I did not have romantic feelings for him, and I made that clear, but he told me that he would be my friend "no matter what." I believed that. He had a look of complete shock when he came in, even though on the phone, I told him, "Dennis, I do not look the same. I am on medication that has made me gain a lot of weight, and I have a lot of scarring from this illness." He said, "That's okay, I am sure you're still beautiful."

Dennis had a mother whom he lived with who was ill with a form of cancer. Whenever I met her, she was wearing a head-wrap. He did not talk about it much, other than saying, "She isn't doing well," or "She had a bad day." His parents were divorced. When he walked in the door that day, I could see the look of shock. He was no longer going to be my "friend." It was uncomfortable for both of us. I glossed over the details of the hospital. My sister came in the kitchen, and caught on to what was transpiring, and became very protective. She said, "Yeah, she had to learn to walk again, and everything. It was very hard for her." He looked at his watch, and said that he promised some friends he would be seeing them this afternoon. He told me he remembered I loved Chinese food, and he would bring some back "tomorrow." I did not see him again.

My mom worked at a local department store at the mall. She told me much later, that she confronted him when he would walk through the mall as to why he would not call or visit. He told her, "I just can't." I became very disillusioned about this. Looks mattered very much. I was his friend, I thought, as long as I looked pretty. Years later, he resurfaced, and he had a different version of this story (fifteen years later, a boyfriend introduced him to me as his best friend, and Dennis stated he remembered none of this and that the reason he disappeared is that I rebuffed his romantic advances. I forgave him, as his life was an unhappy one, and he ended up in the hospital himself, and I sent him a card). But his abandonment of our friendship made me determined never to depend on men, and definitely never take for granted your looks. I always proceed with caution when someone is obsequious about appearance. That may be a huge overgeneralization on my part, but it is what I took with me from that experience at age nineteen.

I also had a female friend who did the same thing. She and I had hung out all through high school. She had gone into the Marines after we graduated, but every time she was home for the holidays, she would visit. The next time she was home, was in the spring of 1987, and she called. She had known nothing about my hospitalization. I filled her in on the phone. She insisted that she wanted to see me. I warned her, "I look very different, Elissa." She insisted that she did not care. She came over in her dress blues, and her jaw dropped wide open. She told me that before she left to go back to North Carolina, she would call. She never called again I have seen her since, also and it has been cold.

My friend Carrie is my sister—we just happen to have different parents. She lived about 50 miles from me at that time (we used to go to the same junior high school, which is how we met). She had a baby as a teenager, and was in an unhappy relationship with the infant's father. She began a new life when she moved with her parents and baby to a small town south of Pittsburgh back in 1985 after her baby's birth.

The miles did not stop her from sending packages daily or calling. Sometimes I would refuse even to talk to her, because I was so ill, or just withdrawing so much, so she would get a report from my mom. This was one of the few friends who did not take this rejection literally or personally, and to this day, I consider her my dearest friend.

She tells me today that from that time, she remembers "talking with you before your lung surgery and you being so afraid." She visited me, and not one look of shock registered on her face. She looked at me the way she always looks at me, like she is happy to see me. She accepts me no matter what. This is why she is family to me. As she says, "I remember visiting you and you had this device you had to blow into that allowed you to test your lung capacity. You were so proud of how far up you could make the balls go, and I didn't understand at that point what a big deal that was!"

Carrie admits, "I remember being afraid you would die. Selfishly, I remember wondering what I would do if you died."

One time, after I got home, she sent me a huge box of chocolates that were unbeknownst to me, filled with cordials, like rum and schnapps. I ate the entire two-pound box. I was still sedated with tranquilizers, that antipsychotic, and narcotic pain pills, and I thought that maybe I was not in need of the dosages that I was given after the room began to spin, and I found the soap operas that day incredibly funny. I thought to myself, if I did not now better, I would think I am drunk! Lo and behold, I was!

Later, after a long nap, Carrie called me and said, "Hey, I wanted to tell you, I sent you a box of chocolates yesterday, but I forgot to put a note in the box telling you NOT to eat them all, because they have liquor in them!" After she heard my laugh, she said, "Oh no! I'm too late, huh?" Some days a little humor added variety to my cheerless routine.

One of my favorite books up to that point had been a true story called *Black Like Me*. It was the story of a white man who lived for a period of time as a black man, back in the times of segregation. I now understood on another level what it was to be treated differently because of appearance. I used to tell my parents about the book, and that I was going to write a book called *Ugly Like Me*. Instead, I decided to not see anyone, just as I had insisted in the hospital. I stayed in that bed for pretty much the next year and a half, only getting out to shower ,go to an old used bookstore, and doctor's appointments.

I continued to have nightmares when I got home, and the night terrors, where I would walk and yell in my sleep. I had a new habit of ending up in the garage of my parents' home, curled up over their drain. This was done while I was sleep walking. Later on this was explained to me as just my body (and mind's) was reacting to the trauma, and trying to run away.

One morning in the late spring, 1987, I woke up and could not move. All my joints had locked up. I tried to get out of bed. It was if my knees had frozen like a Barbie doll. My arms had frozen. My elbows, shoulders, and all of the large joints were locked. It was a Sunday, and worse, it was Easter Sunday—holidays are not good days to have to go to a hospital. I yelled out for someone in the house. My mom asked, "Are you sure you didn't sleep in the wrong position?" I said, "I am positive." She brought me my medicine, and a pain pill. She told me to wait an hour until everything had a chance to work. I waited, sipped on ginger ale, as now a stomach ulcer had developed from all the medicine (I now took over twenty pills a day), but still I was locked up and now from the anxiety, the pain was unbearable. Dr. McCollom had given my parents his home phone number for emergencies. My dad said, "I don't know. This is an emergency. I hate to bother that nice man on a holiday, but I think I have to."

I heard my father out in the hall. "Dr. McCollom? This is Candy's father. Sir, I am sorry to bother you. I would never bother you at home, but you gave us your number....yes. Well, she is locked up....yes, all her joints. Yes we gave her medicine, a pain pill, her arthritis pill. Ok we'll do that." My dad hung up the phone. He said, "The doctor said you should go down to the emergency room at St. Mary's Hospital. I said, "Oh shit. I don't want to go back in to the fricking hospital, man."

My dad, who, despite being a truck driver, never swore, and hated the stereotype of the foul-mouthed truck driver, said, very calmly, "Candy, listen to what that good doctor said, he saved your life, and we called him at home. Now there is nothing we can do for you here."

It took me about a half hour to get out of bed, and I walked like one of the zombies in a George Romero movie. I said, "Let me go get into a warm shower, so I don't offend everyone in the E.R." My mom said,

"That's a good idea. Maybe the hot water will help you." Everyone in the family had very sympathetic looks. This was something I was not used to, as before this diagnosis, everyone was impatient. I thought about this as I stood in the scalding hot shower. It hit me, "They didn't believe I was sick, did they?" And then the guilt hit me, bout what I was putting them through now. God, I am such a F&%ing burden.

I stiffly walked out of the shower. I had managed to put on a large T-shirt and stretch pants, but all of my clothes were now skin tight on me. I had entered the hospital weighing about 125, dropped to around 100, and discharged weighing about 170, because of the steroids. But now, I weighed around 210. I now had stretch marks all over my stomach, and they were red, fresh, and painful, as the weight had just been lost and gained in about a five-month period.

My mom and sister went with me, and my dad and brother in law stayed home with my nephew. My brother in law came over and said, "You take care. I love you." I never heard that from him before. I was not used to this kind of emotion from my family. It was decided that I would sit in the front seat, as it had more legroom, and I could not bend my legs. It was an uncomfortable ride, but with it being Sunday, there was not much traffic, and we made it there in about thirty minutes. We also found a parking spot with no problem.

We entered through the emergency department door, and my mom, said, "This is Candace. She is a patient of Dr. McCollom. The registrant said, "OK. We are pretty full here in the E.R. Sign your name here Candace, and have a seat." We sat, and waited, and a nurse came and sat and got some preliminary information. She saw that I was obviously stiff. She said she would pull my recent chart from my admission. She apologized for the wait. Finally, a wheelchair was brought over for me, and I was taken to a cubicle type of area, sectioned off only by a curtain for privacy. Across from me, was a man in leg and arm shackles who was yelling, "Motherf-----e get me out of here! Take me back. I don't care!" The nurse explained, "He's from the Pen, you know the prison."

Again, an apology was offered for the E.R. being short staffed, and I lay there on the cot. My mom and sister sat there and talked, trying to keep it light, with gossip about the soaps we all watched. I was eavesdropping on the conversation between the doctor and patient behind the curtain next to me. The patient had been retching and puking before the doctor walked in to see him. The doctor told the patient clearly, "John, your liver is cirrhotic. You will die, plainly and simply if you don't stop drinking. Now I would like to admit you today so we can dry you out, then send you to rehab." The patient loudly said, "No f$#* way you aint sending me to no rehab." The doctor said, "Then please do not come back here because you come here every month and I can't continue to treat you unless you help yourself." The patient said, "I'm outta here." I heard him putting his shoes on and belt being buckled and thought, "There he goes, off to kill himself."

Finally a very young doctor entered my curtained off area. He looked to be about fifteen (okay, I exaggerate). He said, "So you have the belly pain?" I said, "No I have the Wegener's granulomatosis, and the locked up joints. My name is Candace." He said, "Oh right, right." He then said, "Sorry, I have been on a 36 hour shift here, let me read your chart here real quick." I laughed to myself as I looked at my New York phonebook sized chart. I glanced at my sister who was rolling her eyes. He looked at my list of meds, and I verified them. He questioned me about the antispsychotic medication that I was on. I said, "That was prescribed because I have nightmares." He said, "Do you still have nightmares?" I told him I do. He said, "So the drug really does not stop the nightmares?" I said, "No, not really." He asked if I was psychotic. I told him, "Yes. I am a nut."

He said, "Do you know what psychotic means? It means hearing voices, and paranoid. I told him, "I can get paranoid in the middle of the night". He said, "The steroids do that, but were you like this before prednisone?" I said that I did not hear voices, and all joking aside, if I were not in this situation, I do not think I would be so nucking futs. He told me that the drug is known to cause muscle and joint stiffness and would I mind if he stopped it? I said that I would not if it stopped this misery. He said he would stop it and prescribe a new pain pill. He asked if he could test my agility and how limber I am right now.When he went to listen to my lungs, he saw the stretch marks, he said, "You have tiger stripes." I must have had a hurt look on my face, because my sister, who had been sitting there silently, piped up. "No she doesn't. That is uncalled for! She has been though a lot, and that is not fair. She has stretch marks, and some things are not nice to joke about. She is very sensitive about her appearance." She then got up and walked out. My mom said, "You'll have to excuse my oldest daughter, she is protective." The doctor said, "I see that, and I apologize if that offended you, Candace." I said, "No hard feelings."

I was prescribed some pain medicine and it was explained that with my Wegener's, my joints may lock up like this some days. Even though I was on the steroids, an anti-inflamatory, I was still dealing with a very temperamental, unpredictable disease, the doctor explained. He told me I could also still take the small yellow pill that I took before the diagnosis was made, the one that helped me to move around before I was transferred to the large hospital. I was discharged from the emergency room, and by the time we got home, it was dusk.

I did not have another episode of joint "lock up" like that until one autumn morning in 1999, when I could not get out of bed. I missed three days of work in a row, which was very unlike me. I do not know what have caused that as I was only taking a thyroid pill at the time. But as I age, my arthritis does worsen, and it pops up in various joints, usually not in all of them at once.

The remainder of the spring and summer, I described throughout my journal as feeling as if my life was "on hold." I turned twenty that summer, and had a feeling that my nineteenth year had been a wasted year. I was definitely not in a place where I could see that you learn from your suffering. I was sick to the stomach a lot. I had migraine headaches a lot. I was in my room most of the day. I had the feeling that I was spending my days and weeks "waiting." But what was I waiting for, I often asked myself? For friends who had promised to come back? For the medication that had changed me to be discontinued? For a magic fairy to come in and give me my old face back? I began to have dreams that I was the person I used to be, and I would dream I was with old boyfriends.

I would wake up from a dream like this, and think, "I will never have sex again, because no one is ever going to want me. I am disgusting." I still had more violent nightmares that involved my dead grandfather, and he was often murdered in front of me. I would dream that my father was in a violent crash in the eighteen-wheeler that he drove, as he often drove a terrible shift of 5:00 p.m. to 4:00 a.m. The steroids made my moods go from intense sadness to rage to actual laughing fits all in the space of a twenty-four hour period. I would see something mildly amusing on television, and laugh so hard that I would be gasping for breath. My sister would come and knock on my door and come in to see if I was okay. Her standing there to even inquire about this, while I was laughing so hysterically would cause me to laugh even more hysterically.

My mother called the local mental health center. She told them she was fearful that I was having a "nervous breakdown." They informed her that since I am twenty, I had to make this appointment myself. I was angry that she did this, but she said, "Don't you want to talk to somebody? This can't be easy, and we don't know what to say to you. These drugs, we think are doing something to you." So I agreed.

I took the number, and called the next day, gave them my information. They set up an intake appointment. My mom and dad went with me. In the waiting room, there were a lot of different types of people. My dad was uncomfortable. The intake worker asked me a lot of questions about my symptoms, and the illness, I was very honest. My parents started to answer some questions, but she told them, "Please let her answer." I told the intake person that yes, I was angry. I was despondent, and felt like I would be better off dead, and that it would not ever get better. I felt ugly, and I did not see a real way out of this hole.

Chapter 11 - Back In The Hospital

I was sent to a therapist. At first, I did not know what to think of this therapist. She admitted, she had never heard of my illness. So she immediately requested medical records. I had no problem with that. She asked what my anger was about. I told her that I was twenty years old, and last year, I had a little bit of control over my life. Now, even if I did diet, I still would weigh at least 170, because that is what I weighed when I left the hospital, so that is why I just gave up and started eating like a pig. But the weight is not so much what bothers me. The doctor promised me that I would lose the weight once the steroids are discontinued. I was really bothered by my face. My face was, I felt, hideously scarred. And I also feel like I am treated like a small child in my home. I am relegated to my room all day. I love my family, but there are five adults and one child. But you'd think there are four adults and two children. I just stayed in my room, and as long as I stay there and shut up, I am okay.

She spoke, and said, "You would change no matter what. You change when you age. You just aged a little quicker. And you will lose the weight. Would it help if we brought the family in? Would you like to bring your parents in?' I said I would, but I did not like that, "You've aged a little quicker comment." I told her that, "Wait I am only twenty." She said, "But with your illness, which I have to learn about more, you are probably equivalent to an older person." I just thought, "Whatever…"

My mother and father came in with me one week, and the therapist brought up the topic, "Boundaries." It was a foreign concept in our family. I had shown the therapist, Jackie, a picture of my "former" self in the first session to illustrate how much I have changed. Jackie asked, "Why did you let your hair color go back to brown, Candace?" My mom answered, "She looked trampy as a blonde. Jackie looked at the whole family and said, "This is what I mean by boundaries. Number one, you answered her question. Number two, she changed her hair color to suit you, and she is an adult. And furthermore, she does not look, as you call, trampy, in this picture. Do you always judge a book by its' cover Mrs. Ross?" My mom was angry, and said, "No, but I don't want my daughter looking like a used up tramp. If she wants to look like that she can live somewhere else."

I made it clear that at this point I had no interest in my hair color, because my face was a bigger issue. My mom was angry that the "pink elephant" in our living room had been talked about, and was silent the rest of this session. Jackie also brought up the issue that I wanted to go to college. My mom became angry again. She stated that they had sent me to broadcasting school, and that they were unable to do anymore. My dad stated that they were very "tapped out" as their other daughter was living with them now with her son and husband. Jackie did not press any more. Jackie asked me if anyone had ever talked to me about "WRAP." I told her that the hospital social worker had. She asked my parents if they had any more questions, and they did not, so they were excused to go to the waiting room.

She said to me, "I can see why you are feeling hopeless. This is a very stressful environment that you are in right now. How badly do you want to go to college?" I told her with everything in my being. She wrote the number down for me and told me to please call WRAP again. She told me, "You have to put your energies and focus on getting educated and out of the house. It will not happen overnight, but try to focus on your future." She said when she got the medical records she was thinking of having me see a psychiatrist to see if I could take an antidepressant, and wondered if I would be agreeable. I agreed, as I felt like I needed all the support I could get now.

Finally the medical records arrived to Jackie, and she told me, "Holy Moses! You weren't lying!" I began to realize that I would probably always have to have proof, as my story is quite unbelievable. She wondered what made me wait so long to get help and how I hid it so long. I told her that I must have just somehow believed it would get better if I ignored it, and she said, "Oh, so the sweep it under the carpet belief, huh?" She asked if that type of thing goes on in my family a lot, and although I had never thought about it, I said, yes, it does.

She had told me that the agency's psychiatrist was a "very difficult" man, and told me that a lot of patients are "intimidated" by him. However, she said that she would talk to him to go gentle on me, and gave me the background on him. She told me he was an older man, and that right away, made me feel better, because, after all, so was my hero, Dr. McCollom. His name was Dr. Bergman. She told me he was a New York City transplant and that he was classically trained as a Freudian psychoanalyst. I asked her what the heck all this meant. She told me that he was going to ask me all kinds of questions about my childhood and also about what is going on now. She took me into his office, which was paneled with oak, and he sat in a chair with a high back, just like Dr. McCollom. I was not intimidated, but had a feeling of deference. He stood up and shook my hand. He was tall, and had wavy, gray hair. He looked kind of like Richard Burton. It was not difficult. I just answered his questions. He focused much more on the present situation. When I told him how I honestly was feeling like I sometimes wish I would be better off dead, he said, "That is somewhat understandable, you have had a terrible event and changes in your life." I told him how I once had been on the antispsychotic medication to sleep and that I had been taking it every night until the side effects caused problems. He asked me about my medical problems and side effects, and gave me insight into my stiffness—he stated that some of the stiffness may have come from the high dose of the antipsychotic that I was on, and affirmed what that E.R. doctor said.

He also explained that the current medications I am on would cause me to feel like I am "bipolar." I asked what he meant. He said, "The steroid you are taking causes some people to have erratic mood swings, sleep changes, as you know appetite changes, suicidal thoughts, mania. But just know, this is the medication. It does not mean you are manic depressive."

At the end of the evaluation, he said, "You are on so many medications, Ms. Ross. I do not feel like you need to be complicated by my putting you on any more. I would like you to tell us if you have serious thoughts of hurting yourself. But keep talking to Jackie. You are a smart girl. And do what your doctors tell you down in Pittsburgh. You still have a long life in front of you."

Jackie was waiting for me out in the hall. We went back in her office, and I said, "He was not difficult! I want to see him again!" She asked if he put me on any medicine, and I told her that he did not, and she said, "Then you aren't going to see him again." She said, "Well let me mark this on the calendar. This is the first time a patient has ever said they liked Bob." I teased her and said, "Bob, huh, we are on a first name basis?" She blushed a little, and said, "Boundaries, Candace. Boundaries!"

Despite the new form of support and having someone to talk to, I hit a high of 265 pounds in the summer of 1987, and I did not even care anymore-that is about a 160 pound weight gain in six months. I developed stretch marks on my stomach and abdomen, arms, legs, breasts. These have never disappeared after twenty years.

I saw Jackie once a week, and my visit to Dr McCollom was now every other week. I was friggin' miserable, hated life, hated myself, hated everyone, hated people who had normal lives. I was so drugged up on the cortisone, and pain pills, that I was a different person. I slept during the day and stayed up at night, watching television or reading to avoid interacting with anyone, even my family—hell, especially my family. I ate, and ate. I would cook a box of macaroni and cheese, and eat it all. Or have my sister buy a one pound bag of fruit chews candies, then eat them all.

Because my sister's car had been repossessed, my parents were letting her family use my old Toyota, so I was not able to drive. My mom felt that I was too drugged up to drive, which in 1987, was likely true. But I felt so trapped. On thing I did manage to do is finish up the correspondence work that was required for Broadcasting school. I received my diploma. However, I doubted that I would work in that field again. It felt like a lifetime ago. Everything prior to my hospitalization now felt like a lifetime ago.

I went out one time to a carnival or fair or something, with a neighbor, one of the wonderful people who did stick by me throughout the whole ordeal. I felt like a sideshow freak, so I ended up just going back to sit in her car, and watched everyone else, walking around, having a good time. That was that. I was in for the next year. I read a lot, so at least my brain was not going to waste.

Although I had migraines since age 5, during that summer, they increased about a thousand fold. I would wake up with the nausea in my stomach, and have that familiar feeling of heaviness, as if a big glob of toxic slime was in the right side of my cranium. I knew that I was in for at least a day of hell. The need to puke would actually wake me from my sleep. The summer of 1987 was one of the hottest and most humid in my memory. Our house did not have air conditioning. I cannot describe the misery. I often would just lie on the bathroom floor and just as I would doze off, the need to throw up would wake me up.

These horrible daylong migraines would occur at least once a week. I inherited them from my father, who was still in his early 50's at the time, and therefore, still getting them regularly. He tells me that after he turned 60, they went away. I met his brother only a couple of times, and his brother told me that he had them also until age 60, and that he would be nearly blinded by the pain, and would lie down on a work bench in the factory where he worked. My paternal grandfather Genovese also had them severely, my dad informed me. My sister got them, and later, her son would get them as he got older.

I mentioned these to Dr. McCollom, and he explained that they were made worse by the fact that my disease was vascular in nature, and also that the steroid medication was making my hormones go haywire. I had not gotten a period for six months or so, and he told me that this might indicate an early menopause. It was at this time that he broke the news to me that the disease and the treatments were also likely going to leave me unable to have children. My few friends who were standing by me at the time asked me if this upset me. And the answer is an honest, "No." For one thing, as a little girl, I never had that desire to grow up and have babies. For another, at the time that this news was delivered, my goal was to get better. The thought of even having a child was out of the question. I could not even take care of my self adequately at this time. How on earth could I even consider a child? It would have been negligent to the child.

As for the headaches, Dr. McCollom was not an advocate of using narcotic pain pills for long, and he started to wean me off these. He explained in very blunt terms, that what little is known about this disease is that unfortunately not pleasant for long term survivors. I asked what he meant. He said, "If you are lucky to live long, you may run into complications with bladder carcinomas or female carcinomas down the road. I am the kind of doctor who likes to prescribe the use of narcotic pain killers for that kind of pain. Because frankly, one day, you are going to need that level of pain killer. This pain you have now is every day pain. And I have to break it to you. You will have pain the rest of your life. You need to bite the bullet."

I look back, and am grateful. I have met some cohorts that are dependent on using pain pills daily. Dr. McCollom also shared my desire to wean me off this steroid as soon as possible, although perhaps not quite as soon as I. My father had recently been given an abortive vasoconstrictive medicine. This is a pill that you take at the onset of your migraine, and it goes to the root of your migraine. It constricts the dilating vessels in your head that are causing the pain. I asked Dr McCollom if I could try that. He said that I could, as it is used only as needed, and not daily.

As I got off the pain pills, that I was used to taking every day since I had gotten home from the hospital several months ago, I went through what felt like a flu, I shivered, then got hot, then threw up. I was only taking one three times a day, but could I possibly be dependent on them? The "flu" lasted about three days. I realized it was possibly withdrawal I was going through.

I still had blood work done weekly, and urinalyses, as well. I was having a problem that Dr. McCollom explained to me as best he could, in which he said I was "spilling protein" in my urine. I no longer urinated the dark blood colored urine, but the urinalysis showed that I was losing a lot of protein, and that affected my "H and H" count, rendering me anemic. I had to take big, green iron pills, which made me so nauseated; I would retch for a couple hours after I took them. I had to do a test at home called a "twenty-four hour urine test." This involved a large jug, a urine collection cup, a little tub, and a lot of ice. You collected your urine for twenty-four hours; you put it in the jug, and kept in the little tub on ice. Then you took it to the hospital, and the lab analyzed it. I was permitted to take it to our local hospital, thankfully. Of all three of our local hospitals, I was not thrilled with any of them, but the one in the little town we lived in seemed to be the best. It was clean, and the people there were very nice. I definitely would not return for any reason if I could help it to the place where I had my first inpatient experience.

This "spilling of protein" occurred until 1990, inexplicably. There was no remedy, and nothing to prevent. Eating more or less protein could not stop it. I had kidneys, after all, that were in failure just months earlier. Now, thank God, they were functioning. There was no longer any talk of dialysis, or transplants. It was just a matter of monitoring. I also was monitoring my lungs by just reporting what my breathing was like. I had to report to Dr. McCollom and Dr. Joaquino if I still coughed. I did not cough any longer. I had more upper respiratory congestion.

This is why, when it began to get cold in September, and my cough came back with a vengeance, and Dr. Joaquino was covering for Dr. McCollom for a few weeks, I was very alarmed by the symptom. I said, "I am coughing a lot." He seemed very annoyed that this upset me. He said. "You are always going to cough." I said, "No, you don't understand. My coughing had stopped." He said, "Candy. You have Wegener's granulomatosis. That's a lung disease. You will always have a cough. Trust me." I now became annoyed. I said, "Sir, I respect that you are a doctor, and I am nothing to you. But I know my own body. And this cough disappeared. " He commented that I had a "bad attitude." And yes, maybe I did. But I was learning, as Jackie had been instructing me, to assert myself. He said, "Very well, if it will make you feel better, I will write a script here for you to get a chest X-Ray. But all they're going to see is a shadow from your old infiltrate."

I saw him as a young, successful, and somewhat handsome man. I did not see much compassion in him. I did not like seeing him when he covered for Dr. McCollom. I could not resist asserting myself a little further. As he was turning to walk out the door, I said, "Dr. Joaquino, do you have any idea what I am going through?" He stopped. There was a silence, and I could see that he perhaps wrestled with whether or not he should reply to me. But he did. He said, "Yes. I do know what you are going through. Maybe not exactly. Because only you can walk in your shoes. And you are a young woman. I can see how angry you are, and I know what that anger is. I have had many operations and problems, too. I have a disease called Amyloidosis . It has been treated with a lot of the same drugs you are on. But your attitude has a lot to do with your healing." I agreed with that, but I think we had started on the wrong foot along time ago when my attitude showed itself with the "foul" language in the hospital room.

At any rate, I thanked him for taking the time to tell me that story. I certainly saw him in a different light now. He was not a perfect person— handsome, educated, one of the doctor-gods. He had an Achilles heel. He knew some of my pain. That took a lot for him to admit that to me, and I never forgot it. As a therapist now, I am careful about self-disclosures: Boundaries! But sometimes, when someone is desperately in pain, and they ask me if I know what they are going through, and I do know, I certainly let them know. Of course if this book is published, my life will be pardon the cliché, an open book.

I went home, and the coughing got worse, and now I was coughing up blood. After a few days, I called Dr. Joaquino's office, and asked if he'd received my results. He got on the phone, and said, "Candy I am so sorry, with covering for Dr. McCollom it has been crazy here. I am looking at your X-Ray here. I am sorry to tell you. You were right. This is bad news. You have an infiltrate now in your left lung. You do know your body. You need to be admitted."

This was happening very quickly. I said, "Will it be a direct admission? Should I just have someone drive me to the emergency room? How does this work?" He said, "Let me get you a bed on the 11th floor again. I will call you back. McCollom is back from vacation tomorrow." There was no car at home right now. The only people home were my sister and myself. I told her what was going on. She said, "What are you going to do?" I said, "What I have to do, Lucy. I have to go back in. I have a hole in my other lung." She was angry. "You told them that! Why don't they listen?" I said, "I know, Lucy, but they have to check things out. They can't just go on my belief."

I called my mom at work and informed her that Dr. Joaquino wanted me back in the hospital tonight, and she said she would leave right away. She had been on a family medical leave for months, and had only recently returned to work, and her workplace understood that I had medical problems that might necessitate her needing to leave. The doctor called back about an hour later, and informed me that right now, there was no space on the 11th floor, but a discharge is being planned.

He told us to hold off until about 7:00 p.m. This actually worked with our schedule.

My mom decided to take me, but she did not want to drive home alone. Lucy was going to stay home to feed her son, and wait for her husband to get home. He also now was driving truck for a living. My father, of course was working, likely until 3:00 or 4:00 a.m. This was in the days before cell phones, so he would not know about this until he got home the following morning. My mom did not want to drive back home alone from the city, so she asked me if I would mind if she took her mother along for the ride. My grandmother, the same grandmother who made some very hurtful comments to me. I looked at it this way. My mom had done a lot for me while I was sick. She had made this trip to the hospital many nights after working. She needed some company. This was her mother. I said, "Go ahead, mom." My grandmother saw me, and said, "Ooh boy. What are you up to now? You have to be over 200." I just shook my head and said, "I don't know, we don't have a scale."

The rest of the ride, I asked my mom if she could adjust the speakers in the back, so I could concentrate on the music, instead of trying to participate in conversation. As promised, when we went through the E.R. and I checked in, the registrant said, "Oh, Candace, you are already registered. Let me call for an escort. We will get you up to 11." I felt fine except for the persistent, hacking cough, and insisted on walking, but the registrant told me it is policy that the patient cannot walk to his or her room. I looked at my mom and grandmother, and realized that they were very cute, and that my mother was now sporting pure white hair just like her mother. My mom was only 48 years old. I said, "Mom, I just realized, your hair is white." She said, "I know. I stopped coloring it when you got sick, and it was more salt and pepper before. Her mom said, "You leave it alone, Yvonne, it looks nice."

I was wheeled up to my room. A young resident, Dr. Nee, very soon visited me. He came in and did a history and physical, and he gave me an idea of what the course of action might be. He said, "My guess is that we will likely increase your steroids."

I interrupted him. "Wait, " I said, "I am now down to 10 mg a day! I was started on 80 mg a day, and I am starting to see a light at the end of this tunnel! I will not agree to that."

He continued, "I am just telling you what the normal course of action is for a relapse of Wegener's granulomatosis, Candace. We will first have to do a lung biopsy, increase the steroids, and introduce another agent, a chemotherapy type agent, because the steroids alone were not enough to combat this illness."

I sat there slack-jawed. An anger and despair set in that was so deep it was in my marrow. I was in disbelief. How could this be? I have done everything they told me to do the first time? He looked at me with an "I'm sorry" look. He said, "I don't know what to say. We will tell you more as we know it, and of course, Dr. McCollom is your main doctor." He then left the room.

My mom and grandmother were sitting there, but I was so consumed by my feelings that I had completely forgotten that they were there. My mom looked like she would cry. My grandmother said, "He was nice. Handsome too. Nice Oriental man." I looked at my mom. "I am pissed off! I am so freaking mad. They are not going to tell me that I am having relapses and shit! I am going to fricking beat this disease, mom!" She looked at me, and said, "Good!"

I still was stunned. I told my mom that she should probably go home, as it was late. I unpacked my bag, and put my soap in the bathroom. It was soap Lucy had bought for me at Clinique. It promised to erase signs of skin imperfections and discolorations. Lucy swore she could see a difference, but I did not know. I knew she had paid a lot of money for the bar of soap, so I was grateful. I was so immersed in my feelings that I did not bother to say "hello" to my roommate. Finally I came over to my bed and just sat there. An aid came in and took my temperature, and it read 102, but it was a false alarm: I had just had a hot cup of tea. She later took it again and it was my baseline, which is 96.8. I am strange that way. My baseline is not the standard 98.6. My cough would not let up, so the staff brought me a strong codeine cough syrup.

Finally, the roommate introduced herself. "Hi, I am Donna." I just looked at her. It took all I had to say, "Hello. I am Candace." Her husband, Bob, said, "Are you from the city?" I told him that we were from Greensburg, 30 miles outside the city. He told me that they also were about 30 miles outside the city, but South. They were people who were in their mid-fifties, perhaps. He said, "I couldn't help, you know,

I overheard what happened here." I looked at him. I was not angry that he eavesdropped. If you wanted privacy, this was not the place. He came over in my direction. I had the bed close to the window. He said, "Look out there at the trees, over near the Arena."

I was not sure where he was going with this. I said, "Okay. I'm looking." He said, "What do they look like?" I said, "They look almost bare." He said, "That's right. It is mid October, and some of them are bare, losing their leaves, or down to their last leaves." I looked at him. He said, "You are one of those trees. You are feeling very bare right now. But you will have a spring again. You have to go through winter. But you will grow leaves. Believe that." He put his arm around my shoulders. I said, "Thanks." But I cannot honestly say I believed this.

I lay there all night, and did not sleep. I worried about my life, about my future. Chemotherapy? An illness that once it starts to get better comes back with a vengeance? What kind of life is this?

Chapter 12 - Difficult or Assertive?

I did not sleep that entire evening. I stared outside the window. I had a clear view of the concert and hockey Arena. I got up and paced up and down the halls. I finally got on the back service elevator and went down to the vending area, where some of the employees hung out, smoked, and ate. I got myself a cup of coffee.

This admission was obviously different from my first lengthy hospitalization, in that I was ambulatory, and had, as I perceived it, one problem: a cough. Yes, the cough originated from a hole in my lung. But, holy cow, aren't these treatments that the resident is proposing a little much?

I went back upstairs after about an hour. I had never gotten into my hospital garb yet. I was dressed in ill fitting pink sweatpants and sweatshirt. I had outgrown this outfit about thirty pounds ago. I did have slippers on my feet. But I was probably able to go downstairs without much notice because of my sweat suit. I was always hot because of the steroids, and felt like I was burning up, so I was drenched in sweat by the time I made it back upstairs, and the hole in my lung made me very short of breath.

A nurse saw me going in my room, and said, "Where were you? We came to check and you were gone" I explained that I needed a cup of coffee, as I had a headache, had asked for aspirin, and had not gotten it, and the caffeine helped. The nurse said they thought I had "eloped." I asked what she meant, and she said, "That means that we thought you left the hospital and didn't tell us."

I told her I would be stupid to do this, as I have no way home and a big hole in my lung. She said that she realizes I am scared and angry about what they are talking about for treatment options, but she is glad that I am being sensible. What else could I say, but "Thanks"? Did they think I would actually do something like that? I later found out when working in the hospital, that yes, people do, in the face of life threatening conditions, "elope." I also thought back to the man in the emergency room months earlier that walked out despite the doctor's warning. No matter what, I always did what the doctors said. I might hate it, but I did it.

I finally took the hospital pajamas, which looked as though they might be cooler, off my bureau, which I noticed were size 2X, and thought that they might be more comfortable than my hot sweats. I went to the bathroom and washed my face again, and I decided to lie down. It was about 4:00 a.m. I was not religious, but I asked God to please look down on me and help me get through this.

I drifted off to sleep, and I woke up to the hand of Dr. Nee waking me up. He said, "You looked so peaceful. I am sorry to disturb you. I heard you had a very restless night. Look, I have Dr. McCollom and Dr. Joquino here with me." I sat up, and suddenly was wide-awake.

Dr. McCollom said, "Candace you have a large lesion in your left lung. That's why you are coughing so much, and bringing up blood. We are going to need to go in the lung and just make sure it is the Wegener's and not something else, like cancer." When he said, "go in there," I had visions of another thoracotomy with a respirator again. I asked him if that is what he meant. He said that this time, I would have a "less invasive procedure," and that this would involve a tube down my throat and a camera at the end of the tube, scraping the needed tissue.

This sounded pretty "invasive" to me. I said, "Wait a second, am I going to be awake or out for this?" He said, "You could be sedated." I said that I would like to be out. I then sounded off very angrily about how I had been complaining about this cough and the cough was blown off at first as being normal for this disease, and "now look!" I was very angry. All three doctors, who were studies in calmness, duly noted this.

Dr. Joquino said, "I apologize for 'blowing off' your concerns about that cough, and as I said, you were right. I am concerned about your being so angry. Would you like for us to send Dr. Sidhwa in to talk to you?" I got even angrier at this suggestion. I said, "No, just do what you have to do with my body. No shrinks this time. Cut me, biopsy me, and discharge me!" They all looked at each other. Dr. McCollom just said, "Okay."

I rolled up into a big angry ball, and tried to go back to sleep. I decided that the surgery details would be provided to me as the days wore on. But as I lay there, I thought, and became more irate. My anger stemmed from the fact over the fact that I had known for weeks that I had the cough, and had, as they said in the medical profession, "complained" about this. I felt that this complaint had been dismissed as being "normal" for my condition, or disease, and knew that this was not at all normal.

The left lung had an infiltrate the size, Dr McCollom told me, of a grapefruit. This would be the reason I was coughing. Dr. Joquino did apologize, and I understood that doctors made mistakes, but I felt like my opinion did not count. I admit, I personalized a lot of this. If I had an education, or maybe came from "the right side of the tracks" I wondered, would they hear me out more? If my father was a professional, and not a truck-driver, would this matter? I was always very class conscious, and this was a result of the fact that my father often imparted that sense of class differential thinking to me.

I decided that I had to be sharp, educated about my health, every procedure, each doctor, each test, each dosage, time it was administered. The first time I came in this hospital, it was largely due to my own neglect, stupidity, and stubbornness. I had, I admit, neglected medical care, and it had gotten ugly. I may have had a large hand in that admission and in my own deterioration.

This time, however, I was upset because I had followed the directions of the doctors. I took each pill. I kept each appointment. As requested, I told them when it hurt and if something felt wrong, and I did feel like I was "blown off." I could give up and feel as if my opinion and words were inconsequential, or I could take this anger and make it work for me. I could become very informed, my own patient care advocate. I decided that I would become the latter. I was unbelievably physically tired. I felt as if someone or something, like a tapeworm, had been sucking the very life out of me, I was so very tired. And sure enough, again, I was anemic.

I rested, and I slept, and because I was ambulatory, I did not require physical therapy, so I also walked the units during this stay. I asked questions. I found that some nurses and assistants still did not like to answer questions. "You have to ask your doctor," they would reply. I told Dr. McCollom I did not want this to be the case any longer. I told him if I were going to have my answers denied, I would sign out of the hospital. Dr. Joquino, a doctor with who I always had a tenuous relationship, showed some anger at me this time, when I made this threat. He said, "Go ahead." This would be the last I would see of Dr. Joquino for quite some time, with the exception of running into him in Dr. McCollom's office. After he uttered this, he walked out, and left Dr McCollom and I in the hospital room alone. Dr M. said, "I will see to it that all of your concerns and questions are answered."

Later that evening, a sign appeared behind my head, above the bed, outside my room, and also at the foot of the bed. The sign read, "Answer ALL questions, per Dr. McCollom."

One nurse said to me, "You know, you are a very 'difficult patient', Candace." I could appreciate this label as I know that it must be a lot easier to have a meek and complacent patient who does not ask any questions. It probably makes a person's job a lot easier. I did not argue with her. I realized then and there that I was not going to be liked by everyone. But damn it, this was my life, and I was going to fight for it.

While I waited for my surgery date to be announced, I continued to pace the halls. I was so wired, and I could not understand this. I hardly slept. I had experimented with stimulants in high school, and this was a similar feeling. I also know that when my thyroid function is off kilter, it affects my mental perception in that I can become almost manic sometimes from too much synthetic thyroid hormone, and when not on enough thyroid hormones, I can tend to get sluggish and at worst almost depressed and even paranoid. Now, I had a paranoid edge. I was still seen as a "bizarre case" by many of the young doctors, and one young doctor who was not even on my case came in and introduced herself to me. She was a Greek immigrant, with curly dark hair, sort of a dead ringer for the actress, Melina Kanakaredes. Since her name escapes me after all these years, I will call her Dr Melina. She said, "Hello, Candace, I heard about you, and I am studying to be an obstetrition, you know a baby doctor. Do you mind if I visit you, just because I hear how unusual your case is?"

Immediately, I recognized her accent as being Greek, because while working in radio, I made friends with some Greek-American announcers (one of the stations I worked at did some afternoons of multicultural programming). I was fascinated by the culture. She taught me some Greek words, and I told her how much I loved Greek food. The answer, of course, was yes, she could study my case.

Every day during this stay, Dr Melina stopped by, some days, brought me in home made baklava, and was very informative and helpful with the latest information on Wegener's granulomatosis. I thought this was hopeful, because it showed me that some of the younger doctors were not afraid to give patients information and provide us with hope. Dr Melina let me know that the increase of the steroid may possibly be the culprit for my sleeplessness, paranoia, and anxiety.

Finally, a date was announced for my bronchoscopy, and they gave me a day to mentally prepare. I was, as I said, paranoid, and anxious already, and Dr McCollom asked me if I would like to see Dr Sidhwa. I secretly did want to see him, but I was being very stubborn, and I also was worried, as I was unsure what the status of my parents' insurance coverage was. So I said, "No shrinks!" Dr McCollom said, "Okay, Gus. So tomorrow, we will have Dr Davies do your bronchoscopy." I asked what this involved. He told me Dr. Davies would be in tonight to answer my questions. I also asked why Dr. Bonzetti (the Burt Reynolds look-alike) would not be doing it. Dr. McCollom told me he was on vacation. Dr McCollom told me that even though I did not want to see Dr Sidhwa, there would be some medication to calm me down ordered.

Later that evening, my mom, and her mother came in. I was getting more anxious. My mom was trying to assuage my fears, when Dr. Davies came in and introduced himself. He was a very pleasant Jamaican man, and he said, "Hello Candace. You are not 20! My God. You look like you're 14!" I thought, I like this guy already. He also made my mom and grandma feel at home by referring to them as "Mom" and "Grandma." He explained everything to me and took my fear down one thousand-fold by telling me that I would indeed be asleep for the procedure. No one had seemed to be able to answer that simple question for me! I would have pictures taken of the infiltrate, and a biopsy taken of the tissue. Dr Davies explained ," At the end of the end of the scope, are little scrapers that we use to scrape the tissue."

I was relieved to know that I would be "asleep" or totally anesthetiszed for the procedure, however, the downside, was that the operating rooms were all booked the next day until 1:00 p.m. I was forbidden to eat or drink anything after midnight. I was very prone to migraines if I had no coffee or hydration, and to go over thirteen hours, would be difficult. But I would do what I had to do, as I had little choice.

The next morning, I was woken early and given a shot of 100 mgs. steroids. I was told that I would only be given this shot one time, because I expressed great alarm over the high dosage. By 9:00 a.m., I had begun to develop the right sided throbbing in my skull, and was only on intravenous meds. I was permitted some pain meds. At that time, the abortive migraine meds were not known, at least to me, so this pain was unrelenting. A sympathetic nurse allowed me some ice chips.

The time came to be wheeled down for pre-op. I was given something before being wheeled down to "relax" me. When I got there, I felt very "relaxed," and without a care in the world. Dr. Davies was there in his scrubs, and greeted me with a big smile, "Every thing is going to be alright, now. Don't you worry," He said in his thick accent. The staff in the O.R. looked at my wristband and then at him and said, "What is going on?" His smile suddenly vanished. "Excuse me, " he said to me. He said to the staff, "I have this broncho scheduled for 1:00. Is anyone prepared? I told you, we had three bronchoscopes today! You are supposed to sterilize the scopes so that we can rotate them! Now we can't take patient in for another half hour!" He came back over to me, big smile intact, "Oh honey, now doncha worry, relax. Close your eyes." I had a fleeting thought about germy "scopes," then I remembered no more.

I woke up in post-op. I felt very out of control, and could not keep my thoughts straight. A nurse was there, and said, "How are you?" I told her, "I do not smoke marijuana, but if feels like I have and I don't like it!" She said, "That's good that you don't like that feeling. Well, we have a shot to counteract this." People were screaming all around me. My eyes felt like they had petroleum jelly in them. I told the nurse, "My eyes have some kind of Vaseline in them." She had a soothing voice. "That's there so they won't get dry during surgery. We will take care of that. Next thing I knew, a warm, wet cloth was over my eyes. She said, "This sounds like Snake Pit. Did you ever see that movie?" I said, "Yes" She was referring to an old, 1940's movie about a woman who was committed to a mental health institution. "Or Frances," she said, "Did you see that movie, too?" I said, "Yes." Nurse continued, "She was so pretty and so talented. What a shame." I said, "I used to be, too." Nurse said, "Used to be what? Crazy?" I said, "No. Pretty." Nurse said, "Honey, You still are. You still are." I felt the palm of her hand on my right cheek, where the scars were, and her other hand stroked my hair, the thinning hair, so much of which that was lost from illness. I never saw the nurse, because my eyes were filled with petroleum jelly and then covered with a wet rag, but I will never forget how she distracted me, talking about movies, and showed me compassion.

While being wheeled up to my room, I began to get sick, and needed to throw up. I was handed the little kidney shaped dish, to puke in. I became convinced it was the ice chips that I had at 9:00 a.m. that did it. When they tell you "nothing by mouth," I have learned since that operation, it means "nothing" by mouth! By the time I got into my bed, I was violently throwing up. Dr. Melina came in to see me. She told me it was not the ice chips, but felt that the 100 mgs of steroids might have been too much. She stayed with me for quite a while that afternoon. I think back on this sometimes and am amazed that a doctor who was not even "my" doctor took such an interest in me.

I was soon given a shot in the buttocks for my nausea which quelled the vomiting, and another shot in my IV bag which sedated me and let me sleep. When I woke up, I looked out the window, and saw the bright orange streaks across the grey sky outside my window. Nina, the nurse who had often taken care of me in my first, lengthy stay at this hospital, was checking my IV bag, and looking longingly out the window, up to the Civic Arena. "Man, I'd kill to be there tonight. U2 is up there. That is supposed to be an awesome show. Do you like them?" I said, "Are you kidding? I love them." She, as usual, kidded, "Let's go. Let's blow this hell hole and go see Bono. God, he's hot!" She took my vitals and said she would be back a little later to see how I was doing.

I was tired, and went back to sleep, and for the most part, slept through the night, I thought, as I fell to sleep, how amazing it was that the one shot did stop my throwing up. I hoped that medicine held similar miracles for me.

The next morning, I awoke to the hustle and bustle of the unit, and went to the sink, washed my face, and felt like taking a walk. It was important to me to maintain my sense of independence by walking around. I went down to vending machine, and got some coffee, hot from the machine. It was better than what came up with breakfast, and only a quarter,

When I got back to the room, a nurse was there, and said, "OK, I have your shot of steroids." I said, "I was told I would only get it the morning of surgery." She ignored my statement completely, and said, "Now honey, I will give it so it won't hurt." I said, "I am not worried about it hurting. I am simply telling you that I was told that I only got a 100 mg. shot on the morning of surgery." She actually let out a sigh, and a "tsk" sound, and then asked if I was going to be "difficult." I said, "If being difficult is asking for this to be checked again to make sure I heard correctly yesterday, then yes. I am difficult."

A half hour later she came back in with my morning pills. She did not mention a shot. She had my thyroid pill, she had my oral steroids, and something for nausea. I asked, "Did you find out about the steroid shot?" She said, "Oh. You are not scheduled for a shot today. That was only for the day of surgery. O-KAY?" She accented the "kay" in a very superficial way, turned on her heel, threw the dosage cup in the garbage, and walked out the door. There was no apology, no, "You were correct," not a word of explanation." It made me feel validated that I spoke up, and advocated for myself, though. And I thought to myself, Nurse, I am sure I just somehow saved you from some kind of medication error.

My roommate, Donna, was hyperventilatimg again. She did this often thoroughout the stay. This often occurred after her mother visited with Bob. We were all watching *Jeopardy* and *Wheels of Fortune*. Donna, Bob, and I were yelling out answers, gleefully. Her mom said, "Shut up! You are all ruining it for me!" "Mom" was a woman who looked like she had stepped out of 1962, replete with beehive, floral dress, and spike heeled pumps.

This was a typical visit, and poor Donna would have what appeared to be a panic attack when her mom left. One evening, after her husband and mom left, she frantically rang the call bell. A nurse came in, and asked what was wrong, and Donna said, "I can't breathe." She was hyperventilating fiercely. Nothing could assuage her fear, even after the nurse took her vital signs and assured her everything was okay. A short time later, a harried looking, young doctor came in, looking annoyed. He brought in a paper bag, and said, "Here. Breathe into this. You are not dying. You can breathe. There are people here that are dying and who are dependent on oxygen for their breath. Please do not waste our time with this. I will consult psych for you."

After he left, I felt embarrassed for her, and you could have heard a pin drop. I had nothing more than a high school diploma, (and was still hoping to finish my radio announcing credits) and that high school diploma was obtained by the skin of my teeth. But what I had witnessed prior to her psychosomatic episode, anyone with a working knowledge of psychology could analyze and determine: she was reacting to the treatment of her mother. After a while, she broke the silence. "He's right. I mean, he could have been a little nicer to me, that doctor, but I have to learn to not take things to heart," she said sadly. We said good night to each other, and I read long into the night. My latest read was the autobiography of Rock Hudson's wife from the 1950's (a short lived marriage).

On the unit with me, was Gerri, the same patient who I met during my first admission at St. Mary's. She was back, as she told me, she had a recurrence of her cancer. "I'm not worried. It's happened before." We talked and we traded addresses.

I woke up the next day, and Dr. McCollom and several residents and interns were with him. Dr McCollom delivered the news. He was very matter of fact, like Jack Webb, on Dragnet. "Well, Gus, we got the tissue sample back. You do not have cancer. What you have is another lung infiltrate from the Wegener's." As much as I liked and respected this doctor, my thoughts were, Yeah, tell me something I did not know! He told me the basics about a drug I would be administered, first intravenously, and then orally. He had told me when I was admitted back in the spring about the possibility of this medication, and I remembered that he told me it was a chemotherapeutic agent, the same time used in fighting some types of cancer. I said to him, "Oh, that chemo you had told me about?" A resident piped in, defensively, and said, "Who told you it's chemo? You don't have cancer!" I said, "Dr McCollom had explained to me when I was first diagnosed that this may be a possibility, and that this is a type of chemotherapy." Dr. McCollom looked at the resident and said, "She is very informed, asks a lot of questions and understands information." The resident stepped back and said no more. That left me thinking that it was unfortunate that there are patients who do not stay informed.

Dr. McCollom told me that there was a chance that I could lose my hair. Many nurses were asking me if I was worried about this. I have to say, I honestly was not. I had been dealing with permanent scarring of my face for many months. Temporary hair loss was nothing. I did not mind the prospect of hair loss. I was also warned about the nausea. I already had experienced a lot of nausea from the steroids, but was cautioned that it may increase as chemotherapy and nausea are nearly synonymous. Dr. McCollom looked at me almost apologetically as he delivered the next statement: Gus, we also have to increase the steroids. I was stoic as I listened to the bit about the "chemo." I was, as so many nurses, and my family liked to refer to taking this kind of news, "brave." But here is where I "lost it." I said, "No, man! I don't want to! I hate that crap! I am already fat and ugly, and I catch all kinds of colds. I can't stand it. It makes my migraines worse. No more. I would rather die." He did not react to my outburst.

"Look, I know that this is not what you want to hear," he said, "But we have to attack this infiltrate and prevent it from growing larger and prevent the disease from getting out of control like it was before. We are arming ourselves with an arsenal—the two best agents that we have in fighting Wegener's granulomatosis." I could feel hot tears stinging my cheeks. He patted my hand. "I promise you, we will keep you on the prednisone for as short a time as possible." I sniffled.

I asked him again for information on this illness, "Wegener's granulomatosis", as I had been unable to find anything on my own. He promised me he would look. I laid back down in the bed, on my right side. About five minutes later, he came back, and said, "Gus, there is one more thing I have to tell you about that Cytoxan causes. You may not ever be able to have kids." This was not a concern of mine at the time, but Dr. McCollom must have thought that at twenty, I must have grave concerns, because he did not send in the psychiatrist, but instead, he sent in a young nurse to see me. Looking back, I realize she had a lot of her own issues, but I understand why both he and she did what they did. They felt that I, as a young woman would have issues about losing my ability to conceive. She identified herself as Ginger.

She looked at my bottle of aspirin on the nightstand. "You gotta get rid of that sweetheart. You are going to be on Cytoxan. You can't take that, and you need to drink loads of water. I am talking big jugs, gallons. You will have a 50 percent chance of developing bladder cancer. Dr McCollom told me to talk to you about how serious you have to take care of this. When I got Vasculitis, I was in nursing school, and my biggest dream next to becoming a nurse was becoming a mother. My fiance and I had my whole life mapped out. When Dr McCollom said I had to go on Cytoxan, I cried buckets, I am talking buckets. We have tried fertility drugs, everything." I sat in my bed, incredulously, looking at this perky, twenty-something woman. She had a job. She had a wedding ring, she had no visible scars. She was a professional. Wasn't that enough? Tears were in her eyes as she talked about mourning the loss of a baby she may never have. I did not get it. I asked her, "Are you in remission from Vasculitis?" She said, "Yes, but I cannot ever have a baby of my own. Do you understand you may not ever have a baby of your own?"

I again told her that I understood. This time, I was actually quite mean, and now the anger came out: "I never wanted babies. I don't care of my uterus drops out right now. I am sitting here, and I was just told that I have to go on chemotherapy for an illness that was starting to get better. Then it got worse because of a cough. I told one of the doctors about a cough, but no one listened to me, because he told me "You'll always cough. Coughs are normal. I know my body. Now I am on this toxic drug. Cy-TOX-in. You act like it is the end of the word that I can't reproduce. I don't even have sex anymore, so big freaking deal, okay?" She looked at me, stunned then said, "Well listen, if you want to talk, I am down on the 8th floor." I felt like an ass, but what was the purpose of the visit? Support for me? Support for the nurse? I was not in any mental form to support another human being.

Anger consumed me. I would take this drug in any way they wanted to give it to me. And it came to me in the form of an IV that burned later that morning. It burned going in my arm, it burned the rest of body's veins, burned my toes, my hands, my gut, and left me with an indescribable taste in my mouth. Well, wait. I can describe it. It was as if you sucked on a piece of scrap metal for several hours. I mentioned this to a couple doctors who said, "That should not be." Only years later when I saw a very intelligent dentist, who was always furthering his education, and also had a degree in anthropology, did he affirm my description. He looked at my medical history, he said, "Cytoxan, I bet it tasted like metal for you all the time, didn't it? He then gave me the chemical reason why it would have.

I then felt very nauseated and tired.   I slept most of the rest of that day, and felt like sleep was the only time I had any escape from the reality of my world. In dreams, I was thin and attractive again. I had friends. I drove, and I had a place to go. I had a job. I was happy. Music was in my dreams. Life was in my dreams. But pain was not in my dreams.

The next day, I received the intravenous drug again, along with the increased dose of prednisone. Again, I felt the rush of heat and burning, in the site of injection, all through the extremities, in my gut, even in my head, and ending with a taste in my mouth, which I now identified as tasting like I had metal in my mouth. Then came the waves of nausea, followed by a good hour of vomiting. This was duly noted by the nurses who came to do morning vitals.

The nurses and Dr. McCollom all told me that this was the Cytoxan causing the nausea and that it was a very powerful drug that was blasting out the "bad" tissue and healing the bad. The side effect was that in the process, I would be very ill. The prescription for this was to continue to try to drink more water to flush its toxicity out of my system, "Don't allow this to sit in your bladder." It was hard to keep the water down, too. But I took the instructions. After ten days of hospitalization, I was sent home. I would follow these directions. What other choice was there if I were to realize the life that appeared to me in my dreams?

This time, going home was less exciting than last. I had lost some of my hopes. I had true fear about my life, as I had met some people (like Gerri) in the hospital, people with chronic, serious health problems. I feared that hospital stays would become a revolving door for me. I was determined to not let this happen, yet I felt this wave of hopelessness trying its best to carry me away.

Chapter 13 - Endless Winter

The days, weeks, and months after I came home from the hospital seemed to jumble into one long day that fall and winter. It was late October, 1987, and it was beginning to get cold. I was very withdrawn, and retreated in my room, and my father checked on me before work, and after.

He would sometimes come in, and check my pulse and scare the crap out of me, and I would literally jump and scream. He later told me he had a fear that I was going to die, and this is why he checked regularly. He drove for a local trucking company, and would sometimes call during the day if he could get to a phone (no cell phones in 1987). I think today about what he must have gone through, as an adult who works long days, without a kid to worry about, and it makes me feel sick at heart. Plus, I have an office job. He was out on the road, grinding gears, often with blinding migraines of his own. And back then most of the trucks did not have air conditioning and all the fancy amenities they do today for some of the local companies.

I did not talk to anyone now other than my mom, dad, and sister and her family. Occasionally, I would accept a phone call from my best friends, Carrie, or Joanna, but I did not let anyone see me. I did not even let my friends from across the street whom I grew up with near me any longer. I spent my days on the bed, in front of television, and reading. I became addicted to the classic movies on all day, and of course, music remained my salvation. I was finding particular salvation in late 1960's and 1970's Punk, and the louder and harder, the better: The Sex Pistols, the MC5, the Ramones. My favorite current artists were an English group named the Smiths featuring a brilliant, satirical lyricist named Morrissey. Morrissey, if you are reading this, you got me though late 1987 and 1988, I kid you not.

My days consisted of taking the full dosage of the chemotherapeutic agent which was 150 mg, then getting very nauseated, throwing up, and lying back down for several more hours. I still saw Dr. McCollom about once every two weeks. His suggestion when he saw my mood, as he still felt that I was depressed over the news that I could not have children, was that I get a dog. My mom also felt that this might not be a bad idea. We started looking in the paper for a dachshund, since that is the type of dog I had when I was growing up, and our last dachshund died over five years ago.

We saw an ad for a $50 dachshund. My mother and I went to see this dog, and the lady who had the dog also had about fifty other dogs in a mobile home, and in kennels on her property. She said, she specialized in schnauzers that she rescued from puppy mills and breeders and that people heard about her and dumped dogs off at her door. One of the schnauzers was only two years old, and had been used to breed, and had already had five litters of pups in her short lifetime. Her belly had a drooping pouch. Another schnauzer was an elderly arthritic male. My mom and I looked at each other, sadly. This made my sad state worse. My mom asked, "Are you sure you don't want one of them?" I said, "No, I want him," pointing to the dachshund.

Kate, the owner, cautioned us that the dog had been owned by an elderly man, and that the dog only favored males, and that he was very temperamental. I still wanted him. He was considered a "toy" dachshund, almost as small as a chihauhau, and was named Barney. I was adamant. Kate still tried to convince me to take one of the schnauzers, with a knowing look. She said, "I'll tell you what—you take him for two days, try him out, and if it doesn't work out, bring him back."

While driving back home, my mom told me, "This will be good for you. It will get you to at least get out, get some fresh air, even if it is around our yard." The dog was bouncing all over the place, and shaking. He was reddish-brown. I wanted a companion who was also slow and liked to sleep a lot, like me. This dog was like a jumping bean. We got him home, and he was like a cannonball shot out of the cannon. He zoomed up our steps, passing me by.

I went to open our freezer, and he jumped up the three feet trying to see what was in the freezer, and I said to my mom, annoyed, "What the hell is with this dog?" She laughed, and said, "Candy, give him a chance! He is checking out the surroundings."

I was tired out by the trip to the woman's house, and said I needed to go lie down. I took the dog with me. He did lie down with me on the bed, but proceeded to burrow under the covers. We never let our dachshunds in the house with us—they always stayed downstairs in the basement before, and I later learned, they indeed burrow. He burrowed and farted. And he bit my butt. My father got home and the dog took to him, as the woman told us, the dog preferred men.

When I would try to take the dog from my dad, he would get angry and nip at me. After two days of farting, biting, and jumping into the freezer, we decided that the trial was over. We took him and a big bag of food back to the mobile home, and the jumping bean never even looked back at us. It just was not time for me to have a dog. I was tired, irritable, and was sleeping most of my day away while on the chemotherapy. My father was very concerned. He was always the active one in the family, and thought that I needed to be out walking every day. And you know what? I wish I would have taken his advice. He was absolutely correct. A walk a day is the best exercise. I know that now, I feel great when I take a walk daily, if I have the time. My pains are lessened when I walk.

But I chose to just hole up in my bedroom, and I became more and more miserable every day. Days turned to weeks, and soon there were no more warm days. It was now late fall. One day, my father came to get me out of bed, and it was late morning. He told me there was a woman on the phone for me. I told him I did not want to talk with anybody. He told me as I walked to the phone that he had talked to a benefits person at his workplace and that I could get my own insurance. The lady on the phone was from medical assistance. My dad said, "You'll get your own insurance and maybe some money, too." I still had some money socked away in my Rolling Stones album double album, *Hot Rocks*, $250, to be exact, from my last paycheck. That was my hiding place. I figured it was my emergency money, if I ever had a craving for Chinese food, or wanted to buy a book.

Having my own money and my own insurance sounded like a good idea, and I had no idea what was going on, so I got on the phone. The woman identified herself as a caseworker. She said that my father had called but that she needed to talk to the applicant as I am over the age of eighteen. I asked what this is all about. "My dad said I could get my own insurance and money." She said, "Well, if you qualify. You may qualify for public assistance or Supplemental Security Income, and if you qualify for those, you will also qualify for Medicaid." I had no idea what any of that meant, so I just said, "Okay." She said, "Now I am going to ask you some questions." She proceeded to ask me if I worked, when I last worked, if I was able to work, what type of work I did, and then she asked me about my health. This took a long time. I had a lot of explaining to do. She often asked me to repeat or spell my illness, and "Are you sure," was asked when I told her I had some procedures done. She asked if I would sign some papers if she sent some to me in the mail. The papers would authorize me to have medical records sent to the local Social Security Office.

I still did not fully understand what was going on. She explained that the information I have given her indicates that I have a disabling condition that prevents me from working again, and I can receive social security payments. I argued, "I am not disabled!" She said, "Now, we will determine, *they* will determine that at the Social Security Administration after reviewing your records. You can expect the packet in about a day or two."

I did receive a thick envelope from Social Security a day later and yellow highlighter indicated where I needed to sign. An adhesive note explained that my signature would authorize them to obtain medical records from the hospital and doctors where I had received treatment. I signed it and thought no more about it, as I did not believe I was disabled, and I did not think that I was entitled to anything, as I was still recording tapes at home and believed that I would be able to get back to work at a radio station one day very soon, hopefully. If only my face did not look so gross and I did not look so bloated from all this medication.

After the dog episode, I seemed to just become more depressed. I felt like a failure. I would still shower daily, but then I would curl up in bed and my life revolved around television, and reading. I did not even look in the mirror any more. I was so disgusted with my appearance. I saw Dr McCollom every two weeks. I would tell him that this was making me feel hopeless, and I wanted to die. He tried to tell me that this medication situation was temporary, and said, "Look, I would be pissed if I was heavy due to medication, too. And I am an old duffer. You got your whole life ahead of you, so this has to be devastating. You just have to hold on, and trust me. I know what I am doing. Don't give up, because I plan to take you off this crap before you know it. Don't doubt me."

The problem was that I was young, and weeks and months felt like years. I had already been ill for a long time, and I had nothing to occupy my time. I had no car (my sister and family were using my 1978 Toyota since theirs had been repossessed and my mom had decided that I was too sick to drive), and my few friends now all worked or were gone. Now even my sister was gone again, out with her family for another shot at living on her own.

Between doctors visits, I ate, slept, read, and watched the television. Around November, something in me snapped. I decided I was done with everything. I stopped my medicines. I locked myself in my room, and I told my mom I did not give a shit if I croaked or burned out my stomach or had a heart attack. This was not a cry for attention. This was a genuine, "I don't give a shit." My thought was, I want off this medication that is making me sick, people my age are out abusing their bodies. I am sitting home like a schmuck. Screw this. I don't care if I die. The problem was that when a person abruptly stops taking meds like steroids, at the high dose I was on, one can have a heart attack. My mom called my sister, who tried talking sense into me. I basically said, "F*&^% this and life itself. I have no quality life. I look like a fat loser. I don't give a shit if I die. Get a piano box to bury me."

My mom called Dr. McCollom. He told her to let me go because I will eventually puke my guts out, learn my lesson, and then I will get back on the medicines. He also told her to bring me down to the emergency room or call 911 if I do have signs of a heart attack, told her what those signs were, and told her not to take the suicidal behavior seriously. He told her that feeding into the behavior would cause it to occur more frequently.

I had my dramatic outburst, and it was over. This lasted a couple of days. I went back on the meds, and Dr. McCollom again told me, "Just trust me Gus. This weight will all reverse itself." I was less concerned about the weight than the scars. I also did not want to have an unproductive life. I explained this to him. He listened to my concerns, as always. He wondered if I had talked to any rehabilitation counselors lately since leaving the hospital. I told him that I had not. He told me, "Call them. The squeaky wheel gets the oil. Call them, tell them you were seen, and no one has called you back. Do you still have their number?" I told him I did. He encouraged me to go for this even when I expressed my anxiety over this "disabled" label that I heard the other day. He said, "What do you think?" I told him, " I don't think I am disabled!" He told me, "Then that's what's important, Gus."

With that defiant attitude, here is the attitude I kept for the next few years: I received a Supplemental Security Check (or SSI) that I felt guilty about each time it came. I discovered that in some banks, it was considered "Welfare." The first bank I went to endorse this check, my father was with me, the teller said, "We don't cash welfare." I said, "It is not welfare. It is a disability." She explained, "No. SSI is for people who never worked. SSDI is disability." She pointed to a sign below her station that said, "We reserve the right to refuse service" and another "NO DPW checks cashed here." This was my parent's bank. My father was with me. He explained very softly, "This is my daughter I told you about who is really sick." She cut him right off. "I understand, but this is welfare."

He looked very disappointed, he told my mom, but they kept their account there, as they had a mortgage there and a car payment. I kept mental notes and decided that I would never do business with people who refused me service now when some day I am a "paying customer." I also admit, I harbored anger toward my parents for not having some conviction, and taking their business elsewhere, too. But looking back, that was their choice. Had it been my child, I would have gone elsewhere, I think.

I also called an eye doctor I had seen for years. It had now been three years since I had glasses and had my eyes checked since those cornea problems started. The receptionist remembered me (she was the optometrist's wife) She said, "Okay now let me get your insurance information"). I told her that I now had my own insurance. When I told her I had the "blue card" which in Pennsylvania, signified "full coverage" Medical assistance, back then, she cut me right off. "No. We don't take welfare. " I asked her, "Even if I used to be a patient?" Her formerly nice tone was that curt, almost disgusted tone now, "No. We do not take Welfare Recipients. We have trouble with them. Ok? Sorry . Bye." She then hung up. I called several optometrists that day, found one who took my Welfare, and I have kept him since 1987, despite my moves into the city and back, and my ability to have commercial insurance.

Although this kind of rejection or not being treated necessarily as fairly as I felt I should have been was hard, I think it was just part of what shaped me. I began to really see, and continued to see over the next several years, how you are treated as a member of the so called underclass. It would get worse when I moved out of the comforts of home, too. But I think it was the best thing to teach me about real life and prepare me for my eventual career, but I am now way ahead of myself.

I learned to develop a crust, and eventually not personalize the rudeness or impersonal nature some people in healthcare have about them, the "abrupt" way that we patients are treated. I never take for granted as a person who pays for my commercial insurance, that I could be one of the masses on public assistance again someday, as I may be a couple paychecks away from that lifestyle again. This is why I never discriminate or treat my "welfare" clients any worse, in fact you could call me "guilty" of maybe treating some of them with a little more care, as I remember those days so well.

I still had a long way to go, however, to get to develop my thick skin.

Enter my second cousin, Angie. This was my mother's cousin. I admired her so much. She was someone I had only seen maybe once a year, at a family reunion, or a funeral. She was married very briefly when I was about ten, and I had fleeting memories of her. She had a new, Red sports car, she had a boyfriend with a boat, and we all went on the boat, and she eventually moved to the city after her divorce. She worked for a telephone company and moved up the corporate ladder. She was, to me, the epitomy of the successful woman who does not need a man or children to make a happy life. She was everything I aspired to be. She was in her early 40's and looked like Liza Minnelli with red hair, and would be the first to admit, "Honey I don't remember what my real hair color even is." She had a map in her spare bedroom with pins in every state and country that she had visited, and I think at that point, there were about three states she had not seen. Angie attempted to visit me while I was in the hospital at my sickest, but I looked so ghastly I did not permit her past the curtain. She understood, and left a card and flowers for my mom.

She called fairly regularly after I got home, and would say, "How are you getting along there with your sister and her family?" I would lie and say, "Fine." She would say, "Really? Don't be afraid to come and stay with me if you want some space. I have a spare bedroom down here, and I know how hard it can be to get along with family sometime. Plus you need your own space. I am at work all day. You would have your own place. You think about it."

I thought about this a lot, and my mom and I were arguing a lot, because whenever I would even bring up the idea of wanting to go to college, she would become very angry. She would immediately think that I was asking her for money and get on the defensive: "I don't know where you think we're getting the money. Why don't you just relax? You have money now. Why do you want to do this? What if going to school shows them that you aren't sick and you lose your money? " And on and on.

I called Angie. No explanation was needed, and I stayed with her. She had a condominium in Pittsburgh. It was a two bedroom, second floor, walkup apartment that she got a few years after her divorce. Sometimes I would stay a weekend, sometimes a week, sometimes, two weeks. I would iron her clothes. She would offer to pay me, and I turned her down, because as I saw it, this was free room and board for peace of mind and some freedom. She also had a dog. I would walk her dog, and explore the neighborhood, and think about how someday, I was going to have my own place, I could dream. I got lost sometimes, and ended up once in an unfamiliar part of the city, near some housing projects. The dog and I just looked at each other. I was so short of breath and overweight, and became kind of panicked. I thought I would never find my way back, and it was such a struggle carrying the extra weight around with my breathing problems. The dog led me back, though, and we were okay.

Over the next year, I would spend several weeks with Angie. Some weeks, I was much sicker than others, and preferred my own bed. Also, my mom and dad were somewhat slighted by my preference of staying there, so it became an emotional juggling act. But I am so thankful for the opportunity. The abandonment I felt by the friends was a pain I did not lose, but I was making up for it with the new support with Angie, and this new conviction that I had about going to school.

This dream was not going away, regardless of how my parents felt. Looking back, I believe it was part financial fear (they were living paycheck to paycheck, had no savings, and could not, as they often put it, lend another child one more dime --they had helped my sister with her ventures); and also, fear for my health (they feared that I would never get well if I took on a stressor).

When I was at Angie's, I had privacy, and could talk with her about my concerns, and she was behind me one-hundred percent. She told me to use her phone, her typewriter, and to start the process and call and write the occupational rehab (W.R.A.P.) people. She said to hound them until I get an interview. So I started hounding. The process indeed was slow. It often was weeks before I got a return call. I finally got an interview with a W.R.A.P. Counselor, but it would not be scheduled until after the first of the year (1988). But at least I had my foot in the door, so to speak. I realized early on, you had to be your own advocate.

By late December, every day, I was still exhausted. Many days, I was nauseated. Some days, I would vomit until I could not believe it was humanly possible to vomit any more. I sometimes would have migraines that would last a day or two. Even though I was prescribed migraine pills, sometimes they did not help the pain, so I just had to turn off all the lights and wait for the pain to subside as well as the nausea.

Around Christmas that year, something felt different. It was not the "normal" vomiting and pain cycle. I was accustomed to my usual, routine. I got up, had some toast, tea, downed my pills, showered. By then my grooming simply consisted of a shower, that is it. My hair was thin (I had lost patches), but I was not completely bald. I had it cut fairly short—chin length. I refused to have anyone take any photos of me at this time, but in retrospect, I wish I had some now. The hair was now to it's natural brownish-black color, all my experiments with color and bleach had grown out. I would put on a fresh nightshirt, and then I would go back to bed. By now, I was routinely warm. I began the year as a very sick person below 100 pounds (I am not sure exactly what I weighed). Now, it was late December, and I busted the seams of my Triple X nightshirts and T-Shirts at 280 pounds. The extra weight was insulation. I had what are known as "striae" or stretch marks all over my body. They were on my abdomen, breasts, upper arms, and upper legs. I had fat distribution from the steroids in my face (know as a "moon face") and in my upper back (known as a "buffalo hump").

On December 25th, I was burning up with what felt like a fever, then I would shiver so violently, I was searching for something that would warm me—I only had a few size 3x pants and sweatshirts that were reserved for when I went to see the doctor. It was apparent that something was very wrong when I began to throw up blood. I had become accustomed to now dealing with my suffering again like I did when I initially got sick. I did not report every change or discomfort to my parents or doctor. I felt this was not necessary, because after all, this was chemotherapy, and it was explained to me that I was ingesting a powerful chemical daily, and it was expected that I would be sick. I just learned to, pardon the pun, swallow it.

The first time I threw up the blood that morning, I thought maybe it was a fluke, and I went back to bed. My parents were planning to go to my sister's house (she had moved and was settled in to her new place, and now talked to me more than when she lived under the same roof). They had heard me in the shower and thought this meant I was also going.

I went back to bed, and I buried myself under the covers, alternately shivering, and burning up. I would be woken up by the powerful wave of nausea deep in my gut, and just make it to the bathroom. It was apparent that this was not a fluke, that I was still throwing up blood. Soon, my parents realized that something was wrong when I was not getting dressed and joining them.

Dr. McCollom had given us his number for emergencies, and my dad had asked if anything was wrong. I finally broke down and told him what was going on. He told me he planned to call the doctor, and I begged him not to, because it was Christmas Day. My dad said,

"The doctor told us if it is an emergency, to call. I would say this is an emergency."

This made me very upset, as I did not want to have the doctor disturbed on what might be his only day off. I went back to bed, and could hear my dad making the call. I had fallen back into a sleep which was kind of fitful, as the waves of nasusea came back now about every twenty minutes, followed by my need to go and throw up so hard that my abdominal muscles hurt, abdominal muscles I had forgotten about, underneath all the layers of fat.

My dad came in, and told me the doctor needed to talk to me. I went out to the kitchen, and the doctor was on the other end, asking me, "Hey Gus," of which I interrupted, apologetically, "I am so sorry to disturb your Christmas." He said, "That's Okay. Listen, were you throwing up blood the first time you vomited or did this happen after the second or third time today?" I told him it was the first time."

He instructed me to stop taking all my medications for a week, and that I should see him January 2nd. My parents went ahead to my sister's home. Later that evening, the phone was ringing off the hook (these were the days before we had cordless phones and answering machines) and I went out to get it to stop the shrill noise. It was my sister. She told me that she missed having me there, and she had made a great dessert. It was a creamy pudding with whipped cream—and at that point, thinking about this, I felt the wave of nausea start and I had to lay the phone down, and I had to be very rude and go throw up. I came back a few minutes later and my sister was still talking, and saying, "Well, what do you think?"

I told her, "I am sorry, I didn't mean to be rude, I was sick there and usually I love dessert, but I had to throw up again. I have to go lie down." She said she heard from mom and dad, and that she knew the doctor stopped my meds, and wondered if they were being discontinued for good. I told her this was doubtful. I remember going back to my room, and watching (or actually listening to) *Back to The Future* for the first time that night. The shivering, burning up, and throwing up, continued for the next three days.

I felt like I was missing so much "normal" life, being shut inside the house, and not having a social life. My life was all about television, and radio, and I was just so ashamed of being seen. When would it ever change, I worried and wondered?

Chapter 14 - Up Against the Professionals

The days that followed the acute sickness that I had at Christmas, 1987, after Dr. McCollom told me to stop meds caused me to feel my body withdrawing from all the medication. I had spells of being very hot, then very cold, and I perspired a lot. By New Year's I felt as if the medicine was gone from my body, and I had a sense of hope, maybe even some kind of euphoria. I planned to stay off the meds (except my thyroid pill), whether my doctor knew it or not. When I saw the doctor after the New Year (1988), I told him that I felt fine, and that I did not need to remain on the medication any longer, because, I was still living, and in fact felt better.

I was keeping a journal at this time, and noted that I had resolve to get this poison out of my system and that I was finally done "kicking." I felt "wonderful, as if a weight had been removed. Since I began chemotherapy, I have been paying attention to my nutrition….(now) I (am) vegetable crazy!" This "craze" lasted for twenty months and I did not touch any meat, including chicken or fish. After ten days of being off all corticosteroids and cyclophosphamide, the two powerful drugs, I saw Dr. McCollom, and told him I felt wonderful.

My journal reflects the disappointment: "He ruined it!. He told me I must continue my medication. I could have screamed. I addressed my concern about my looks, and he said, "I know you are upset about your appearance. It would upset even an old duffer like me. I'm 56, over the hill, but we all have some concern about our looks. But you must remain on this . Otherwise you will have to start from scratch.'"

The journal continued, "I am logical, yes, so I understood his reasoning, but I did not gladly accept it because I was finally 'clean' from all this medication, and I did not die without it!"

For the next six months, the first half of 1988, I withdrew into myself even more. I was very susceptible to every germ, and it never failed that whenever anyone would visit, even if they were not ill themselves, I caught a serious cold, or some sort of stomach "virus," and would be throwing up for several days.

My best friends were my books and my music. I was self taught in very old theories of psychology. The used book store that my father drove me to got my patronage once a week, and I would buy several twenty five cent paperback books. I devoured books on Freudian psychoanalysis, Jung, Skinner, Erich Fromm. I assumed this is what people studied in college if they were psychology majors. Very early in that year, 1988, is when my interest in mental health began, I suppose. I learned that when I did go to college that modern professors scoffed at those old ideas, but I still respect them greatly. They were our forefathers of the study of the mind.

The days in the first half of 1988 were so uneventful. I passed my time with my books, my television, and music. I learned to be alone. My parents worked. I did not bother them much with my concerns any longer. They drove me to my appointments as I did not have a car. The old Toyota that I had before getting sick was on loan now to my sister, whose car had been repossessed. It was not a great car, but it got me around, and I missed it. I now had to beg to go places and my parents tried to tell me I was not stable enough to drive. I asked Dr. McCollom about this, and he disagreed.

I met with the W.R.A.P. Counselor, Jake, early in 1988 as scheduled and announced my plans to go to college and help others, possibly to become a nurse. The counselor's office was located smack in between the bathrooms at the local hospital, and the smell was awful.

It seemed to me, from our first meeting, that his job was to discourage me from all of my aspirations. He chuckled at both of these statements. "You think you can go to college? You have no formal education beyond high school other than a certificate from a broadcasting school. We got your records from high school that you signed a release for. Your grades were not stellar. As far as nursing, I have to say that you are not a good candidate for that because I have your medical records. You have arthritis, and you could not complete the basic training and lifting that is required for a nurse."

I was not impressed with Jake. He seemed sarcastic and also, although, I had learned my own hard lessons about judging a book by its cover, he was also someone who I just did not like from the beginning from the outside as well as inside. He had long, unkempt hair, and long, dirty fingernails. I thought he looked very unprofessional. And he literally laughed or chuckled at everything I said in our brief meeting, as if I was delusional or putting him on. I knew that this was going to be a difficult battle, but I also knew that I needed to have funding if I was going to go to college. So I had to be polite, and I had to be respectful. I "yes sir"red him.

He explained to me that I would need to undergo an aptitude test as well as a psychological test to determine my readiness for vocational and/or educational placement. He stated that this would be done in about a month, and if I did not hear from him with a date and time, then please feel free to call him.

We shook hands, and I left. I patiently waited the month, and even gave it an extra week. I did not hear from Jake. I started to leave him messages once a week in February. He never returned my calls. I sent him letters asking for him to return my calls. My initial impression of this counselor, a person whom I was to have support from, was proving to be correct. I did not like him at all. He was not supporting my goal nor did he believe that I had any chance. Much later, my first impression of him would prove to very correct. I told my parents about this, and even though they were very wrapped up in their own problems at this time, for some reason, when I explained this to my mom, it rattled her cage, and she said, "Gimme his number!" She called and left a message, and said, "Uh, yes, you are the counselor for my daughter and she has left you messages. Why aren't you returning her call? She is waiting for an appointment."

I also told my therapist, Jackie about this situation, and she had some dealings with the man, and she was not impressed. She called him in my presence, leaving him a message, as well.

One day while my mother was home, Jake called back and told my mother that he had been avoiding a Candace, but there was another

Candace he was confusing me with. Somehow, I did not buy this story, but still, I was at his mercy for now. He did not have a scheduled appointment for me, but gave me the name of a psychologist: Donald Jennings , PhD. He instructed me to call the doctor and explain that it was for the W.R.A.P. evaluation. I did this right away. I got an answering machine, and had to wait for several days to get a callback, but I had a scheduled appointment: May 31st, 1988. Dr. Jennings told me that I should be prepared to be there for about an hour at 1:00 p.m that day.

My cousin, Angie had me to her place about once a month to stay a week, and I would take my pile of books, and during the day there, I would watch her dog, read, sip tea and if I was bold, venture out for a walk.

One of my other biggest goals was getting off the steroids, as it made you retain weight—a puffy, unnatural looking type of weight. Dr McCollom finally gave me the good news in May, 1988 that I would be able to stop the prednisone! Angie and I celebrated with nonalcoholic champagne and a Chinese dinner, my favorite food! The doctor felt that to take me off both meds at the same time could cause a relapse. That was fine, because the steroids caused most of the weight gain. I had already started losing some of the weight. I had hit an all time high in late 1987 at about 280 pounds. Now in May, I was down to about 260. After I was off the steroids, I dropped 30 pounds in one month.

I was exited about the evaluation I had on May 31st with Dr. Jennings, the psychologist, as to me, it was a step closer to going to school. My father drove me there, and was going to wait in the waiting room as he had to be at work by 2:30 p.m. I felt so bad for Dad, because since he lost his 25 year job with the one trucking company, he was now working for another company, and was never on daylight anymore. But often with unforeseen traffic problems or problems with loads he was carrying, it turned into twelve hour days. This was a job that the company did not want to give him, as he failed the company physical. He was nearly fifty years old when he got the job, and already had a fake shoulder (replaced in 1981) and arthritis in his back—and this is why they told him , "No way." He told them that he was worth their while, and he proved it to them for the next fifteen years. I later inherited my work ethic from my father.

When I arrived with Dad at the office that day, Dr. Jennings came out, no one else was there, and he said, "Candace? Dr. Jennings. Who is this?" I introduced my father. Dr Jennings said, "Are you going to come back for her?" My father said, "No I am going to wait, sir, I have to be at work for 2:30." Dr Jennings said, "She will be here until 5:30." I immediately, feeling defensive for my father and also for myself, said, "But you told me that I should count on being here an hour." Dr. Jennings denied this. The doctor said, "Look we can reschedule, but that will put you back a few months as I am booked with the State rehab evals until September." My father then got very anxious, and said, "I can't call off work. Maybe I can call your mom, or your sister." He asked to use the office phone, and after several attempts, was able to get in touch with my sister. A ride was secured with my brother in law with my old Toyota. I was still anxious at the way this whole evaluation began. My father was also very anxious, and asked several times before he left, "Will you be okay?"

Dr. Jennings explained that the evaluation would be several parts: I would have an evaluation in which he would ask me my history. This was a psychological evaluation that involved questions about my life, childhood and my more recent past. I remember answering very honestly about how I felt about the illness and how I believed it had robbed me of precious time, and how it has had destroyed my looks. I admitted that I was very angry about how I was treated by many of the doctors, nurses and several providers, and how I was repeatedly blamed initially, when in fact it had been proven that I had an illness that was not "my fault." I admitted that I was having a difficult time coping, but that I was slowly making my way back, through therapy, and by having a dream and that with that focal point, I would, by God, get through this, and I believed, be a much better person than before the illness struck.

The next part involved some motor skills, in which literally, I took round pegs and attempted to put them in round holes and square pegs and put them into square holes. I was timed as to how long it took to do this, and was very anxious as he was using an egg timer.

I was given arithmetic testing (which after the basics-addition, subtraction, division, and multiplication—I was not skilled) and then verbal and language testing. I can clearly remember racing through that section and having a lot of time to go back and obsess over my spelling of the word "embarrassment." Does it have one "r" or two? I clearly finished this section in the quickest period of time.

I took a personality test. It is a test that I now know looks for evidence of personality disorders. It was lengthy and asks you to answer true or false to items such as "I like to be in charge," or "I like to be taken care of."

I then took a career assessment. The questions assessed what type of work I might want to do. I do remember answering in the affirmative to a lot of the helping career questions.

I finished the testing. Dr Jennings told me that his evaluation would determine whether I was able to go on to community college or even pursue a bachelor's degree. My brother in law came to pick me up. I had no idea that this day of testing and that evaluation would have such an impact on my funding for years to come.

I always had a dream to go to New York City. Angie told me that it was a possibility. She said that we could go for a few nights and that she would pay for the hotel and she had "frequent flier" miles. I had never flown before. On my 21st birthday, this is what we did. I was now receiving a disability check every month. I spent it on my medications, my own food and personal items (toiletries) and my phone calls, etc. I paid for my food on the trip, and I realized that this dream could really come true. Angie told me that many people have dreams that they think they can never realize, but they really are just a matter of saving a few dollars and getting over the fear to do it.

She is/was twenty-two years older than I, and she was someone I idolized while I was growing up. She was single most of her life. She was successful without having a man support her. She was married very briefly in her twenties, but she divorced him in a year, and she supported herself. She never had children, and she never wanted children, and was not afraid to admit that. I realized that I was not alone in that lack of desire in wanting children.

The flight was not scary to me, but the hustle bustle of getting ready, flying, the cab ride into the city, and still being on the oral dose of chemotherapy made for a, as I put it in my journal, "a sick chemo day." By the time we got to the hotel, I was throwing up. Angie saw my whining as wallowing, and she promptly told me so. She told me, "You have a sickness. You have been given this terrible illness. But you are going to be okay. I will not listen to this F%$#ing wallowing. You wanted to come here and see this city. Now what works for this nausea at home?" I told her in my whiny voice, "Coca cola. Crackers." She said, "Then let's get you some "f&^%ing crackers and coke and go walk. When that city excitement hits you, you won't remember how sick you are. C'mon." She told me "Life is short, and you might not ever get to come back here again."

I was secretly thinking this was so mean! But you know what? I have had countless, I am talking hundreds upon hundreds of sick days in my college, graduate school, and employment life since then. My work attendance is good. And now I ask myself, "What works for me at home?" Many times you will see crackers and coke on my desk or Tums in my desk, or Tums in my car. The only time I stay home is when the migraine has me so that I cannot lift my head from the pillow or if I could potentially infect others with what I have got. Life is short and I remember that, God willing in eight hours I can drive back home again. I might not get that chance again see this day. I do not want to spend it face down in a pillow.

We saw the city, I took pictures of the Twin Towers (when the horrible tragedy occurred in 2001 I was so glad I had taken that picture) Brooklyn, Harlem, the Statue of Liberty, some break dancers in the street. I turned 21 in New York, and I even drank enough to get drunk, and yes I paid for it, but you only turn 21 once. Of course with my low tolerance, it only takes a few drinks, but still!

I was still on the cyclophosphamide (oral chemotherapy). I decided to start looking for a reconstructive surgeon for my right ear. It had never healed properly from lesions that occurred and the ear lobe was essentially gone from the granulomas that were on the earlobe and neck area. The right side of the face was also badly scarred. A Plastic Surgery Department was recommended to me by Dr McCollom. The town I lived in outside of Pittsburgh (a small town about 30 miles away) was not an option, as one doctor told me, "No doctor out here is going to touch that." A medical resident carefully looked behind the ear and agreed that this was the area that needed to be tended to first as it was still seeping from not healing. It was not an active granuloma, but it was flaps of skin that had formed over other skin, and was very unpleasant. It was unhealed, and increased the risk of infection. He looked at the area on my face and said that he could also see potential for smoothing the scars there, too, and that first there would need to be scar excision and perhaps some dermabrasion.

Some people that have Wegener's granulomatosis have another disfiguring facial problem called "saddle nose deformity" which is a collapse of the bridge of the nose. I did not have this condition. I instead lost part of my earlobe and had the facial scarring. My left ear was very minor and has a tiny flap, but did not require any corrective surgery.

I asked some doctors if it is anything more than coincidental that so much on the right side of my body was affected by the illness (right lung, right ear, right side of face) and the answer is , "No."

In early autumn, 1988, I had some bloodwork done to prepare for the potential plastic surgery, and was told to come back in a month, as my case would be "considered" during that time. I did go back in about four weeks, and the resident who had promised to make me "just like new, " a phrase I had heard many times over, told me emotionlessly, "While you are on chemo, we can do nothing. Then we can only do the ear. The face. Well, you'll have to live with it. It just looks like a case of bad acne scars, anyway." He then rolled up his sleeve and showed me a gash. He said, "See this scar? I had a tumor. I had Non Hodgkin's Lymphoma. I know what it is to be sick. We could start hacking away at your face and it would be never ending. Do you want this on your face? I don't think so!" He was perspiring and red in the face. I was speechless and nearly in tears and could not respond because I was a plethora of emotions: stunned, angry, disappointed.

I just walked out. My father had driven me there. He asked me what happened, and I just grabbed my coat from the waiting room's coat rack, and Dad had known me for twenty-one years to gauge that when I was red faced and speechless, to just follow me. The receptionists said, "Thank you. Have a nice day!" My father, always so polite, said, "Ok. Thank you. You do the same!" I stormed past the people wearing green , white, and multi-colored scrubs, got on the elevator, and when I did, the elevator bounced due to my girth. I was still not talking. We got into my dad's vehicle, which was an older model VW pickup truck. Our 30-some mile drive home was mostly silent, which was my choice, as it did not seem fair after all this family has seen to have my dad hear the story and how angry and frustrated I was.

My mind was working overtime, though. Acne scars? I never had acne! Wegener's scarred me. That doctor lied! You promised me you would make me "just like new!" You lied! I wanted a cigarette for the first time in a year and a half. I sat on the cold porch when I got home, contemplating my entire life's purpose. I survived this illness, but I am told continuously by doctors about the "long road ahead of me." I am now facing a lifetime of being facially scarred. I was beginning to feel hopeless again. I drank some vodka from my parents' liquor supply. They did not drink at all. It only took a few drinks before I was in complete oblivion in front of the television, but the next day I had a horrible headache. I learned over the next several years that drinking and my migraines did not mix well.

Another thing I learned about drinking in 1988, is that drinking might make your worries go away for a few hours, but then you wake up with the worries, and you feel horrible.

I also began to put two and two together, in that I realized, just by seeing (mostly on television, as this was really now my connection to society) that alcohol and drugs do not lead one to success and achievement of dreams. Those that are "successful" at least by my definition (able to support themselves) who also have drug and or alcohol problems end up sacrificing their successes and or relationships. I could not sacrifice my dream. Even though, my dream to go to college and support myself seemed to be something very far away and frankly, not supported by my family, I had to keep my eye on the prize. I had to envision what my life would be like someday, calmly. Acting impulsively, and hurting my body was the old way. I would have my own apartment, and I would be able to pay for my own way and I would also be able to work every day, just like all those people that I saw driving back and forth to work outside my window all of those months when I was cooped up in my room in the Pittsburgh hospital.

It had been a big decision to talk to someone outside the family. Early in our family history, we tried the therapy route. This did not work. When I was a child, I can vaguely remember talking to a male therapist one time. We never went back. I later asked my mom about this, and she said that he asked too many personal questions. I have now worked many years as a therapist, and have tried to explain that we do ask personal questions, and this is how we try to understand what makes a family tick.

Now, at age twenty-one, I was trying to find answers, and mainly, support. I needed someone who would support my plan, or quite honestly tell me if I was "crazy" for having the plan that I had. Was it realistic?

The next time I saw Jackie I told her the story of this plastic surgeon, how the first time I saw him, he promised me he could help me, and the second time, he was red-faced, rolled up his sleeve, told me that I could have a scar even worse, like the one on his arm. I admitted I coped poorly, by drinking and pouting. She asked if that coping skill worked, and I told her I quickly figured out that it did not.

She then told me something that I was not seeing. She said, "Candace, it sounds like that doctor has mental health issues. " She asked me if I would sign a release so she could call him." I did and she called him. The next time I came back to see her she told me she had talked to him and told him that she had been trying to prepare me to go on with my life and he had effectively attempted to dash my dreams. She revealed to me that he told her his whole story of the Non-Hodgkins and how this affects him when he sees a young person like myself. She said "I sympathize, but this patient came to you for help and it sounds as if you laid your issues on her. Could she have the surgery to correct some of her scars or not?" And he told her he would not do it. Jackie advised me to go back and get a second opinion, as I still had the problem with the ear scar that was a health issue, as it drained continuously.

I was naïve. I asked Jackie how a person could get through "the screening process of "being a doctor" or "other person who helps people" and have such issues. She just laughed and said, "You'd be surprised."

I had certainly met my share of rude doctors and nurses. But in our family, we still had that self esteem issue that "they" know best. Now I was learning that it is okay to ask for a second opinion and to spot that something may not be right.

Candy Marcus-The only picture I have of me while sick

Chapter 15 - Focusing On The Positive

I began to focus on some of the more positive aspects of my life. The most positive thing was that I no longer felt ridiculously bloated, like I was literally walking on water balloons. My face was no longer round like a pumpkin. This was a very liberating feeling, and made me feel as if I could now begin to conquer the world. I was still very overweight, but I was watching what I was eating. I was also still very tired, but I was determined to try to get my body on a regular schedule, instead of the sleep all day, and eat whatever I want routine that I was in for nearly a year.

One day in October, 1988, my father had taken me to the library so I could stock up on some reading material. It was then that I found the Consumer Handbook that is published in Pueblo, Colorado. Inside, is listed several topics, from tax information to information on disabled rights, to Patient Rights, etc. I wrote the address and asked for information on my illness, Wegener's granulomatosis. Dr McCollom would patiently sit down with me with a large Merck manual, and try his best to explain to me the medical terminology. But there were no patient friendly pamphlets that he could just give to me. He also gave me printouts of all my blood work, explaining what the normal ranges of my blood levels were, where mine fell and why mine were either normal or abnormal. I appreciated that so much. He would show me what a normal TSH (thyroid stimulating hormone) level was and say "Now these TSH levels are bass-ackwords, you see. A high level means you have a low thyroid. And when you were your sickest, your's was up at 64, no wonder you were tired."

I wanted anything and everything in print that I could obtain, especially to show Jake and even my therapist, because when I first told them about my illness, neither of them had ever heard of it, and both had, I felt, questioned my voracity.

I also looked not healthy, but robust, and frankly, fat. I was judged. Now especially, being obese, I did not look ill or frail. I was treated differently, and at times, poorly. I had to really rely on being informed and become my own advocate. My mantra became "I no longer have my looks, so I have to develop my brain."

I received some information on Vasculitis from an organization called "N.O.R.D," or the "National Organization for Rare Disorders," several weeks after I wrote to the database out in Colorado. I had to pay $5 for a printout about Vasculitis. I paid the $5 because it was almost exciting (yes, my life was very boring in those days) to see if not my "name", my disease in print.

It was a paragraph and it was a very poor copy. It was grainy and hard to read. I was also sent more information on the National Organization for Rare Disorders. Kindly, someone had stuck a handwritten note in and the note said, "Wegener's granulomatosis support group, Platte City, Missouri." I was almost frothing with delight. I wrote to the address immediately and explained that I was diagnosed with the illness a year ago and had no one to talk to about it.

Exactly one week later, I received a nice handwritten letter from a woman named Carolyn Hampton. In her letter, she introduced herself, and stated that she had been diagnosed with the illness in the 1970's and that it had completely disabled her from her job as a registered nurse. She had lost most of her hearing and also had saddle nose deformity. She was still taking a low dose of steroids and had chronic kidney problems. She apologized for not sending me the full "packet." She promised that the packet would be forthcoming. I already had more than I had ever imagined. There was actually someone else out there!

One week after the initial letter, the "packet" arrived. It was a large, 11" by 8" envelope, stuffed full of information, including a People magazine article about a young woman my age who had Wegener's (how had I missed that? I read my sister's *People* every single week!)

Jackie, the therapist I was assigned to was kind of quirky, but she did confront me. I do not think she had a modality, per se. She listened, and I asked for feedback. She gave it. She did not give me the answer I wanted all of the time. In mid to late 1988, her help was very effective. She asked me simply, what my goals were, and I said that someday, I wanted to make enough to have my own apartment, and that I would like to have a college degree and be able to help others someday.

She was able to speed things up with Jake and was even able to obtain the results of the psychological evaluation. She told me that she could not give me the results of the I.Q. test or the full evaluation, but if she were me, she would go ahead and take a class just to get the feel for a classroom again. She truly encouraged me. I decided to take that advice. I registered for my first non-credit college class as an adult learner that I would not take until early 1989. The class was conversational Italian language. I looked forward to it.

I let Jake know I was going to take a class, and he promptly informed me that neither he nor the W.R.A.P. people would endorse nor pay for the class. I told him that was fine.

I just knew I needed to do this in order to "get my feet wet," as I had not been in a class room," and had doubts about my ability to learn despite my burning desire to obtain a degree. I had a question in the back of my mind. Was my brain affected by all of this?

The other issue I was still dealing with very much was the issue of my changed appearance. Jackie advised me to look at it as if I was someone who had aged. "Your appearance changes as you age." I understood that reasoning, but aging is a gradual change. My appearance had changed greatly in a span of less than a year. I went from what some people had considered "beautiful." I became frankly, what some people would consider "ugly."

It was odd. I used to get catcalls from men while walking, while driving before I got sick. Depending on what color my hair was, I would get "Hey Blondie!" Or "Yo Red!" Now, after the illness, and with the presence of scars, and being a large person, when I would venture out alone (which was rare) I experienced a couple of occasions from teenage boys where I was called "whale," "dog", and once while driving, a carload of teenage boys drove alongside me and yelled out nasty insults to me, some unintelligible. In McDonalds, fresh out of the hospital, at age 19, I was slowly walking, with a limp, and coming out of the bathroom, and going back to the table where my parents were waiting. A bunch of teenagers mimicked the way I walked and made big outstretched arms to show the universal sign for "There's a fat person." They were laughing and having a great time at my expense.

I did feel "old." I no longer felt like a teenager or a young adult. I felt as if I had been through a war, or a terrible experience and I realize now, I was still a young person, I was fair game. The teenagers saw me as a young woman who was not attractive, so they could attack her with insults for not keeping herself attractive. I now had let my own hair color come in, and I looked in the mirror and saw someone I did not recognize any more. I looked like a blown up, overinflated version of what I looked like as a child. I experienced similar bullying when I was an overweight child. No matter what age you are, it is upsetting.

I was reading the Sunday paper one day, and came across a column in which teenagers and young adults send in letters about problems that they have had, and how they have coped, in order to help other young folks. One caught my eyes, as it was written by a young woman my age, 21 from Florida. She wrote:

> "When I was 14, I contracted a rare muscular disease that changed my appearance drastically. My eyelids drooped, my speech was slurred, and sometimes I drooled. Before that I was athletic..beautiful..many friends…with the illness I felt like I had lost more than my appearance. I felt like I had lost my life. People shunned me…..made fun of me…to them I was no longer the same person…I was the same person..longing to be treated the same as before…Now I'm doing well. Thanks to medication, my health and appearance have improved. I'm still being treated differently, but I've learned much better to cope with people saying stuff…with losing friends, your mental attitude is the key…I'd never do this to anyone else. No one knows how much pain it causes."

I still was a hermit, for the most part, and had long accepted that I had long lost some of those friends. Some called occasionally. But they were moving on with their lives. Many were having children, or going to college, or getting married. I focused inward, and read, and kept my eye on that prize, the day I would have my degree, but I did still want to have some corrective surgery as I had very rough areas on my face, as well as that ear that was unhealed.

I took Jackie's advice and called the University's Medical School. I asked for the Plastic Surgery department and I soon was going to get that second opinion. I explained what was going on in my initial phone call, that I had some unhealed skin that was causing drainage and also scarring. I got an appointment.

In early October, 1988, my mother and I went back to the University's medical clinic. This was a much different experience than before. This resident came in and introduced himself by his first and last name, "Hi my name is Jack Peterson. I am a plastic surgery resident. Tell me what brings you here" I told him I had Wegener's granulomatosis. I also presented him with a detailed case history, to which he said, "Very impressive!" I told him that I was very troubled by my facial scars, but that the biggest problem is the fact that my right ear is draining and had not healed. He carefully listened. Then he explained that the priority is indeed cutting the unhealed flap of skin and suturing the wound so that it does heal.

The first consideration was that he would not operate while I was on chemotherapy, because it is immunosuppressive. I was scheduled to see Dr McCollom soon, and he had indicated in my last visit that he was going to be taking me off the drug. Dr. Jackson said, "Great. I would like you to be off the drug one week before I would do this operation."

I saw Dr. McCollom a week later, on October 12, 1988. This time, I went alone. I was tired of going with my parents. For months I had been telling them that my doctor had been saying that I am safe to drive. My father relented, and let me drive his car that he used to drive back and forth to work: a 1985 Renault. I realized I would never see my old Toyota again, as my sister was not going to get another vehicle any time soon. I needed some independence, and despite my parent's protestations, I explained that this was something I had to do, as I had driven into the city frequently before I had gotten ill. When I got to the doctor's office, I explained my plan, and he listened to me. That day, Dr. McCollom said, "Well some people might call me a renegade. There are schools of thought that say that a patient should be in remission for a year or two, or even more before you take them off immunosuppressive drugs. But you want to get on with your life. I know that. I will monitor you. I also think keeping people on these drugs is just more harmful than beneficial. Frankly, it's just bad medicine. You can stop the cyclophosphamide today. You might feel a little sick because your body is used to being on this drug.

I went home, and braced myself for the worst. I had been through abrupt "withdrawal" before ten months earlier when I had the acute episode of gastric bleeding, and the flu-like symptoms, followed by the sense of healthiness.

I had none of that unpleasant withdrawal. I felt fine. I still kept up with my old habits of drinking a lot of water daily, as suggested by Dr. McCollom. He suggested this for months to follow, because he told me that the risk if bladder infections and even cancer remained high, but he said that he did not want me to be afraid or "paranoid" about this. I drank the several water jugs full of water a day, and remained on my diet, which was still mostly vegetarian, as I could not stand the thought of eating animals, getting to a reasonable 160 or so pounds eventually, by the time I started college in the fall of 1989.

A week after I was off the chemotherapy, I followed up, as ordered by Dr. McCollom, with bloodwork and a urinalysis. I continued with this for years to come, until 1995, usually monthly. I had also received a letter from Dr. Jack Peterson, thanking me for meeting him. I had never received a thank you letter from a doctor before. The letter said that it was delightful meeting me, how he had been impressed by my typed history, and how he encouraged me to call when I have been off my medicine a week. When I received that letter, I called the plastic surgery clinic and explained that I stopped my Cyclophosphamide last week. I was put on hold, and I heard, "Hi this is Jack Peterson." I said, "Dr Peterson?" I then told him the whole story. He said he would go ahead and schedule a surgery date for me. He would request the records from my last visit with Dr McCollom ("Not that I don't believe that you stopped taking the drug, but we have to have it for our chart.") . The surgery was scheduled for November 22, 1988. Dr. Peterson told me that he would have someone call me two weeks prior to surgery and again a day before surgery, and there would be a packet sent in the mail. I began to have a feeling that things could work out for me.

Two weeks prior to the operation, I did get a packet explaining that

I should stop taking aspirin, ideally stop caffeine (this is when I really had withdrawal symptoms). I considered myself to be like a fighter in training. This would be my first surgical procedure that I could prepare for. They were the lung operations that I had to have for diagnostic reasons, and had no time to take care of my body, and I was not given any type of choice. They were more or less life or death.

On November 22nd, it was 25 years since the death of John F. Kennedy, and on the ride down to the hospital, this was on all the radio stations. Dr. Peterson came out and introduced himself to my parents. "Hi, I am Jack. I guess I don't have to convince her not to be afraid. "Let's do it!" I was not afraid. I considered this the first step in looking somewhat normal again.

I had the option to have a local or total anesthetic, and I had told Dr. Peterson that I wanted to be awake. I wanted to be alert, and under control (or at least as in control as possible), and I also wanted to recuperate in my own bed. He told me I was "brave." I never could comprehend how I got the "brave" or "courageous" label, as I just was trying to make the best of the situation at this point, and I was in the acceptance mode.

Dr. Peterson explained absolutely everything from the beginning to the end. I received shots in the cheek, all around my right ear, and down my neck. It felt like Novocaine, but ten times stronger. He had medical students with him, and I know he was speaking with them, but he also was including me in the conversation. "OK. I am severing the nerve now. Hear that noise? That's just some cartilage, don't worry. " The procedure took about an hour.

At times, it was uncomfortable. But by this time, I had read about a process called "visualization." I now used this, and use it to this day whenever I have a procedure, or a test. I imagined myself floating in a warm, water filled chamber. I imagined my favorite record album was playing, track by track, from beginning to end. I now no longer heard Dr Peterson, only when I willed myself "back" into the room. I allowed my senses back to reality to remind myself that I was in control of the situation. But the smell and sound of burning nerves was a little too much for me for an hour, and my "chamber" was a safe place.

It was over, and Dr. Peterson and the nurses told me how "brave" I was. He told me not to take the bandages off or the stitches out. I was to return in two weeks. He instructed me to return "straight home and get some rest." I had a bandage directly over my ear, and another head wrap. I looked like a stereotypical cartoon character with mumps. There were a couple of ways to get home during the "off" hours when not at the height of rush hour. The direct way home normally only took about forty-five minutes. The circuitous route took over an hour. My parents decided on the latter with stops. I fell asleep in the back seat after about ten minutes. I woke up and looked around and wondered, Am I home?

I realized that we were at a car dealership. They had stopped to look at Cadillacs. They got on kicks now and then to purchase things, often things they could not afford, and this would be one of those things. They might have had the credit, but then the bills would roll in, and they would say how they were "back against a wall." I had heard them talking about this new kick, and put my two cents in, which my mom promptly told me to mind my own business when I did. She said that after having her oldest daughter move in with her several times and me being sick, they "deserved" the car.

I sat in the car for a while, digging in my tote bag for a magazine. I tried to lie back down. It had now been several hours since my surgery. The pain was intense. Imagine a toothache or dental surgery and your Novocain has worn off. Essentially the doctor had removed my ear lobe to do his repair and sewn it back on. I now was feeling that pain. The sensitive skin on my neck felt pulled and stretched, which it had been. I figured that my parents were just looking at cars. How long can they take? I decided to go look for my mom and dad and remind them that I needed to go home and lie in bed, like the surgeon had instructed.

I went to get out of the back seat, and felt a little bit light headed. I saw stars, but I got out of the back seat, and went to look around. Usually, when they went to look at cars, they "window shopped." They looked at the lot, and read the sticker, but if a dealer approached them, they said, "No, we are just looking." I walked all over the lot, and did not see them. It was about 25 degrees that day. They were obviously inside.

I went in, and looked around, and did not see them. I was feeling very groggy now. A well dressed man approached me, looking aghast. "Excuse me? May I help you?" I said, "Yes, I was looking for my mom and dad. I was asleep and I woke up, and looked for them and couldn't find…" He interrupted me…"What's your name Miss?" I told him. He went into each salesman's booth. I was standing where he left me feeling like my head was now spinning. He came out still looking at me as if I was an undesirable, or some sort of bum that wondered in off the street. He brought my parents out. "Are these your parents?" I said "Yes." He said, "Your daughter came in here looking for you." The salesman who had been with them looked confused. He said, "Maybe you can stop back another time." My mom and dad looked very embarrassed. My mom said, "Oh this is our daughter. She just had a little bit of surgery." The two salesmen were not smiling, and just looked shocked. I was feeling as if I could lie down on one of the leather couches in the showroom.

The salesman gave them his card and the sales manager (I assume that is who he was) ushered them out with "You can stop back." I imagine my presence was not great for business. When we got to the car, I told them how I was not feeling great. We still were an hour from home. I also crossed the boundary and asked what on earth they were doing looking at Cadillacs.

Obviously, I was well enough to go home, but, I was supposed to go straight home but I just had my earlobe removed, repaired, and sewn back on.

I was in pain and a high risk for infection. It was the day before Thanksgiving. I headed straight for my bed that early afternoon. I slept until about 11:30 p.m. I watched the tributes to J.F.K. the rest of the evening.

I do not remember much of Thanksgiving, so it must have been uneventful. I did visit our neighbors across the street, who had been very supportive throughout my illness. They commented on how I was starting to look so much better. It was great to spend time with old friends and get some self-esteem boosting.

The Sunday after Thanksgiving, I took the bandages off, and examined this scar. It was pink. It was not at all red, and there was no scabbing. I had some net adhesive bandages left over from when I had my lung operation (thoracotomy). The pulling sensation was very bad. The stitches were black, strong thread. I took some manicure scissors that I had, and I took them out to the kitchen. I boiled some water in a small pot. I dropped the scissors in the pot. I let the scissors stay in the boiling water for a long time.

I then turned the heat down, and waited until the water cooled off, drained it, carefully picked them out with a paper towel, and took them into the bathroom, and swabbed them down with rubbing alcohol, just to make sure they were sterile. I carefully cut the thread that was sewn around the earlobe. The thought did occur to me while I did this that this might not be healed, and that I would be in deep water, but there was no turning back at this time. I pulled all the thread out. I took some of the rubbing alcohol, and a cotton swab, and rubbed up the back side of the earlobe. It was a clean, healed scar. I still dressed it with the net bandage to be safe.

When I saw Dr Peterson three days later, he saw the bandage first, and said, 'Where'd you get this?" and I told him where it came from. He laughed and said, "You pack rat!" I was just relieved he was not angry. He just looked at it and said, "This is incredible! It's completely healed! It looks like it was done a month ago. It is pink, and smooth. You did this yourself? How?" I explained to him how I boiled the scissor and swabbed them down with alcohol. He laughed and told me that it was certainly a "Don't try this at home stunt." I explained to him how it was pulling and itching and I knew that it was time, and that it would be extremely uncomfortable to wait almost two weeks. He shook his head and said, "I would never recommend this to any patients, but you did a great job, and the most important thing is, you are healed!"

I never saw Dr. Peterson again, but I received one more letter from him. The letter wished me well and good luck in my health and pursuit of college one day. I never forgot him, and although he was only my doctor for a very brief time, he made a difference. I have since had a few doctors who have also touched me in that way, but I have to say, none who ever wrote me personal letters. I felt such exuberance for life. Nothing was going to stop me from pursuing my dream. There were still going to be detractors, but the most important factor is that I believed in myself.

Another very important factor is that I had support from the Wegener's granulomatosis support group. It is very difficult for some people to imagine in today's day and age, but there was no Internet back in 1988. My connection was the mailbox, and now I received letters every week, thanks to this support group. I was beginning to meet regular "pen pals."

Carolyn Hampton, the support group leader, sent me regular letters, and they were full of love and support. But she also sent me lists of names of people close to my own age. I began communicating with a young woman overseas who was in her 30's. She was diagnosed in the 1970's when so little was known about our illness. By the time her diagnosis was made, she lost vision in an eye, lost her entire nose, lost a lung, and lost her larynx. She had since also had numerous joint replacement operations. But her letters were upbeat and she was grateful to still be alive after eleven years.

Carolyn recognized in my letters that I was a good writer and asked if I would like to contribute to the newsletter somehow, sometime. I would regurgitate, in my own words, as I learned when I worked in radio, what I had read about coping with illness, and about hiding scars, about hiding the bloating, and camouflaging the weight gain caused from steroids. I was featured in many of the newsletters with my "beauty tips."

I had applied to the local branch campus of the University of Pittsburgh, and waited for an acceptance letter. My WRAP counselor felt that I would have no problem getting in, he told me, based on my IQ test and aptitude test. I asked him what that was. He laughed and said, "We don't like to give that to people because it will give them a big head." I just thought, huh? I still was very worried about it because I never took SAT tests in high school and was not aiming for college at that time, because it was established in my family that we (my sister and I) were not going.

I do not remember Christmas, nor did I journal about it that year, so it must have been uneventful. I do know that I looked forward to 1989.

Chapter 16 - Armed With A Purpose

I started out 1989 with a sense of hope, and that hope lasted much of the year. I continued to read as much as I could, and I also continued to lose weight steadily. The hair that I had cut off before chemotherapy had grown back. It was now my own, natural color, and I had not dyed it since late 1986. It was a beautiful dark brown, and thicker than ever before, and down to my waist. I left it alone until graduate school, and never thought about hair all through college. I was determined to put beauty at the bottom of my priority list, and now when I look at the few pictures of me that were taken during college, I envy my carefree, natural look. I still cared about my appearance (and went through periods where I fretted the scars) but hair was not an issue.

In February, 1989, I was ready for more reconstructive surgery. Since it was not "cosmetic surgery" (i.e., surgery that was being done simply for vanity such as getting breast implants), but surgery that was done to reconstruct damage that was done by an illness, I was able to go to the University and have the repair done under my medical assistance. Dr. Peterson was no longer there. Another young resident was there who was equally dynamic, and she was also quite dramatic in her first impression, as I recall.

I was sitting in the same room where I sat when I first met Dr. Peterson. I heard a young woman outside the door having a loud argument, with a man, It sounded like a lover's quarrel. "You don't want to commit. Screw you. I am in for the long haul, and I will find someone who is in it with me, not some asshole who is just out for a good time." She started to open my door and he said, "Wait," I looked out and saw two people in green scrubs, and she said, "Excuse me, I have a patient now!" and closed the door on the man in scrubs.

She said "Hi, Candace? My name is Dr. Jennifer Welsh. I am the plastic surgery chief resident." She had my chart in her hand. She was wearing very high heels, and had her scrub shirt tucked in to her pants. I thought she looked pretty cool. She asked what she could do to help. I explained that I had corrective surgery on my right ear back in November, and now would like to have corrective surgery on my face. She looked at it very closely and asked what was most bothersome, and I told her that the deep scars on my right cheek were most upsetting to me.

She explained that these look like bad acne scars at first glance, but are much more severe. "You have been scarred several layers. What we will have to do is something called scar excision. We will have to cut out the scars, then sew the top layer. What I am thinking of, is making maybe one or two scars here rather than the twelve or so deep acne like scars. What would be worse for you? One or two large scars that look as if you have had a knife or surgical scar or twelve large pitted acne scars?"

I decided that I would rather deal with two scars. Who wouldn't given this choice?

I was scheduled to have the surgery on February 28, 1989. This time, my mom drove, and I did the navigating. I was not fearful. I saw this as another step in looking "normal," and regaining confidence. I arrived early, checked in and again, was not put under, but only prepped with the local anesthetic. Dr. Welsh was dressed again in scrubs that were not baggy, but tight, with the shirt ticked in to the pants, and high heels. She was wearing a colorful, print hat to hide her hair. When I was wheeled into the Operating room, the radio was blasting R&B music. I laughed and said, "Can you operate with that music on?" She said, "Oh yeah! Can you handle it?" I said "Yes." She sang along to every song. This was the era of songs like "My Prerogative" and "Me, Myself and I." I felt some pressure on my right cheek, but no pain. I declined any prescription pain medication.

After the operation, my mother and I stopped for Chinese food in a Pittsburgh neighborhood. I had grown immune to stares over the past few years, and realized that a giant bandage on my face may be off-putting to some people. Oh, well. After this, I went home and napped.

Later that evening, I came across an article that nearly ripped my heart out. Here is what I wrote that day:

> *Today I underwent some scar revision. I was awake throughout the procedure, as I was during the last procedure. I have little discomfort now, twelve hours later.*
>
> *I was told so many times today how "brave" I am. To me, that is not so. When I was ill, fighting to live, I was called brave, courageous, and strong. At that time, I did what I had to do. Live or die, it is that simple. It was not easy fighting all the time, it was not easy waking up to a new day. Now I am called brave because I "suffer" through plastic surgery. I chose this "suffering." I am vain. I sat down tonight all smug and comfortable with a magazine, and saw a photograph of a 41 year old man who was horribly disfigured and blinded ten days after arriving in Vietnam twenty years ago. He wore a mask in public to spare others, not himself.. He now does what he can to help others who are disfigured. On his lap was a cat he stroked lovingly. I am not brave.*

I was starting to feel that I could get out, and have some pride. Yes, some people would stare. Some people might ask that dreaded "what happened?" question. But I was now armed with a purpose. My purpose was to provide help and support to other people who have been ill, and also to treat those people with the respect that often I was not treated with throughout the times that I was sick.

I did very well in the Italian class I had enrolled that I began in April 1989. It was held in my old Junior High. Most of the people that were taking the class were people who were planning trips to Italy. I took it because it was my grandparents' first language, and although, I never knew my father's dad, I wish I had. My mother's father was now also deceased. I remember him speaking this language. I picked up the conversational Italian well. I earned an A in the six short weeks, every Wednesday evening. I talked to myself in Italian. I read aloud to myself in the language, and purchased a "Learn Italian" cassette tape.

There was now another used book store in town. It was named after its owner, Penny. Penny was so painfully shy when the bookstore started that her husband sat in the store with her, and she would not make eye contact with her customers. She had long, brown hair. Her hair practically covered her entire face. I went to her store once a week, because I could pick up books for a quarter a piece and trade ones I had already read. After several visits, she began to know me by name. She would become a fixture in my life for the next several years.

Jackie said, "I knew you could do it." Jake, my WRAP counselor, was not impressed. "That is very different than what you will encounter in a college classroom," was how he reacted when I showed him the grade. I still was not discouraged. I was going to do this. Jake and I met in Spring, 1989. By now, I had gotten my acceptance letter from the branch campus of the University of Pittsburgh, and he informed me that I was approved but I had a budget of $2000 per semester. This was fine. This would work out well, as with my disability benefit of less than $300 per month, I do not think I could afford to live in the city, and also purchase textbooks. Since I could not pursue my desire to earn a nursing degree, I expressed my desire to study psychology. He stated that this was not recommended. I asked why. He stated that because of my medical history and also because of my "personality profile," I would not be able to pursue that type of degree. "You can pursue an English or communications degree. You have a high aptitude in writing and English. You do not have a high aptitude in math. We will fund a college degree for you in an English degree. If you want a psychology degree, you can find funding elsewhere."

I was stunned. What "personality profile?" What do I do? I felt backed in a corner. I wanted a degree. I could prove to them that I could pass and do well in psychology. It sounded to me like they were telling me I was "crazy." I will just start college, and perhaps things will change. I decided to just go with the degree. Besides, things change. Nothing can be this rigid, can it?

I told Jackie about this. She said, "This is crazy. Once you get to the university, you can schedule your classes. When they see that academically you are doing well, we will cross that bridge when we come to it. Just focus on getting to college first."

I could barely stand the wait, and I enrolled in a class at community college that would begin in the summer, and decided to take an Introduction to Psychology Course. I informed Jake about it, and he said that he and WRAP would not pay for it, as they refused to endorse any plan for me to pursue a degree in psychology. I explained that I wanted to take the course to get my "feet wet" and that it is a credit course. He said that I could pay for it myself or withdraw from the course. I decided to take my own money and pay for it myself. I took Jackie's advice and decided to "cross the bridge when I came to it" about the major. She told me that by the time I had a few semesters under my belt, maybe Jake and the rest of the WRAP people would change their tune.

In May, I was able to have the second part of my scar excision with Dr. Welsh. She had excised all the multiple scars on my cheek. Now came the part where she would try to sew the work up to make it look as though I had two smooth little scars. She warned that I still may need some dermabrasion to smooth the rough surface eventually. She now was at another Pittsburgh hospital. I liked her work and liked her bedside manner and was upset to learn that she was not staying in Pittsburgh. I returned to her for my follow up appointment and, was healed. I surprised her with a present I had gotten for her at a candle shop. I did not know what they were called. All I knew was that they were candle holders shaped like stars and vanilla scented candles. She opened them and hugged me. "Oh, these are beautiful sconces! I will put them above my mantle! I already picked out my apartment on the beach in Tampa. If you ever come down there, look me up. I will finish your plastic surgery." I thought she was a bit of a wild and crazy free sprit, and I wonder what happened to her!

I began my class at the local community college. It was something I looked forward to with trepidation. Could I really pass a real college class? Jake had planted that seed of doubt in me. It was held two nights a week for six weeks early in the summer. After my first evening, the doubt disappeared. I read the textbook from cover to cover, and I sucked this information up, and the instructor was wonderful in the way that he presented the information to us. He was a former police officer from Miami, and he explained that experienced "burn out" while working the that job, seeing drug trafficking, violence, and also a lot of corruption in many areas, and decided to get a master's degree in counseling and taught part-time at the community college.

This class offered an introduction to Freudian, Behavioral, Social, Cognitive, and Abnormal Psychology. Some of this I was already familiar with, because for the past two years, I had been reading all of the cheap, used paperbacks that the local bookstores had to sell in the psychology section. I particularly appreciated Freud. I came to learn that Freud was often not given a lot of credence in modern times, particularly by feminists. But without Freud, where would we be today? I also came to appreciate one of his students, Carl Jung.

One creative thing that I remember the instructor doing is that he showed a film entitled *Koyaanisqatsi.* He came in to class one evening and announced that he was showing this film, and he wanted us to write an essay about it after we watched it. The title of the film translated to mean "life out of balance." It was nearly ninety minutes of both slowed down and sped up images of people going to work, getting on commuter trains, in traffic, sun rising, sun going down, etc. We race through our lives, and it is the same thing, day in, day out, and we look like lemmings crammed into small spaces.

I wrote my thoughts about this film as I watched and spoke about it after the hour and a half was over. The professor always complimented me on my efforts, and this class lifted my self-esteem to new heights. I ultimately did very well, earning an "A" in this course, and the credit transferred to the University.

After this class was over, I accepted an invitation to visit an old high school friend of mine who had moved to North Carolina, in Charlotte named Chloe. She had moved out of our town immediately after high school to move in with one of her older sisters in a town further east. She had greatly objected to her father marrying a few short months after her mother's death. Her mom had been ill with cancer all through Chloe's high school years.

When I went to visit her while we were in high school, often the house was as quiet as a library and dark, and she would say, "Shhhh. Mom is really sick today. She had chemo." She would show me the room where her mom was sleeping and on the dresser, were Styrofoam heads with wigs of all different styles of hair. Her father was infrequently home, and he would sometimes be dressed up in a suit, and have cologne on, and would drop us off at the mall on Friday night. When Chloe asked where he was going, he would say, "Oh just to meet some business partners."

Chloe confronted her dad when he announced he was getting married and demanded to know whether or not he had known his bride-to-be prior to mother's death, and he did tell her that he had. He told her that her mother was sick for years, and that he needed to still have his needs met. He told her if she did not like it, she could move out. She did just that, and started a pattern of moving from apartment to apartment with her older sister for about a year in a small college town an hour east of our High School alma mater. She had once had solid plans to go to college herself.

Chloe was one of the girls I had considered "privileged,' and certainly not like myself. She lived in one of the nice middle class homes in the area. After she made her decision to move and stand her ground, she was essentially cut off from support, emotionally and financially from her father. One time we went out after high school, and she was literally, just like me, scraping coins together at the fast food restaurant, and the passenger seat in her vehicle was a milk crate. We were praying that a policeman would not stop us for anything because I was sitting on the milk crate.

By the time I got sick, she had gotten tired of Western Pennsylvania, and moved to North Carolina for the promise of better employment opportunities. She would write to me and tell me how beautiful it was there, and send pictures of the great looking men she was dating. "It's green here all the time!" She then sent me her wedding photos, from October, 1987, which barely hid her swollen belly, and then the letter that announced the birth of the baby girl, Amber. She drove all the way up from North Carolina once overnight with her infant to see me once when I was sick. I was really too sick and medicated to interact with her, but that meant so much to me. Her life sounded so exciting to me, even if some of the choices she was making I knew I would not make. By the time 1989 came, she was in the midst of a bitter divorce.

She had married a young man a year younger than us. He was from a very wealthy family, and they eloped. His family disapproved of her. The marriage suffered from the strain of her in-laws and it collapsed just about the time she was giving birth to the couple's baby. The in-laws tried to take full custody. Sometimes when people tell you things like this, they become self-fulfilling prophecies. Chloe agreed to a settlement and shared custody, and her spiral had begun, although I did not know how bad it had gotten.

I wanted to see her, as I was beginning to feel better. I had a little money each month that I received from disability, and I had a small savings bond that my parents had given me for my 18th birthday. It had not yet matured, so I only got it's face value of $100 but I managed to scrape together the $250 air fare. I set aside a week in August. I had a large tote bag and several outfits, and that is all I took! How simple I packed in those days. I wish I could be so simple now. I packed basic black and white. I rolled my clothes so that they would not wrinkle. Chloe had asked for a Pittsburgh brand of Sausage and when the bag went through the security X-ray, the security checkpoint people saw it on the screen and laughed.

My parents were concerned and could not believe that I was flying alone. I was insistent that this was something I had to do, and wanted to do, because I was starting school this year and would not have any time or money to go anywhere or see my friend.

My mom drove me to the airport and was worried and I told her to "Stop!" I was also a little scared, but when I was afraid, I faced my fear. I was determined not to go through life fearful and wishing I had done things and not doing them out of fear.

When I got there, Chloe was there waiting with her little girl, Amber. Amber was only 18 months old but already was walking and talking. She was like a miniature version of Chloe. Chloe told me the story of how her ex-husband's "rich parents" broke them up because they did not think she was good enough. She said that she had tried to get her father in Pennsylvania to come to her defense and to tell them that he had money, too, but he reminded her how she had made her choice. I listened to her words, but they were so incomprehensible to me. I really could not imagine having a child, having a husband, and then an ex-husband. I wanted a future, and she already had so much of a past. I had such sympathy.

I tried to put these thoughts behind me as I looked out the window and looked at the different state. I now had been in New York, and North Carolina in the past year. I felt so lucky! We really did not have a whole lot planned out for the week, because neither of us had much money. I had a budget of $50 for the week. (I received $250 per month, and although I lived at home, I paid for whatever expenses were mine). Chloe had a life much tougher.

She was not working a regular job, and was hosting home interior products parties for extra money. She rented a half of a home, and the landlords seemed very nice. They were a mother and daughter. The daughter was about fourteen, and she spent several days that week coming over and practicing braiding my hair. We also went to visit Chloe's other sister who lived in a remote location in a wooded area about a half hour away.

The first day I was there, I had a terrible migraine, and needed to lie down. There were no beds anywhere in the house. One room had a mattress, and Chloe explained that this would be my room, since she knew I probably would be uncomfortable on the couch. I thanked her for that consideration. She checked on me several times. She asked if I needed any aspirin or anything. I said that I did. She brought me two small pills. After I took them, I realized that these were not aspirin. My reaction to narcotics is very distinctive—my migraine does go away but then I feel like I can lift a house afterword, there is no relaxation feeling for me. I get very anxious.

I asked her what type of pill she gave me, and she giggled. "You were in pain." I told her not to do that anymore. She always meant well, but that is how she was.

She had other children that she watched during the day, as a sort of makeshift "day care." The mothers dropped the kids off and she would smile and greet them, and then put them in one of the rooms of the house and basically ignore them, and say, "easy money." I was not a fan of children. I knew I did not want children and did not have the patience for children. However, when I saw this, I knew this was wrong. Chloe left them screaming and went back to sleep. I sat up and tried my best to entertain them, as best as I could. I had a nephew who was once a young toddler, so I was able to talk to them, and I fed them the bread and butter and water that was in the house. There was little else to eat.

I questioned her, but she had an attitude that she had to do what she had to do for money. She had her home improvement party the Saturday

I was there, and that evening, she had her boyfriend over. They smoked, drank, and I watched the little girl. He had a heavy Southern accent. He referred to her neighbors as a "a bunch of Yaaard-dawgs."

Chloe said, "You're going to make something of your life. We'll live like this the rest of our life, you know that? I asked her what she meant. She said, "You have stuff planned. You want to go to school. We are just scrappin' and can't even pay rent half the time. You'll be a rich psychologist someday and we'll be stuck here on Tobacco Road." They both laughed and pitched another beer in the garbage.

Early next morning, Chloe drove me to the airport. Back in those days, security was not as tight as it is today. You could wait at the gate with people, and she and Amber did. As I was getting ready to board , Amber came running over to me, and grabbed on to my leg, and said, "Take me home with you! I wanna go home with you!" This tugged at my heart, and I thought for a moment that I would actually consider taking her if she had no other biological parent given what was going on.

I never saw Chloe again, and lost touch with her after many "Return to Sender : Address Unknown" Christmas Cards were returned to me.

After being on the plane for about a half hour, the pilot made an announcement that he would have to make an emergency landing in a very small airport in West Virginia, and that we would have a layover. The "airport" was about as big as a garage. I later found out it was a "resort" town and airport. It was one large room, and we were actually stuck there for two hours. I had my one big tote bag, and one magazine that I had already read cover to cover.

I went to the small "gift shop." I was very surprised by a couple of items I saw for sale there: some handblown glass items that were done by Jeannette Glass that were definitely made by my maternal grandfather back in the 1960's. My mother, grandmother and aunt owned some of these unique, signature swans, gondolas, and shoes.

I had about two dollars to my name. I wished I could buy the items, but could not. I sat and flipped though the magazine. A nice looking man in a suit came and sat next to me. He flirted and talked, and I thought he was very handsome and was a dead ringer for Mark Harmon, the actor. It was difficult for me to get past the fact that any man this handsome could talk to me, as just a year ago, I was 260 plus pounds and felt like a whale and no one this gorgeous would even look at me.

I was pleasant to him, but I excused myself to go to the restroom. I looked at myself in the mirror. I guess I did not look very bad. In fact, I looked okay. We shared a bag of peanuts. He asked if I wanted something to drink, and I turned him down, but he came back with a bottle of Coca Cola classic for me and I was secretly thrilled as I was thirsty! I thanked him profusely. He asked where I was from and I told him I was from the Pittsburgh area, and he told me he was from Charlotte, and heading to Pittsburgh for business.

I thought that it must be so cool to travel on business and see the country. Finally after sipping the coke, and saying very little, the announcement was made that we would be taking a small plane to Pittsburgh. The plane, I later learned, was called a charter plane. It was very loud, and rough riding. I sat with the man the entire way home, another hour or so. What was supposed to originally be a one and a half hour direct flight home, turned out to take several hours of waiting and stopping over. But it was an adventure. The man and I could not really talk over the loud engine, but we shared another bag of airline issued peanuts.

When we got off the plane, we said "goodbye" to each other. My mom, sister, and nephew were standing there waiting as I got off the plane. My mom yelled, "We were so worried! We just found out that there was a delay!" She then said, "Who was that man? He was good looking." I told my mom the whole story, and we began our drive home.

That evening, I was scheduled for my one of my last classes and I still went, even though it was a long day. It was raining and chilly back in Pennsylvania, but now I was even more determined to get back into a routine and move toward my purpose after having experienced a little bit of Chloe's life in the South.

Chapter 17 - Keeping My Eye On The Prize

Sometime before I went to North Carolina, I began to pester my WRAP counselor, Jake, as I felt I needed to get registered for classes for my first full college semester. He had a laid back approach and assured me that there would be plenty of time to register as late as August for the Fall semester, even though in my student manual there was a deadline that stated I was long past it.

I will admit it. I am a "bit" obsessive-compulsive. When I preface things with this statement, friends and family members laugh at me and say, "A bit?" I feared if I missed the deadline with everyone else, I would not get to pick classes I would like to take. In this case, I was correct. As I went to the registrar's office in late August to register with the instruction from Jake to tell them that I was a WRAP student, I was pointed to the big registration book and it was explained to me that the classes that were highlighted were "closed."

The pickings were slim. I was registered as an English major as Jake had registered me. He insisted that this is all WRAP would fund, and I had to sign on that, and I felt that at some point, perhaps my grades would prove otherwise. As it turned out, even Introductory English and Introductory Journalism were closed. I did not get to take those classes until my very last semester in college, because of the way that WRAP's last minute registration worked.

I ended up taking Introduction to Sociology, Intro to Anthropology and an Advanced Writing Course—Newspaper and Magazine Writing, among others. I carried 18 credits in all. I loved Sociology. It challenged my thinking and gave me new ideas about the world, and helped me to think outside myself. I learned about Erich Fromm, B.F.Lonergan, Erving Goffman, and more. I devoured the old sociologist's books.

But before I get to how I delved into college, I have to be honest about my first few days. Late August, 1989, was hot, humid, a typical Pennsylvania summer. I had reconnected with an old high school friend who had recently graduated college herself. Chrissie was back, living in her grandmother's house. She was, what I believed to be, worldly, as she had traveled to New York several times to visit a very chic cousin, who now, also was back home from NYC.

I caught her up on the last four years of my life since she had been away at college. She apologized that she had not written or come to see me, but she was living hand to mouth at a college clear across the state, waitressing, and even told me a story about how she had been gang mugged on the street. "I was pissed off that it was my good Anne Klein purse," she said in her characteristic fashionista flair, but I could see she had been shaken by the experience. "I screamed after them, Take my cash, gimme the purse you morons!'"

She herself had obtained an English degree and she advised me, "Don't do it. Get yourself something useful. If you are a good writer, it does not matter what type of degree you have. You can get published or a writing gig. Now I am pegged as a copywriter or proofreader because of this degree. If you go for the psychology degree you want, you can work in that field, but you can write for fun. I am thankful for that advice.

Chrissie and I used to go to concerts a lot as teenagers. She was one of my non drug using friends when I was a teenager, so this is why we reconnected so easily, and now my obsession was education, and here was a real, live, college educated person to talk to. We attended a Stevie Nicks concert right before college started for me. I remember us wondering why Stevie was just standing there and then we read in the newspaper that she had a broken foot.

I had the support of Chrissie. But here is the truth: I doubted myself after the first full day of class whether I could do it. For starters, although I was only 22 years old, I felt extremely old. I seriously considered myself a "nontraditional student." I looked around and saw eighteen year old boys and girls who lived on campus, who looked as though they had not a care in the world. I looked at the syllabi (schedules) of the six classes

I had taken, went to the book store, tallied up the cost of all the books, and was overwhelmed by the hundreds of dollars texts would cost, and all of the requirements expected of me, and I ended my first day with one of my blinding migraines.

All I could think was, I don't belong here. My parents are right. We are working class people. Maybe I am not cut out for this. Who am I kidding? This is crazy. I am never going to get a degree. I am going to be sick every day. It will be a miracle if I make it through one week, let alone one semester.

It was a hot day, and I drove home (only three miles or so) and went into my bedroom and lay on my bed, and turned on the window air conditioner that I had begged my parents to let me install. (The doctor had asked them to allow me to install it for better breathing, so my brother in law put it in. My mother was against the idea because she did not like how it looked on the front of her house). As I lay there, I obsessed about what I had gotten myself into. Had I taken on more than I could handle? The more I thought, the more my head hurt. I finally realized that I just had to put a cool rag on my head and go to sleep.

I woke up the next day and braved it again. And I did it again, and again, and again. I stopped worrying about others. I was not 18, and carefree. I was not living on campus. I had experienced a lot of pain, and still have a lot of uncertainty ahead of me. This was true. But I realized when I sat in those classrooms, the world outside, and more importantly, my own problems, my inner worries, dissolved, melted away. I was becoming a thinking, developing, logical person. I can do this. Every day, I realized I can truly do this.

My confidence grew as I passed "pop quizzes" and I heard some of the younger cute kids outside talking about how they "bombed" the quizzes and heard a lot of them talking about how they got "bombed" last night.

The anthropology professor looked like Jerry Garcia from the Grateful Dead. He had a laid back style. In fact he was so laid back, that in some classes; he literally would lie across the desk and talk about Aborigines, Hunters and Gatherers, and other people that were not like those of us in the Western World. This was all like learning a new language. He did not have an organized way of teaching. A lot of students would say, "He doesn't care if you show up. He just lays up there and shoots the breeze." On the first day of class, he said to us, "There will not be any homework. No papers. You are adults. Your grade will be based on a final. It is easy."

On the night of finals, there were 28 people. On an average day of class, there were maybe five of us. He handed out a sheet of notebook paper to all of us. He said, "Well, four months ago, I explained to you that you were all adults and that your grade would be based on this final. I have heard about how easy this would be because I am so laid back. I have heard I look like Jerry Garcia. I hear that I teach a blow off class. I am going to write your question on the board. If you attended on October 30th, this will be no problem for you." Those of us who attended religiously looked at each other relieved and smirked. He wrote the question: "Describe a typical Day in the life of a !Kung San."

He looked at the 23 or so students who did not attend. Many audibly said, "Oh shit," some had their mouths open, and a few just walked out. The professor bellowed and said "Fooled your asses!" He then said, "As I said, this is easy, and you're adults. Part of being an adult is showing up where you are supposed to be. Let it be a lesson."

I did not understand why he even had to verbalize such a basic fact.

I took a pause, thought about the question, went back in my mind to a day sometime in October when he talked about the !Kung San, and looked up at the chalkboard again. The professor took his usual place, lying on the desk, with his belly protruding out of his green sweater. He looked out of his paperback book that he was reading occasionally to see if anyone was looking at anyone else's paper. I felt that I gave a good answer, as I described the basics of the lives in that culture.

I handed in the paper, and he said, "You should do fine. You were here." I attended all of my classes and did all the required papers, devoured every book that was suggested. If a professor mentioned an author, I wrote the name down. If they cited a name, such as the sociology professor, citing Erving Goffman, I went to the used bookstore, and bought all the used paperbacks I could find authored by Goffman. I wanted to learn all I could.

My first semester in the writing class, I did the paper based on Studs Terkel's classic 1970's book, *Working*. The book was written in a very casual, first person account in which Terkel interviewed people on the job, and they told their story giving you a typical "day in the life of" their occupations. We were given the assignment of spending a day with someone who has a job and reporting their story, all in first person account, but editing it so that it could be published. That is when I decided to choose Penny, the owner of the used paperback store that I frequented.

It was November, 1989, and I had just gotten Marcus. Marcus was an eight month old dachshund. I saw the ad in the paper, and it said, "Lovable, male red dachshund. Housebroken." I told my mom and she said that she would go to look at Marcus with me. We went to the home, and it was a girl whom I had gone to high school with named Suzanne. She had three children: two toddlers and a new baby, in a swing. She told me that her new baby was allergic to Marcus, and that her husband was making her get rid of Marcus. Suzanne looked petrified. I asked where Marcus was. I heard her husband yelling at that time, and he came in the living room and was yelling at the kids, at Suzanne, and Suzanne looked as if she was going to cower in a corner. He lifted up the sofa, and there was the little dachshund hiding under the sofa. My mom said, "We'll take him." Suzanne said, "Good. You can have his crate, his bed, bowl and everything. Thank you so much. Are you writing a check?" My mom wrote a check, and we took him.

My mom and I thought we got a deal—all his belongings and the dog. That evening, I was taking a bath, and I had Marcus in the bathroom with me. He walked around and he came over, stood up on his hind legs and gave me a kiss. I thought, "This is it. He is my best friend for life." And he was. No "one" has ever surpassed the love I have had for Marcus. I realized over the next few days that Marcus had severe asthma, especially when he got nervous. The first few nights were horrible. I thought he was choking on his bedding, so I got rid of it..it was a fluffy, down like material. I gave him some of my sheets instead. It did not go away. His breathing calmed down a bit after he stayed with us for a while.

I was overwhelmed by the thought that I had this responsibility: the dog. I also was still having the fear that I could not successfully complete school. But every day I just did it, and I actually had the "support" of this little dog. He did not care how I looked. He did not mind if I had a migraine. He was amazing. One morning he was wrapped around me very protectively and I could not shake him off. It was actually quite annoying. I did not understand what his problem was. Soon, about a half hour later, I felt the waves of nausea, the squiggly lines that occur in my lines of vision, and a full blown migraine occurred. Had he sensed my migraine before me?

I later read about dogs who could sense when their owners were going to have seizures and diabetic comas. Maybe I had a special dog, too. For the next 13 and a half years, Marcus and I were there for each other, and this might seem crazy, but he knew, sometimes before I did, that I was getting a migraine. If I was sad, or had a broken heart, he was there.

For the writing assignment, I took Marcus into Penny's store, and saw a different side of Penny, as she got down on the floor and frolicked with Marcus. Marcus was, effectively, the icebreaker, and she allowed me to voice-record her conversation. She spoke about how she was so sheltered and shy that her husband purchased the store so that she could get over her fear of people.

My confidence was still shaky about college. I was "getting" some of it, and some of it was literally a foreign language to me. For example, I took Spanish the entire first year. I became so obsessed with excelling in this language that I purchased books in Spanish, opted to rent videos in Spanish, and listened to Spanish radio broadcasts on the overnight radio on a.m radio. Overnight, you can pick up all kinds of cities on a.m. radio. I got radio stations from New York and Florida featuring Spanish speaking broadcasters (the Pittsburgh local market did not have daytime Spanish broadcasts).

Soon, a strange thing began to happen: I began to dream in Spanish. I began to speak to my professor in Spanish. She was from Venezuela. It was rusty at first, but she was pleasantly surprised. She would correct me as she said I had an Italian accent and used the soft "c's"—as in "change." It was a habit I could not break—it was how I heard my grandfather and his mother speak when I was growing up. I became obsessive about most of my classes in this manner. The result was mostly A's and an occasional B. I made the Dean's list.

I had fun with my classes. I enjoyed writing, and enjoyed learning. I looked around and saw people griping about "having to go" to class, and felt that it was a privilege.

For the second semester, I again took two Psychology classes. One was very advanced (It was called Learning and Cognition) and another was Creativity and Psychology. The latter was a psychoanalytic course in which we explored the meaning of art, music, and other expressions of art, especially works done by artists who have had mental illness.

For the Cognition and Learning Course, I was forced at that time to enter the world of computers. This was scary to me. We had to go to the computer lab and program data into the IBM's and analogize this to how our brains functioned and write a thesis based on this. I was having a difficult time with this. I went to the psychology professor and voiced my comprehension block. It turns out that this man had a fascinating background. He had a PhD n Psychology and left the field, but got a Master's in Information Science, explaining to me, "In ten years, this will be the wave of the future, Candace. It will infiltrate all aspects of life, including psychology. If you are in a private practice somewhere, you will have to be proficient on a computer. I personally left that field because I would rather deal with a machine than people." I liked his honesty. He told me, 'Don't be anxious. The computer is not your enemy. There is no such thing as a computer error. It is a human error. Just go down in that lab and practice, practice, practice!" I did it. I spent hour upon hour in that lab until I got it right. I learned on IBM and Macintosh. I admit, I loved Macintosh. It was easy to play with, it had MacPaint, it was fun. I made friends on University of Pittsburgh's Intranet.

College was fun and I learned. I met a friend in the bathroom in 1990. It was someone I had recognized walking everyday along the side of the road. She said later that she was scared of me. I don't know why. I may have had a kind of hard nosed edge about me that I built up as way to protect myself from being hurt, as the last three years, I had lost many so-called friends.

My meeting with Anne is described by Anne like this:

"I saw you walking...and we began filling our friendship epic of an ongoing conversation that has been incomplete for the last ....decade and a half (or more).."

The combination of learning and building connections boosted my self confidence. I met with my WRAP counselor, as we WRAP funded people had to do each semester. He asked how I was doing. I told him

I was doing very well. I showed him my mid term grades, and as we sat in the cafeteria, many people walked by and said hello to me. He could see I was pretty popular and commented on the fact. He said, "Why are you taking all of these psychology classes?" I told him that I felt what I was doing was a calling. If I could not help people through nursing or medicine, I would help them this way. And my first step would be to obtain a bachelor's degree in psychology! He said, "You sound pretty sure of yourself in just your second semester. Do you know how difficult it is to complete a psychology degree? You have to pass a statistics course." I explained to him that I was aware of this and that I was willing to find a tutor, take a math course down at community college, pay for it myself, do whatever I had to do to accomplish this dream. He said that I seemed determined. There was no indication that he was going to oppose it. I felt very good about this whole thing! I was riding the wave until one day, I came home and opened the mail.

The letter was from Jake, my WRAP counselor, dated April 2, 1990, and it read:

> *Dear Candace,*
>
> *I reviewed your case with my supervisor and we both feel that it would be inappropriate for us to agree with a change of major. The results of your vocational testing indicate that you have a talent for communications type of activities, however, it does not support a career as a psychologist. In particular, your relative low aptitude in arithmetic skills would mean that you would have difficulty passing a course in statistics which would be required of anybody seeking a degree in the field of psychology.*
>
> *Furthermore, your overall personality profile leads us to believe that you would have trouble dealing with many of the issues that would confront a psychologist on a daily basis. If you wish to continue on your original area of study, we would be happy to continue funding you at the University of Pittsburgh. If, on the other hand, you switched majors you would have to find some other source of funding.*

I am sorry to disappoint you in this regard but I honestly feel that you have a much better chance of success in your original choice of job objectives. If you would like to talk with me further about this, please feel free to call.

I was stunned at this letter, as he was indicating that he did not support this choice. He did voice that I "might have trouble" with" statistics when I met him a few weeks earlier. I showed the letter to my mother, and asked her what I should do. She said, "We can't help you. We are tapped out. You proved yourself. You did it. Maybe he is right. Maybe you can't do it. Why fight city hall?" I could not believe this reaction! This was not about "proving myself." This was about a feeling that I had that I wanted to help people, and going after it through learning, and obtaining an education.

I called Jake the next day. He actually was available, which was a rare occurrence. I explained that his letter said that I should call if I wanted to talk about this further. He became defensive. He said, "Candace, there is really nothing to discuss. We staffed your case. The decision was made, and you are not appropriate to be a psychology major." I again explained how well I was doing academically, and he said, "Academically I have no concern. I am concerned about your personality. You are not suited for working with other people." I said, "You indicate in your letter that you do have academic concerns and you saw how well I get along with many people at the college." He cut me off. "Candace, we have made our decision. You can find your own funding if you do not continue the pursuit of an English or Communications degree."

I talked to my Academic Advisor, the Psychologist, turned Information science Professor about this matter. It was with much embarrassment that I told him the whole story, because I did not want anyone to know I was the status "disabled." He did not show any sign of shock or judgment. What did surprise him was that I had been so sick, just three years earlier. He said that I look healthy, and did not appear to be in any pain. I told him I still often am, but that I manage it well, and do not let it get me down, as I want to have a life that is not focused on my illness twenty-four hours a day. He had a very pensive look. He then said, "Look, play their game. You are obviously intelligent. You can still take the courses and also English course. The main objective is that you want a degree. If you do go for a graduate degree, then let's cross that bridge when we come to it. Do not do anything right now to mess up your funding. Just continue to take your courses and know that you are certain you want to pursue this route."

I thought about it, and he made sense. I do not have to tell WRAP. How does that help me? I actually though that I would prove myself and even pay for and take an algebra course over the summer at community college to prepare for statistics, mentally. Then I would show WRAP that I could "pass statistics" as they were predicting that I could not. No one was going to stand in the way of my dream.

I just stayed focused. I kept visualizing, just as I had when I had reached my lowest point a few years earlier, when I was sick, homebound, grossly obese. My visualization at that time was picturing myself slimmer, picturing the nodules/tumors erasing from my lungs, and in control of my situation, attending school. Here I was, now in the situation I dreamed of. Now I had to tackle this hurdle. Life was a series of hurdles that had to be tackled, one at a time. I attended my classes, put forth effort in my papers, enjoyed learning, enjoyed writing my papers. I researched each subject I wrote about, citing references diligently. I had my old manual typewriter, and many professors did not tolerate whiteout on their papers, so mistakes were not permitted. I became a perfectionist.

In the second year of college, my parents did see how hard I was working, and they did reward me with an electric typewriter. The manual typewriter may have kept them up at night, as it was loud, it had a loud bell that rang at the end of every sentence, and I had to manually move the arm at the end of each sentence. I taught myself to type on that model, and some of those old habits still remain. Some of that "hunt and peck" behavior and hard pressing of the keys remains, but the job does get done!

I made honor roll again, the end of the second semester of college. At the end of the first year, I did take my own money and enrolled in a summer course of algebra at community college. My goal was to become familiar with the complex math that I did not experience in high school (I regret this) and prepare myself for statistics. It was difficult. I only took math until tenth grade. It was frankly remedial math, and the high school math teacher actually brought in a check book and said, "You guys are here for a reason. You are not mathematicians. But I want you to be able to go out in the real world and do basic math. This is life skills math." He often would shake his head and look at me and say , "Candace, why are you here? You are too smart to be here. You are not living up to your potential, girl."

I knew that, but something about math scared me. Math and driving stick shifts. My dad took me out at age 16, and I stalled his car out and he yelled at me that "broads can't drive sticks." He then told me to try to drive it home. He was yelling the whole time. I stalled and stalled. Math and sticks seemed like impossible tasks to me—the insurmountable. Anyone who could do these things seemed like geniuses to me. These were two things I wanted to achieve more than anything in the world, and it would take a long time to get the driving down. I stuck to automatics and did that well, but always felt like a failure. I finally achieved the stick shift with patience (and buying my own manual car) at age 38.

Summer of 1990, two nights a week I attended three hour classes. Algebra was a new concept to me. Why were letters and math being mixed together? What is the purpose of this? I began to slowly understand. I took my book and workbook to bed, to the bathtub, I read it and practiced it all the time, just as I had with my Spanish. I began to dream math problems. I was determined to prove WRAP wrong. I withdrew from it. It was not an A. It was going to be a a C+, and it would not go on my transcript if I did not ask for it to be transferred (I did not) as I did not want it to affect my GPA.

I began the second year with a new confidence. I had problems with scheduling in the second year, just as I had the first year, with late registration and WRAP. They were late in providing funding, almost a week before classes started. When I went to register, I was asked to make one third of a deposit. As tuition was up to about $1800 a semester, I admit I got a little sarcastic. I said, "Here let me see what I have in my pocket. I pulled out the three and some odd dollars of change and put it on the counter along with my completed registration." I was told that without the one third deposit, I could not register, no exceptions.

I explained that I received funding from WRAP and also applied for state grants. Both were late in arriving. I was told, "Sorry, we cannot register you." This was how it went every semester. I went home, deflated, called WRAP, left a message for Jake, that probably had the tone of frustration, and explained my plight. I had to sit and wait for him to get back to me. It took two days, and he explained that they preferred for me to get some from the state first, then they would provide the rest. It was a game that I played each semester. I also now had to make sure that I registered for English classes each semester so that my funding would continue with them, as they made it clear that they would not support my desire of obtaining a Psychology degree. This was quite stressful.

But once the wait was over, I went back with my check for the tuition, went the registrar, saw what classes were still open, picked my psychology classes, followed by sociology classes next, and then, picked my necessary English classes. Statistics, disappointingly, was closed for the Fall semester, in 1990. My tactic to pretend I was planning to go ahead with my goal to gain an English degree was dishonest. I did not get enough grant money to complete my education as they calculated my parent's income and wrote me a letter that despite my disability, felt that I should get parental support.

I explained to my parents that they had to stop claiming me as a "dependent," as they continued to do, or that they had to help me with my education, which is what my academic advisor told me. They were putting me on their tax return as a dependent, which screwed me from getting financial aid other than WRAP. WRAP was not "allowing" me to claim the major I wanted. Technically the state, even though I lived under their roof, saw me as independent of my parents, as they gave me an income, a disability income. My academic advisor frankly advised me, "Move out of their home if they are not supportive of your goals." I told them I would do that, and my mother told me that I would not be able to take the old Renault Alliance that I was now driving. I relied on that vehicle to get me to and from class. There were not any dorms available on campus. It was mid-semester. I was really in a bind. I had to push the case of having them not claiming me as a dependent any longer, and finally that was the ticket to getting some grant money, but it would not be to my benefit until my junior year in college.

I was unaware that at the time, my parents had financial problems. They made statements like "We helped our kids enough. We got burned." I felt that this was apples and oranges. This wasn't a purchase of an item, or cosigning on a house or a car that I would default on. This was an investment for my future. I planned to work. I look back and I realize I could have given up, but I had a visual –to just keep my eye on the prize; the pot at the end of the rainbow—and that pot was not money, or fortune, but just simply making a difference in the loves of others one day, while being serene, and being able to support myself, and not being caught up in the day to day drama.

Chapter 18 - Fighting For What I Know Is Right

I began my second year of college with different anxieties than I had in the first year. My first year's anxieties were all about whether or not I could do the work. I now knew I could academically do this. Now it was all about getting caught, or found out by WRAP.

Despite my academic advisor and the Department head of Psychology's reassurances that I should concentrate on just doing well, it was not that easy. I could certainly do well, and I did. I had classes that year such as Gender Psychology, Logic, Public Speaking (I used my knowledge from the old radio days combined with the new information I was gaining in psychology and did well), and Sociology of Aging. I got one B in the fall Semester. I look back at my papers, and they are works that I am still very proud of, as I put my heart and soul into them. College was not party time for me, as that time was ten years earlier in my mixed up life.

Some people dread writing papers. I loved it. I loved reading. I immersed myself in some of the more personal papers that I wrote for the psychology classes. We were asked to know ourselves so that we could understand what others are going through. I already knew that I was affected greatly by my years of isolation, and rejection, and that this was either going to make me better at helping others, or unable to deal with others at all. I felt very confident that my own suffering was going to prepare me better to help others who were suffering. It was very hard to relive what I had gone through.

I continued making friends, some which proved to become lasting. Anne, was someone I spent pretty much every day with, sharing laughs, dreams, hopes. I dated a few people, but my main focus was getting this degree. Something in my soul never allowed myself to get too serious in a relationship. I analogized it to a pot at the end of a rainbow. I would see people get side lined by relationships in college just like they did in high school. That scared me.

I knew that my only ticket "out," and on to complete independence and the freedom I needed was to get a degree and then be able to make the decision to work or go to graduate school was to get the bachelor's degree. It was very calculated and I knew it would take extreme patience. But I had to stay in control.

The second semester of my second year, Anne had a party at her boyfriend's house. We all were non drinkers, so it was a very sober party. It was there that I met another lasting friend. I did not know any of Anne's friends. I was sitting there, observing. I can be social if needed. At work, nowadays, I must be social. I have to market programs. I have to make appearances, and speak publicly. Intrinsically, I am a very socially backward type of person, who prefers little interaction. I was that way before I got sick, and out of survival, and habit, when "holed up" for three years when ill, became extremely solitary. This was an evening when I suppose that true, authentic part of myself was showing.

I sat there, and I looked in the other corner, and saw another person, and recognized a kindred spirit. Something clicked. I got up, and slowly, made my way over, sort of like a crab would make their way across the sand, and said, "Hi. I am Candace." I could see that she was as uncomfortable in this environment where people were laughing and talking as I was. We talked about books, authors, and I realized, this person, Sarah, is one of the most literate people I have ever met. She could talk me under the table when it came to literature. She was up to speed on modern and classical authors. She was currently into Ezra Pound, having "been over the Jack Kerouac thing" at the ripe old age of 21. I was not into fiction, further proof that being an English major was not my bag. I introduced her to a few of my heroes, like Lenny Bruce, and some musical heroes, like Phil Spector, and Otis Redding. She had a middle class, and more financially stable background than I did. She began college initially at age 16. I envied that, but a similar wild teenage ride.

Sarah is still someone I turn to when I need a verbal, logical, literate kick in my ass. I trust her completely. She has sound judgment and is funny. And I do not think she even tries to be—she is just so gifted with the English language.

It helped to have supports. I had people whom I could talk to intellectually, share some laughs, and who did not think that my goal was outlandish. The second semester of my second year of college started, and I almost did feel hubris, as if everything was going to be alright, that I was untouchable. My grades continued to soar. My ability to reason abstractly was increasing. I look back at some of the papers I wrote, and I was very confident:

> *While many believe that it is only the masochistic type who is overly dependent on others, without the masochistic type to follow the sadistic type, the sadistic type would also be alone. The two are interdependent upon one another; each needs the other for survival. The sadistic type therefore, is also dependent.*

I loved writing, and expressing my views. My grades, at midterm were all A's. (That entire semester they would be all A's). In the middle of the term, I had my obligatory meeting with a WRAP counselor. He came to the campus. I took the opportunity to proudly show all of my mid-term grades to him. Of the five classes I was taking that semester, three were psychology classes, one was an advanced English (I still could not get into that Basic English class due to my inability to register early), and one was a sociology class, which would become my minor). I talked to this WRAP counselor about how well I was doing, even showed him a couple of my papers, talked to him for about a half hour about some of the different theories in Social Psychology (I had paid for a Social Psychology class over the summer with my own money and now was in advanced Social Psychology), Clinical Psychology, and some of my favorite writers in sociology. I expressed how well I was doing, and how this was my dream to have a career in this field. He asked if I would want to practice as a clinical person or a researcher. I said that I had a burning desire to help others, even though I enjoyed my research class, and research was necessary. He wrote a lot of notes. He said he was pleased with my grades and wished me luck.

I had also met another person in college at the time who received funding from WRAP. We met while in class and happened to see each other waiting in line to see the WRAP counselor. Neither of us could believe that the other had a "disability," because the other looked so "good." Her name was Pammy. Pammy told me she had been diagnosed with a degenerative disease, but was asymptomatic. She received WRAP funding and was approved for a psychology degree and had been attending college since 1986 (it was now 1990). She told me she would go until about midterm, long enough to declare an "incomplete," then get a refund, and then pick up the next semester. I listened, incredulously. She said that this was her way of getting some extra on top of her disability check, then she could also get a degree, eventually, at her own pace. I began to see this as a scam, and here I was, trying to prove myself! (By the time I made it to graduate school in 1993, Pammy was still "working" on her degree)

I felt good knowing that I was going to have my degree in four years, and actually maybe less than the projected four years, because I was getting in a couple classes each summer and managing up to 21 credits one semester. To me "scamming the system" was not being a winner. I would see Pammy over the course of my time at the branch campus of the University and she would show off a designer handbag and say, "Check it out, I bought it with my refund." I grappled whether or not I should report this, but I thought to myself that I was already not on the best of terms with WRAP, and would they see it as some sort of ulterior motive on my part?

Inevitably a second letter arrived from my WRAP counselor on March 18. 1991. As I suspected, my worst fears were confirmed, and all of my hard work did not pay off, as the letter said:

Dear Candace:

> *I understand you talked to (the campus WRAP counselor) recently and reiterated your request that (we) allow you to change your major to Psychology. Your case was staffed in our office this past week, and reviewed by myself, my supervisor, and our medical consultant. It is our feeling that this would be an inappropriate change of objective for you, and cannot agree to this kind of change. You of course have the right to take any*

courses you want, however WRAP funding can continue only so long as you are enrolled in your original major (English). If you are dissatisfied with the decision to close your case, you may submit a written request for administrative review within 30 days..."

I read and reread this letter, and grew angrier at the injustice. I attended every Class. I was a serious student. I was very goal directed. I paid for my own summer classes, so I actually saved them money. I had a plan for my life. I was 23 years old. I was not partying through school. I absolutely was going to appeal this decision, because I knew that, as per the first letter they sent, they were basing this on a personality test that was done while I was very physically ill. I knew just enough about this that you cannot judge a person's personality on testing done when a person is ill and on powerful medications.

My next move was to speak again to the Head of the Department of Psychology and also to the therapist that I still saw monthly so that she could attest to any progress I had made. I could apply for a student grant for the fall semester, but I could not jeopardize losing the funding for the spring term which was already in progress, the term which I was academically excelling in.

I shared the letter and the brief history of the story with Dr. Jane Lash, the Department head, and she listened, aghast. She said that it was unbelievable. She asked to read the letter and again said, "This is unbelievable!" She picked up the telephone in her office and telephoned the WRAP counselor, and spoke to him. She said, "I have this young woman in my office. I have had her in my classes, I have seen her on campus, and it is my understanding that you are basing a decision on a three year old aptitude and personality profile. Do you realize that medical illness can skew results?"

I heard a lot of "Uh huh."s and "Yes,"es, and sat there with my head down, or looking at her book shelf. Dr Lash finally hung up the phone. She told me, "This man is not budging. He really has something in for you for some reason, and does not want to change his mind. Do you want to go all the way with this appeal?" I told her I did because I had no other means to pay for this semester. She said, "I will help you. I will administer the psychological testing myself or have the university counselor, who is also a licensed psychologist, do it. This is an outrage!" I could not believe that someone was in my corner!

She then told me to get to work writing my appeal letter because it was time sensitive, and to get in touch with Jackie, the therapist to also write a statement. "We have to move on this since the term will be winding down." I told my mother about this, and she said simply, "That's good."

I was nervous about all of this, because I expected the worst. What if indeed this MMPI (Minnesota Multiphasic Personality Index), a personality profile did show that something was inherently wrong with me? Maybe I was seriously defective! My Intelligent Quotient was also going to be tested. I was scared about this, too.

The University Psychologist scheduled the IQ testing and the MMPI in two separate sessions, unlike the first time I had this done in one marathon afternoon. The MMPI revealed "no elevations on any personality or clinical scales" per the letter written by Dr to WRAP. She further attested that the initial testing was done "in light of a presence of a serious medical illness, Wegener's granulomatosis….at the time of her initial evaluation by Dr. Donald Jennings, she was having considerable difficulty dealing with the nature and implications of the diagnosis, as well of the symptoms of the disorder. Standard personality tests cannot distinguish between psychological problems that are reactive to serious medical problems or those that are more enduring personality problems. ..based on the results of her current personality assessment, on her academic performance, and on the report of her psychotherapist, it is recommended that Candace be permitted to change her major to psychology."

That letter by the therapist stated that I have shown a concern because "WRAP placed" me as a journalism/English major, and that my ability to "confront and resolve stress has grown and is focused on growth and development, " and that there are no indications that she could not pursue a career in psychology," as clinical work would not begin until the graduate level.

My own letter was an exercise in restraint and humility. This was my life on the line. I explained how I read not only all the required books, but also outside the required reading list, how I attended class regularly, how seriously I took school, how I was placed in a major that was not of my choosing, and that it was "quite a Catch 22", as I wanted to obtain a degree rather desperately, because it was explained to me that if I wanted the degree, I needed to agree to the major, but that this was my only chance of funding as my parents had still claimed me as a dependent at the time of starting college. I explained how I believe I had proven myself academically and interpersonally.

Now, it was a waiting game for the hearing to be set. I still had to concentrate on my studies, which I did. Next, I received a letter from the Director of Program Operations at WRAPS Regional Offices. They informed me that they may not have a hearing. They again would "staff" the case with all of the information that they had, which included an "Informal Administrative Review." They asked me to return a postcard indicating whether or not I would be able to attend a hearing, should one be necessary.

In late May, I received a telephone call from Jake, my WRAP counselor. He was very curt and to the point, but said that , "We have reached an agreement based on a staff meeting that you may change your major, to your chosen field of study, psychology, but this depends on your ability to maintain your grades at at least a C average. I still have concerns that you can pass Statistics." I thanked him. What else could I do? He also encouraged me to still apply for student state grants as a "back up."

I received a letter from Jake dated May 28th, which indicated that I needed to meet with him to change my educational plan. I received a letter, dated May 30th, that his supervisor wrote. He wished me good luck in my studies.

When I met with Jake, his attitude toward me was still unchanged. He had a very condescending demeanor, and mentioned again that he was unconvinced that I would be able to do well in Statistics, even though I did "better" in the IQ testing. I did not dispute anything he said. I did not understand or even want to analyze this man's anger toward me. He obviously, as Dr. Lash stated, have "it in for me," for whatever reason.

I thought back to when I first met him, and I expressed my desire to obtain a psychology degree and he said something to me that to me, showed that he had some real problems of his own. He said, "Really?

Well, I would like to study music, but I can't carry a tune in a bucket. But this is what we have decided for you."

I was just thankful that now I could go on with my choice and not his, and to go with the plan that continually he said "we have chosen" but it was obviously his own plan.

I vowed early on, before I had any clients of my own, never to force my choices on people, and also to try to help people the way Dr Lash helped me and the way that my physician, Dr McCollom helped me. I hope I have been able to do that in my career. If someone asks for something and they are in need, and I can do it immediately, I try to get it—if that means making an important telephone call or writing a letter, then I do it. If they can find it within themselves, I try to help them find it.

Sometimes, people really do get screwed by the system, and it may just be because of one disgruntled person.

Chapter 19 - Bumps In The Road

My health was not without issues in college. I tried to take preventative measures and although I was not able to do serious aerobics, I did some stretching, walking, weights.

One evening, I was doing my routine, and I felt my lower back go out of place. I treated it with heat. This was in 1991, and my second full year of college. After two weeks of serious pain, I went to the local E.R. The first thing they did was come in and asked me the questions that I always got asked because I was on medical assistance. They assumed at the hospital that I was a "high risk" because I was low income, and asked me about venereal disease, illicit drugs, etc.

I felt they were stereotyping me and not everyone fits that profile. He x-rayed me and stated that I had a "bulging disc." They recommended that I follow up with my regular doctor. This caused me concern, because my fear was that my plan for my life would be thwarted.

When I followed up, he recommended I continue to do the same-light exercise, but that I need to be careful as this disc is fragile, and he is not surprised as I have the history of long term thyroid hormone replacement, and the high doses of steroid and chemotherapy in the recent past.

I also had seen a local doctor for a simple infection, taken the time to provide my medical history, and was prescribed a commonly prescribed older antibiotic. After a few days, I began to have a serious sharp pain in my lower right side. I called his office. I was told it is normal, as "all antibiotics cause GI distress."

After 5 days, I woke up and it felt like a knife was in my right side. I called my therapist, whose first career had been nursing. She said, "Get to the E.R. That could be liver, gall bladder. Don't mess with it." I went out to the kitchen. It was a hot July day, after I had taken my shower, and I asked if I could use the car. Although I was sweating from the heat, I was alternately experiencing chills. My father looked at me and said, "You are not driving."

I got there, and told the triage nurse that I believed I was having a liver problem. I was greeted with a smirk, as I was talked down to because of my medical coverage, "Oh really? And what makes you think that? How much do you drink?" I told her I do not drink, but I believed that I was having an adverse reaction to a medication that I have been on for five days now.

I explained what medication I was on, and what was recently added. I explained my medical history. The nurse explained that this was a "safe medication" and "hardly anyone" has this type of reaction. I had a doctor examine my abdomen, and he asked me, "are you sure you did not drink cold water? It is, after all a hot day?" I said, "No I drank tap water when I was brushing my teeth. I am sure this change came about when I started this medication." He asked, "are you sure you don't drink alcohol? I assured him I do not drink alcohol at all. I asked him again to please check my liver functions. Finally he said, "OK, to humor you, I will." He left the area, and I let loose with a few choice words. I thought, why does a person who is honest, and seems to know what they are talking about and what they are dealing with have to do somersaults to get relief?

I had my LFTs (liver functioning) taken and the results came back. I was informed that they were "extremely elevated." Next thing I knew I was going for a liver ultrasound. The doctor came in and said, "You were right. You have very elevated liver functioning and we believe that antibiotic caused it. You have drug induced hepatitis. You need to be admitted." I refused to be admitted to that hospital. I did not trust the local hospitals. Even though this was not the hospital that had diagnosed me with pneumonia four years earlier, if this E.R. treatment was anything like their inpatient treatment, I decided I would wait and speak to my doctor in Pittsburgh.

The E.R. doctor told me that this was against medical advice. I told him I understand what this means. He explained that I could die. I told him that I do not come into the E.R. unless I am in serious condition, and that although they have a habit of stereotyping "low income patients," I do not use the E.R. as my health clinic. I had a good idea what was wrong days earlier when I called the prescribing doctor. I will wait to call my Wegener's doctor, and if he wants me to be admitted, I will go to the hospital in which he has privileges.

I said from what little medical knowledge I have because I am only a second year psych student, there is nothing they can do for me anyway, because if I have drug induced hepatitis, I cannot take any more medications anyway, right? He said that was actually correct. He again apologized for not hearing my concerns initially but stressed the seriousness of going against medical advice.

Customer service is important, and this was my issue. I felt a huge lack of trust here. I felt like I could go home and not take medications. I called my doctor. This was a Saturday evening. I told him what I knew. I had written down the results of my LFT. The local hospital had scared me as they had told me that with the elevation, I am "close to cirrhosis." He told me "Yes, but what they didn't tell you is this is acute. You would be close to cirrhosis if this was chronic. You don't drink and this was an asinine situation." He stated "I would not go to my hospital tonight. It is a Saturday night. Skeleton crews are there on weekends. Give me the name of these docs out there. I will call the E.R. I want records. I will authorize a direct admit for tomorrow night, and we will go from there. Didn't they know not to prescribe that medication to someone with a history of kidney disease? Did you tell them about the kidney disease?"

I told him I had, and he said, "If things get worse, find a way down to my E.R." I told my parents what was going on. I went to lie down that night, and began hallucinating. I was really sick, and spent half the night in the bathroom, throwing up, the same way I had when I was on chemotherapy (the ugly green bile that seems to come from deep in your gut even when you have not eaten for days), and the time I spent lying down, sweating, having chills, and hallucinating visually—and the colors I saw were purple swirls—and I hate purple.

The next day, I spent the whole day doing the same thing: throwing up bile, hallucinating, sweating. I finally dragged myself into the shower, packed a bag, and my dad drove me down to the E.R. in Pittsburgh. As promised, Dr McCollom had me as a direct admit. I was back up on the

11th floor. I was not allowed anything but water, and my thyroid pill. I was yellow. His team were angry about this situation as I explained that I did give my medical history, and one of the cautions were to not give to someone that particular med with a history of Wegener's or kidney or liver complications. I was there three days into this stay and decided to sign out.

Just when I was about to sign the AMA (against medical advice papers), one of Dr McCollom's residents came in and said, "Stop right there. You don't want to do that. Until the LFT's stabilize you do not want to go home. Be patient. C'mon. Rip it up. Yes, this is stupid. That was a stupid mistake. But let's get you back on the road of health."

Dr McCollom had the resident place a sign above my bed that read, "Answer ALL questions."

I agreed to stay, and this was a seven day stay. They could not give me any medication at all during that stay. I had toxic (drug induced) hepatitis. I was ill because of overdosing or allergic reaction to medication. I needed to be cleansed of medication. I basically had to wait this out and be monitored. Once my liver functioning tests lowered to a point where I could be discharged medically, I was sent home.

I was not "right" until about September. After I was discharged, I was still throwing up after eating certain foods, exhausted, nauseated. That summer was a bust as far as energy. I took a few classes, and spent time with some of my friends, but it felt, like a setback, and I had fear about my health. I took a class on drugs and alcohol that summer that was actually extremely helpful as the psychologist who taught it used to be a nurse, and explained how drugs are oxidized in the body, and how allergic reactions occur. This helped me to understand my own situation more. However, my own fears were not dissuaded: would I ever be independent, and would I always be "low income?" The fears would run though my head as I was going to sleep at night.

My last years of college were more of the same academically. I remained very focused on my reading, and I am probably certifiably mentally ill because I enjoyed writing papers. I loved doing my bibliographies, footnotes, the obsessive, compilation of providing my resources. It was now good to know that I was going to have the funding and did not have to live the "secret life" of pretending to be an

English major and trying to convince my sources of funding that I was worthy of majoring in psychology. That anxiety was luckily gone.

I had also found a way to make money that I continued through graduate school. I had quite an interesting collection of music on vinyl, and also a lot of video tapes—just a lot of music performances I had recorded from television. Also, I had recorded a lot of concerts from the radio when I was growing up.

I occasionally picked up a music trade paper, and perused the classifieds. I found that some of the things I had buried on the old tapes were worth money. I decided to compile them in an ad on the old typewriter. I sent an ad in (they charged by size of the ad) and I began making duplicate copies of these videos, and cassette audio tapes. I could charge more if I used a higher "grade" tape. Videos were $20 to $25, and audio cassettes were $5 to $8. I soon had connections in New Jersey, Texas, and Florida: three men who between the three of us, ran a brisk business. I made up to $375 a month. This paid for my textbooks. I later found out when there was a raid in local hotel that this was not on the up and up-that is the video tapes, not the reselling of albums.. This scared me as the three guys and I had quite a business going on. I ceased this as soon as the raid occurred. All I knew is that I was willing to do what I had to do to supplement my income for my education, and my parents could not help. My video business stopped in 1993, but not the resell of albums, as that was still lucrative.

I also would scour old record shops, and with my love of old music from the 1950's and 1960's knew what was rare. I would resell the albums in trade papers. I did not sell my last album until 2003. It was a difficult one to get rid of, a rare Bobby Darin find. The most I ever made from one 45 record was $50. It was due to a label that was a different color than what the other labels were normally printed. It also was in "mint" condition—meaning it looked as though the 1962 record was just purchased that same day. I recently looked in one of the trade papers, and saw that one of the guys I used to trade videos with is still selling a lot of videos and DVD's. This is not something I would feel comfortable doing nowadays. Back then, I had no idea, and I would have sold everything but my dog to pay for my education. Well, I take that back, I tried to sell his "services" once, but he would not uh.. perform. All it did was confuse him, and he howled for weeks. I got

$75 for his time. And whenever I talked to my father (who has a very sarcastic, at times deadpan sense of humor—and those who have met him, say "A ha! Now I see where you get it) would call me up and say, "How is it going, you pimp? "

I still had a lot of underlying anxiety about Wegener's returning. Again, I have to stress, in 1992, the internet was not in everyone's home. It was not even available widely on campus. It was only known to the "computer geeks." I was slowly becoming one of those people. I was able to access some of the databases and find some key contact people in the research of Wegener's and I began to send for all the available research studies from NIH (National Institute of Health) and wrote to almost every physician, posing the question of whether the disease can go into complete remission, and what the longitudinal complications would be of users of cyclophosphamide.

I got one reply from a Medical Director of Rheumatology in California in early 1992 that eased my anxiety, and allowed me to let go some of the fears I had for each cold, flu, joint pain, etcetera, and hopefully will ease some of yours' if you suffer from the disease:

February 8, 1992

Dear Candace :

> *Thank you for your letter. The answer is yes, the disease can go into complete remission…however, relapses can occur, and you will need to be checked for an indefinite period of time. Secondly we do not have exact numbers on long term complications of cyclophosphamide. They do occur but are rare. We do follow the bladder for a decade or more with routine checks of the urine, In summary, remissions can last forever.… but since relapses and side effects occur rarely, your doctor must continue to check, probably over the next 10 to 15 years.*

I maintained a few close friendships with people I had met in college, and my main focus was my school work. Men were also on my mind and I did have a fling with a classmate who was very nice. I sometimes wonder what became of him. But I did not allow anything to get in the way of my goal. The goal was now becoming to get the degree, and now my professors were starting to encourage me to go to graduate school.

Graduate school would not be funded by WRAP, as I asked them. I had aspirations of even going further as my passion was sociology, particularly social class structure, and this is still my passion, and I thought about obtaining a PhD in this field. However, back in 1992, this subject was being "phased" out in many Universities.

A couple of my professors talked to me candidly and reminded me that my mission was to "help" others, and that the wave of the future was to obtain a Master's degree In Social Work, as soon, people with this degree will be able to be licensed, and if you choose the course of study to do psychotherapy, you will be able to do so with the master's and license, and will not need to go all the way to the doctoral level.

As becoming gainfully employed and independent as quickly as possible was my goal, I listened to this suggestion. I still held the hope that I may get a PhD someday, but I needed independence.

I took some computer classes and began to spend all of my extra time in the newly built computer lab. I had spent so much time doing papers on my old typewriter, laboriously typing papers, and many of the professors had strict rules about "no whiteout" on their papers. This meant if I made a mistake on my old manual Olympia typewriter, I had to take the paper I was working on, pull it out, and retype it. Even my newer electric typewriter had a correction ribbon that was obvious to professor if a mistake had been made. Everyone makes typos! If I were writing this book on that old manual, it would have taken me twenty years, instead of the eight that it has taken me (I wrote it in my free time) thanks to the use of my desktop and laptop.

Now, I was thrilled that with the new Macintoshes in the lab, that there was another way to do my papers. I learned Macintosh and the pre-"Windows" MS-DOS IBMs. I preferred the Macintoshes. My last two years were much easier, thanks to those computers.

I got to learn what "chatting" was thanks to the large University wide "intranet" as well, and made a friend in the graduate chemistry department. He and I then dated off and on (up until I got to grad school and he was then working on his PhD).

But again, my focus was on this education, and I was never too serious about anyone. I had seen women getting so focused on relationships that they actually dropped out of school, or took semesters off. I vowed that this would never happen to me. In fact, I vowed that a relationship would never get in my way of my career aspirations or my desire to take care of myself. I had a desire to be self reliant that was so strong; I could not wait to get to the finish line. I was willing to do just about anything. If I believed in the devil, I used to tell myself, half jokingly, I would sell my soul.

I had always had a fear of math, but in the third year, I did tackle statistics. It was scary, and I did have to work at it very much, but, did it. I also did Research methods, and learned to understand it. All of it made sense. I decided to take what I learned from these classes and devise a survey for the Wegener's support group.

I designed questions aiming at both the physical and emotional symptoms and such as "did you ever smoke?" and "Were you ever exposed to chemical lawn services?" and asked if the person felt relief when the diagnosis was made. That question was asked as when I was corresponding with some of my cohorts, the sense of relief was felt by many of us, as so many were sick for so long, and many were even labeled hypochondriacs, and even were given anxiety medicine who started seeing doctors when they began seeking medical treatment when they had complaints such as excessive runny noses and were told that they just had "bad colds" and were dismissed as being complainers.

I even had my Research professor look at my 20 question survey, I developed a hypothesis (my hypothesis was that we were exposed to some sort of inhaled antigen or toxic agent) and that this was all that we had in common. I asked for demographics, because I was curious about our genders, ethnicities, ages. All the information I had read thus far had us as being on average, as 40 something, Caucasian men, and I wanted to see some up to date information!

I thought I had lost my survey and surprisingly found in buried in a file while writing this book, and added it at the end of this book. It still looks great, if I may say so, all these years later. I put this survey up on my "myspace" page and got a few hits from some of my Wegener's friends online while still writing this book. So the results that are at the end of the book are from recent participants after the new millennium, and myself included.

Back in1992, I proudly shipped my hard work off to the Wegener's support group, and awaited a reply. My reply came back from the support group "No, you can't do this. We may be merging with the Wegener's Foundation, and they will not approve." I was disappointed. I thought about mailing out the survey anyway, using my own postage, but then decided, no, I need to concentrate on my own assignments for college. My research professor asked me about it later, and said that this reason did not sound like a good one, and then told me that if I would ever go as far as the PhD level, I should get used to getting shot down like this.

So far, I have not gotten a PhD, but even at the graduate level, I have experienced getting shot down, academically and in my professional career with good ideas (or ideas that I sure thought were good), so he was right.

Again, my goal at that time was to finish my degree, and move on, (toward the bigger goals) of helping others and helping myself to be self sufficient. Now I had to begin to investigate graduate programs.

I started to study for the GREs (graduate school examination) as well as doing my usual studies. I studied for the general GRE and the psychology GREs. I was keeping my eye on the pot at the end of the rainbow, no matter how many roadblocks were thrown at me. It was always something. Life will always hand you something.

I saw people dropping out of school due to breakups and breakdowns. I refused to let this happen to me. I saw the light at the end of the tunnel. I visualized myself on my own, and nothing could stop me. I did not feel that I was betraying my family by wanting to be different from them. You can love your people by trying to break away from them. Do not let that stop you from trying to obtain your goals.

The day I was scheduled to drive into Pittsburgh to take the GRE's was a typical Pittsburgh snow day: snowy and icy. There is a hill that goes into the city's Oakland section that I slid down into sideways. I was taking two separate tests. The general and psychology. The tests were very long and tedious. I had not taken S.A.T's, so I imagine that this is what they were like. (By the time I got into community college that summer of 1989, I had to take a placement test) I was there when it was dark in the morning. When I left town, it was dark, probably about 5 p.m.

I began to compile applications to three graduate programs I had picked out at that time, and rounded up the professors whom I would use as references. When I took the tests, I had signed releases for them to send results to two universities: Duquesne and University of Pittsburgh.

I did apply to the School of Social work, as it had been suggested, although I had my hopes on the Master's in Psychology. I also applied to a Master's in Rehab Counseling. The professors who acted as my reference gave me the simple words of wisdom: "if it is a thick envelope, you are in, if it is a thin envelope, you are rejected."

I did receive a thin envelope in early April, 1993. The end of the first week, I graduated from college. My parents were busy with a new plan: they were trying to sell their house and looking for a new one, in order to help my sister also to settle down with her family. I was trying to also think ahead. With this type of uncertainty in my future, I could not do anything but plan for my education and stay focused on that. I did go to my commencement. One of my friends attended: Sarah. My parents did, also. There is only one picture of me in my cap and gown. My mom was never too good at taking pictures and unfortunately, she aimed poorly, and you only see half of me. But I swear, I did graduate!

We came back home and ate and my mom had an appointment to go look at a house. I decided, I was going to send in my acceptance to the graduate program, and I also had to start thinking about what I needed to do in terms of a living arrangement.

The graduate program was in the part of the city of Pittsburgh known as Oakland. This was where at least two of the major universities are located, and I would be attending University of Pittsburgh's main campus.

Chapter 20 - On My Own in Graduate School

My friend Sarah had moved into an apartment building with a male friend (whom she would later marry) in Oakland, and she told me that they were renting there.

I visited her, and looked at the apartment.

She had a very large, one room apartment. It had a sink, built in book case, refrigerator, bathroom, and was about 15 feet by 15 feet. This was perfect. I could already envision my stuff in it. It was about three blocks from the University of Pittsburgh.

I knew I needed to move, as I did not know what my family was going to do. Every day, they were changing their minds about staying in the house they owned, which was about 30 miles from the University. The one property that they were looking at was also about 20 miles south of the city, and if I drove, I would need to drive through a tunnel. Actually, where they currently lived there would be another tunnel that I would be stuck in.

Pittsburgh is infamous for its morning traffic congestion of tunnels and bridges. They were going to let me keep the car that I was driving, which was a piece of junk by now, as it was not always reliably starting, and I also had been side swiped by a drunken driver. Luckily, I was not hurt.

The drunk driver paid the $500 out of pocket to avoid turning into her insurance, and my mom and dad took the money and agreed to pay on the insurance for the vehicle. I would never have been able to afford the insurance otherwise, because the disability money I receive was $290 a month.

I made an appointment with the rental company that rented the apartments in June. They were located in another part of town, in an area called Shadyside. The company managed several buildings around the University, and their corporate office was located in their most exclusive building by Shadyside Hospital.

When I went in to sign my lease, I looked around and wished I could live in this building, with its marble foyer. Someday, I thought, maybe I can live in a nicer place. I explained my needs and my income. I expected that they may be judgmental. I received a lot of prejudice from all angles—healthcare, the local bank, when I went to cash my check back home, when once a teller referred to my disability check as a "welfare check."

Unbelievably, the male and female rental agents were not taken aback by this information. They said, "So you have a steady monthly income? This is great news!"

I explained that I was very quiet and my "partying days" were long over. I said that I just wanted to be close to school so that I could focus on school not a long commute.

They were treating me well. I believe that they could see I was an upstanding person, not a wild and crazy partying type. They drove me up to the building, and showed me a one room apartment in my price range. It was smaller; a lot smaller than Sarah's. It was about 8 and ½ feet by 9 feet. It had two windows, a very small bathroom, and closet. It also had a small refrigerator and range, and sink. (My one friend joked that you could "sit on the toilet, watch TV, and cook dinner at the same time").

Hell, I needed a place to live. It would be $265 a month. This would leave $35 extra until I got an increase after the following year. Could I do this? I decided I had to. I knew my car could not make it 65 to 70 miles per day. It was old, used, with a lot of miles on it, and was vey unreliable. I knew in the field I wanted to work, I needed this master's degree.

I decided I needed to do this. I was old enough, and needed to forge ahead. I knew that this was all I could afford, even though I could barely afford this. They presented me with a lease to look over. It was about ten pages long. I could not bring Marcus with me. This was going to suck. There was no security deposit. They had what was known as a "broom sweep" policy which they described as making sure that when you leave the premises, you sweep out the room, and not leave anything behind. I looked puzzled, and they laughed, and said that many people leave and also leave behind their belongings. I later would meet people in grad school who did that, explaining to me that it was too expensive to move their furniture back home with them.

The asked me if I had ever rented before. I had not. I did have a credit card, so I had some credit history. They were able to do a credit check. The said it looked good. However, without a rental history, they would need a cosigner. They gave me the paperwork to take with me and asked if one of my parents would be willing to sign this. I said I would ask.

It was a beautiful, sunny day. I was scared, excited, and hopeful about my future as I drove back home. I thought about how much of a struggle this was going to be. I knew I was not going to get any financial help from my parents. They still fretted daily about their future-should they sell or should they stay? I could not get caught up in it any more. I know if I had stayed there, I would have lost my mind.

I explained to my father that I would need a cosigner on the lease. He said, "Well I guess we'll sign our life away for this kid, too." I was insulted. I said, "I just need a cosigner. I will pay my rent every month, no matter what. He said, "Yeah, Okay." I was not thrilled at this point that I needed to ask for any help, and I realized that after this, I would try to limit asking for any at all, even more than I did at this point.

He signed, but I could see he did not trust that I would not default or fall behind on this. I knew that this would be the first thing I did each month when my disability check came in, come hell or high water, as the cliché went. I took the completed lease paperwork back later that week to the rental agents. They explained that I would have the key to my apartment the 31st of July, as long as I paid the month of August.

I had been gathering all of my belongings up ever since I signed the paperwork in June. My family was in a sort of state of denial. Their house was now for sale and they were making plans to go ahead with moving, all, including my sister, and her family to a town south of Pittsburgh. My parents were purchasing land and moving some mobile homes onto the property. They hoped that this would be a panacea for the family to be together, and hoped that it would help financially as well so that my sister and her family would not move her son any longer. He was in junior high school now.

I packed up my Renault, and several plastic and cardboard boxes. My lower back pain was beginning to hurt more as I moved my boxes up and down the steps to the third floor of the creaky steps of the old Victorian.

I just wanted to get all of the belongings into the big room. I had a lot of books, and they took up most of the space. I also had record albums. I had a small book case, one dresser bureau, an old turntable and am/fm radio combo, a microwave, and a day bed.

I spent several days scrubbing the apartment with bleach and detergent. The bathroom was a blue tile, and the toilet looked like a public toilet, with the moon shaped black toilet seat and kick flusher. My friend, Sarah said the toilets were great as you could flush anything, including rotten take out meals, and doubled as garbage disposals. The tub, which I wish I had now, was one of those great, big, deep ceramic tubs, which you could soak in for hours.

My first night at the apartment, among all my boxes, I lay awake for a while, with my two windows open for air. It was August, and Pittsburgh was hot and notoriously humid. A few blocks away, were several University Hospitals. There were sounds of sirens in the street from ambulances, and police cars.

I lay awake listening to all of the different sounds. I heard distinct "pop pop pop" sounds that sounded like gunshots. I lived in a part of town that was in the middle of a gang war. Some parts of town had young gang members who wore red clothing and they were known as the "Bloods," and other parts of town were known for their blue clothing and bandanas and do rags, and were known as the "Crips."

On the news the next day, it was broadcast that on the corner where my building was, a young man was shot, by a member of a rival gang. That year was a year of record numbers of gang deaths and something that the city had not heard a lot of, but that other big cities were unfortunately not strangers to—drive-by shootings.

My building was across the street from a high school that was plagued by a lot of youth who had members in gangs, and so forth, so in the mornings the noise outside was a rumble. As my friend Susan , who later had a job at a daycare center notes, the students who attended the high school would often break in to cars, while the preschool kids looked on. (Luckily my car had nothing worth breaking into to steal. I believe I had nothing but an a.m radio!)

It helped to build my awareness of the problems that go on in the inner city. That school was "shut down" since I lived there. In graduate school, some professors told us "Whatever you do, don't wear blue or red when you walk the streets." This sad violence is still often occurring, a decade and a half later.

The refrigerator was shorter than me, and was pink. It had one door. It had a sticker inside the door that said "Enjoy your new Frigidaire," and the date was 1956. I had a faucet in the "kitchenette" area. The pipes were so rusty, I made sure to have a few gallon jugs of water in the old refrigerator, as Sarah had warned me that once after drinking the water, she and her friend had gotten very sick. I had a stove top that did not work, and something that looked like an oven, but it was actually a storage bin. I never used it, as the inside was so dirty, that even after many heavy scrubbings with Mr. Clean, it still was very dirty.

I instead got a hot plate. I did my cooking on the hot plate and in the old microwave.

The day bed was not comfortable as my back was hurting terribly, and I asked my brother-in-law to remove it, as it was taking up three quarters of the space in my apartment.

I slept on the floor after it was removed and kept my legs elevated. I slept this way for several months until I could not stand it anymore. I was never thin, per se, but after about three months of living on the very limited income I was living on, I was losing weight, and it was hard to get comfortable with hip bones, shoulder bones, and other bones jutting out, and with my arthritis on the floor getting stiff.

I had seen Dr. McCollom, and he said that the discs were bulging and required support through a comfortable sleeping environment and sitting in a comfortable position. He said that there was likely a nerve that was being pinched between the discs known as L4 and L5. When I woke up in the mornings it felt like a tennis ball was in my left buttock. My left calf also was contracting. The only thing that alleviated it was walking. I walked around the neighborhood. I was up on a hill, and several blocks from classes.

I finally called a mattress company in November (I moved there in August) and had them deliver a mattress and box spring and charged it. I did not want to charge much, but with an income of $290 a month, and the rent itself being $265, it was a stretch. I did not receive any food stamps, as I had been told that I was above the income line.

About a month after I had been living there, I did receive a letter in the mail, from the Department of Public Assistance. The letter was from the county where I had lived, and it had said that I had failed to notify them of my move, so therefore I was going to have my medical assistance cut off as well as my disability benefits of the $290 a month if I did not go to the Allegheny County Office within ten days of the date of the letter. It instructed me to call the number to see which district in Allegheny County I resided in.

After being on hold for about 45 minutes, I was directed to a very rude person on the other end, who sounded like she could not wait to end the call. They determined my district by zip code. I was determined to be in the Hill district zone of Pittsburgh. I was advised to get to the DPW (department of public welfare) early in the morning as the service there was "first come, first serve." They opened at 8:00 a.m.

My father was down that morning and offered to take me. I told him I could do this on my own. I had been to the other welfare office in the other county before. I knew how they treated consumers (often poorly) and knew what I might be in for. But he insisted.

This building in Pittsburgh was much larger, and the elevator had a security guard. The first thing you had to do is take a number. You were then told to sit down. After about a half hour, you were called up to an opaque window, which opened up, a woman handed you a very lengthy form to complete, with no instructions. The form is one I would later, in my job on inpatient units, help clients to complete, as it was very difficult to understand. It was about 20 pages long, and asked about assets, cemetery plots, home ownership, retirement funds, car ownership, and other money that you might have.

I was able to complete the form very quickly. My father sat there and looked around and was appalled at some of the language and carrying on. It was 1993, and many people there had mobile phones and were talking loudly, laughing, carrying on. I found nothing celebratory about being here. Every time I was in a DPW office, I was quite frankly, ashamed that I was there. I kept thinking that one day, I will be working again. I verbalized this every time I was there, and I would get a chuckle from the caseworkers as they looked at my file. "Do you uh…have any skills?" Then when they would see that I had been determined "permanently disabled" I would be reminded of this fact. It was almost as if I was getting a message to not try to succeed or get off "welfare" or disability.

Two people, one male, and one female, came in and were wearing business suits. I tried to keep my head down, and avoid eye contact with anyone when I was in the office. It is not that I ever thought I was "better than" anyone. I just had a belief that I would get out of this situation. I had to believe this. I just had to. I never look down on anyone today on disability or welfare, because now I still remember just how others do look down on you.

The female approached my father. "Excuse me. We are from Plus Medical. "My father looked at her like she was out of her mind. He said, "I don't want anything." She said, "Oh I am not selling anything. We are here to talk to all medical assistance recipients about how in the next two years, there will be a switch over to managed care and you have to choose a plan."

He looked at her and had a kind of insulted look, "I am not on medical assistance." She apologized and moved on to another person. When the male in the suit came to me, he introduced himself, and gave the whole spiel, and explained that in 1995 all medical assistance recipients would have to have an HMO (health maintenance organization). He explained that it would be best to pick one now, and explained that theirs was the best as it offered the most providers. I asked some questions, such as what did they mean by "offering the most providers?" He said that other plans restricted who you could see. I passed on picking a plan, as I explained that in two years, I would be working with a master's degree. He just looked and me with a wide eyed expression, and said, "Okay." But I believe he felt that I was delusional.

I finally was called back to meet with my caseworker, a well dressed, polite (an anomaly) woman. She asked for the form, looked it over, and said that it was all filled out correctly. I explained to her that I had been living here for a couple of months, and showed her the letter I had received. She explained that when a person moves to a different county, you have to notify DPW that you are moving. I explained that I was unaware that this was the process.

She understood, and she stated that this was not a problem, and she would note that this was unintentional in my file. Furthermore, she notified me that I was eligible for an increase in my disability payment by $100 a month, as I was living independently. She would notify the Social Security administration of my move as well. She let me know that if I changed addresses again, I must make sure that I notify Social Security and DPW. She smiled and was kind.

She also notified me of something else that I had been never made aware of: that I was eligible for Medicare. I did not know about this. She explained, "whenyou have been disabled for a period of two years, you are eligible for Medicare.. Didn't anyone ever explain this to you?" well no one had. I have found that any times people do not volunteer information to you. She asked if I would like to apply for this benefit. I did not, because I reiterated that I was going to be working in two years and would just stay on medical assistance. She said, "It is there for you, if you change your mind." To this day, I still get Medicare reminders in the mail and every Medicare HMO's flyer in the mail ton sign up for their plan.

I always appreciated anyone who was kind to me at this low point in my life, as when you are on medical assistance or on "welfare," you sometimes do find providers who judge you. I vowed never to be one of those people.

I was lucky to find, during this time an optometrist and dentist who treated me well, and conversed with me, and who I have stuck with ever since. They listened to me, and treated me with respect, and encouraged me, and did not judge where I was at the current time.

An assignment that we had in our first semester to "go where your clients are" and to sit in a welfare office, a social security office, a public health clinic, or an AA meeting and write about how you were treated.

I now saw Dr McCollom at the Public Health clinic, and was treated extremely poorly, as were all the patients, and of course had spent many times in the welfare office and SS office. The staff weighed us out in the open, shouted the weights down the hall (I once verbalized my disapproval about that, and was told, "Where else are you gonna go for your care, honey? You have a problem?")

The only option left was the AA meeting. We had to go and "pretend" we were a client. Many of the students were "appalled" at how people were treated and broke their cover, and told off the staff who were rude to the clients in the waiting rooms. It was hard to stay silent when some of them said, "I know how it feels to be on welfare," when they clearly did not, because they were not. I did not want people to know! I was ashamed. I could have taken the easy way out and wrote about how I sat in the offices, also, but I searched the Alcoholics Anonymous listings and found an "open newcomers" meeting, and went, and passed on telling my story when the other members asked me if I would like to speak. I learned a lot about how AA is a helpful program, and I recommend it a lot to my clients. The exercise was a good one, as it did give the students compassion as to what an impoverished or consumer deals with on a daily basis in pubic, instead of sitting in the "ivory tower."

As a student loan borrower, we graduate students were all asked to meet in the auditorium for a meeting prior to classes beginning. We were shown a film and were spoken to with caution about how we could face fines and imprisonment if the loan were not paid back. We were given the option to back out now before classes began. This was scary, but not as scary as backing out on my lease and moving back to my family. I have not had to back out since. It has just been all about moving ahead since then.

My day to day life now consisted of combating pain that was becoming progressively worse, and attending classes. When you are that kind of pain, you build your world and your day around it. Until I got my bed delivered, I had a comforter on the floor with a throw pillow on the floor for my mid back, one under my knees for support, one for under my neck, and tried not to move throughout the night.

Because I was in an unsafe neighborhood, and heard sirens, and even shots all night, I tried to make my surroundings and the apartment as safe as I could. My bathroom had a window that did not lock. Outside of the bathroom was a fire escape. I walked to the hardware store several blocks away, bought a Phillips head, and regular screwdriver. I then reversed the lock on the bathroom door. I figured if someone breaks in my bathroom at night, then they are going to be locked in. I also bought a chain lock for my apartment door and a "draft dodger" to keep anything from being slid under my door in the hallway. There were also some strangers in the building, including a prostitution ring. The pimp lived on the second floor, and several prostitutes lived on other floors. Sarah and I took note of this pretty early on.

I did decide to splurge with my increase in my income on cable as in my building. I could get basic for $10 a month. I called the local company and could get the basic 12 channels for that low cost on my 12 inch set. The cable guy came and came in and said, "OK, where is the room I am supposed to set this up?" I told him, "You are in *the* room," after I offered him a cold cola. (I always offered service people a beverage, and even the older man who ran the vacuum out in our hallway got a drink from me. I figured I will always treat hard working people nice, and am still that way) He thanked me as he said no one had offered him a drink all day. He said, "Holy hell, you are shittin' me! You live in this two by four?" I said, "No this is it. He asked me to show him the garage of the building.

(In the garage, there actually were some nice vehicles. There was a Porche Carrera and Corvette. In the building's Penthouse, a physician resided there, who took the private elevator. One day, when I was home, the maintenance guy who was painting my apartment asked me, "Do you wanna see something cool? Promise not to tell? Seriously, I will lose my job! We went up on the elevator. The whole top floor was done in black marble, black appliances, and black leather. I thought , Now I could live like this. The view was incredible. You could see all of Oakland, Downtown, and it was so awesome.)

But now, I was satisfied to have clearer television reception, and a bed!

The cable guy, once we were in the garage, proceeded to splice some wires and hooked me up with several premium channels expanded basic, and had me sign on the dotted line that I would pay for $10 a month. I looked at him wide eyes. He then said I would get a survey in the mail. He said, "If anyone asks you how you got premium service, you don't know my name, got it? I just feel really bad about you living in this shithole!"

I kept pretty much to myself. Now at least I had hundreds of channels of entertainment for the cold fall and winter. We had no individual heating in our apartments. I had also a door jam or club to secure the lock even further. After all these measures, once I got inside, I felt very safe inside, and after a while, the sounds of the street actually lulled me to sleep.

I really had to keep to myself, as I had very little, and as you now know with my financial situation, only 30 dollars for food or books, after rent. Oftentimes professors would encourage studying in groups and when they would do this, I would groan, because people would get all giddy, and want to know whose place we were meeting at.

Once a classmate's (we will call her Buffy) boyfriend picked us up. He did the driving. She had talked about him among the study group in class. My opinion of her was not very high, as she had gone on about how she was only sticking with him because "there is no way I was going to live in the city in some bad neighborhood around a bunch of black people, so I suggested we live together. I would never marry him because you know, he's like, blue collar. After I get out of grad school, I will probably dump him."

She lived in that building where I signed my rent papers, and I walked and delivered my rent check diligently every single month, no matter what the weather, because I wanted to make sure that rent was paid.

Chapter 21 - Icy Winter

People would ask "Hey Candace, how come we never meet at your place?" All I could say is there is no place to sit." Buffy's boyfriend, Chuck, once insisted on walking me up to make sure I was okay. I told him, "Really, I live here, I know the building. He looked inside, and his eyes got big, and he said, "Oh my gosh, Candace. Aren't you scared living here?" (at this time, I still did not have a bed). I told him I am not because I have a lot of precautions in place.

The next day his girlfriend, Buffy, had a million questions, and I could see her feigned concern, and I answered very few. I was very proud and very private about how I lived. She said, "Oh my God. Chuck told me how bad it is. You should have told us." I said to Buffy, that is my home. It is not, as you call it, 'bad'. "I focused back on the board. I thought, here we are trying not to pass judgment on people in this program, and what are you doing? Buffy is someone who later worked for a private practice I also did some contract work with. She pretended that she did not remember knowing me from graduate school. She then said, "Oh yeah, I remember. You lived up on the hill." She was still, frankly, a snob, who only would see "certain" clients.

This is why I never gave details to people about my living situation. Even one of my lifelong friends, Susan did not ever see my apartment. We talked on the phone every night, and some of our observations of how graduate school was not maybe as academically fulfilling as we had thought it would be; and also, some of the people maybe should have been psychologically screened could go on for hours. Still, she did not see the inside. The only reason she could afford an apartment with one bedroom is that she had gotten married, he was supporting them on her "lifelong savings of $2,000," plus working with developmentally disabled children. Her husband worked at a hardware store.

We once did a class survey of the student body income (and other demographics) in our Graduate Research class. My yearly income was $4,800. I skewed the result so badly, I was considered an "outlier." The results were anonymous, but some of the comments from my fellow students were, "Oh my God. Who is that? Is that person, like, on welfare?" I decided that I would just keep to myself, and had two close friends and only studied in the groups when it was absolutely ordered by the professors.

I had dated a man I had met in college who was now a police officer, and the dating did not last long. I just had gotten so isolated and also the pain became so bad, I stopped returning his calls. He had seen "the inside" of the shameful place. I just had this idea that no one would believe that people could live like this. It was really unbelievable, but for me, it was fine. I could not get into trouble, and I really focused on my studies. I just did not feel like explaining or being social at this time.

There was another male friend I had known in college who was attending some graduate classes, who if you can believe it, actually stayed in this room. He would bring a sleeping bag and sleep next to the 1956 "new" Frigidaire. He stayed on nights when it was subzero or snowing, and would buy pizza. Two people in that room was definitely too much, and as much as I liked my friend Logan, I was wishing him well when it was his time to go until the next snowstorm.

When the money I received was raised to $400 a month, it felt like I hit the jackpot. I often went without textbooks. I had asked one time for $45 for a loan from my mom for a textbook. With all that was going on with her and my father at the time, she flat out said "no." She was in a very bad mood, and said she had given enough to her kids (she was still trying to get my sister to agree to move to the property that they now had moved to) and she also said, "You made your bed, you lie in it. You wanted to take out the loans and go on for more schooling. You figure it out." I did. I figured out where I could make free copies or the cheapest copies on campus, what exact chapters the professors truly required, and did that 90% of my time throughout graduate school.

I spent a lot of time in what was known as "the stacks." These are the archives of the Hillman library at the University of Pittsburgh, as when a book or article was cited, I would look this up, read that article, and even read the turn of the century history of social welfare. Then I got familiar with the University's Medical school and Law school libraries, as well, so that I could do the most thoroughly researched papers. I decided, if I cannot own the books, I need to read, and know what I am talking about—so I read the books, a well as ALL of the citations. Yes, it was a tad bit obsessive. Plus, living in the one room place caused me to become a bit claustrophobic. I spent all day alone, in the libraries, doing work but before sundown, headed back up the hill to my place, as my neighborhood was not one you wanted to be out as darkness fell.

I was one of ten students who concentrated in psychoanalytic theory, a dying form of psychotherapy. I decided to do this specifically to get the most well rounded educational experience, as I was paying for this degree, and wanted to get the most "bang for my buck" so to speak. Others concentrated on either cognitive behavioral therapy or family systems. I had a grand goal, but decided to go for it. I had already been accepted for my first year into St' Mary's Hospital for my first year's graduate internship, hoping to see if working with people who had medical illnesses might be a career choice for me. For my second year, I decided to start to apply to the University's Psychiatric Hospital. This was the most coveted placement among graduate students in our program, and they really screened applicants (for example, if you had ever been a patient there, you were rejected, one student had told me).

I was excited about my placement at St. Mary's as I interviewed with Kathy, the social worker who helped me several years earlier. She could not believe that I was in graduate school and doing well. She was thrilled to have me. She looked at my academic records and recommendation and said, "My God, you are a success story!" I told her I did not see myself as such, as I still had a long way to go. Success to me would be when I was not struggling hand to mouth , helping others, and not in pain every day.

I knew that I had broken down on the way there, gotten a jump on my battery from a stranger and had to cover the battery with an old rug I kept in the car, because it was a trick I had learned: as long as the battery was kept warm, it was more likely to turn over. I had learned a lot about patience in graduate school, but it was from time spent in solitude, just as I had from the years when I was ill. I think that how a person handles his or her solitude helps him/her develop coping skills. If they use it to cope poorly (with drugs or alcohol, or not facing their problems) then they are not going to cope effectively; if they use their time to look for solutions, or to try to find what may work if the problem confront them again, it becomes a learning experience.

One way I coped was through keeping a journal consistently in those days. I wrote throughout my illness, and this was very helpful in recalling details of my time in the hospital, names, tests I had to go through, and it certainly was helpful in recalling this period of this very bitter cold winter of 1994. According to a recent article I just saw in a Piitsburgh newspaper, that winter was a record breaker as several days that January 18, 1994, the mercury stayed below zero. I wrote: "I am not getting what I need intellectually from this academic program....it will, in the long run, cost me less to stay , as it will avoid entanglement with the landlord, the University and the government whom I borrowed money from to attend the University." This was a dark time, I would not live over again, but I also would not change, as it has made me the strong person I am today. It has made me better able to understand clients that I help.

As I wrote earlier, not only was I living in a very scary place, but I was now getting to be in such severe pain, I did not know what my future was going to be. My true fear was that I going to be disabled and unable to ever work. That feeling started every day as if I had "a tennis ball of raw nerves" as I documented in my journal. My doctor still did not believe in prescribing any kind of medication with any narcotic pain relievers, as he felt that was reserved for end of life type of pain. He knew I did not "maximize" my pain, and knew from my X-rays I had a bulging disc.

I was scheduled to start the graduate field placement in January, and after a couple of weeks of actually doing social work on the 11th floor of where 7 years earlier, where I had been a dying patient, I wrote, "The field placement has brought out misplaced fears and anger...I do enjoy the patients. I have taken on the attitude of fake it till you make it. It's funny. I felt safe and secure falling asleep last night. But my future looks so uncertain."

Dr. McCollom would make rounds on the floor, and he was known by the nursing staff as being a difficult doctor to get along with. Kathy was not hands on as a field instructor because she was so busy. I had, in her defense, put her on a pedestal for many years. Now in day to day, insane work life, she was abrupt, not immune to sometimes judging people, and she saw me as being someone who could aid her in mundane tasks.

She expected me to complete assessments and discharges, etc. I had no training as they were "self explanatory." I found that this was often the way at many later jobs in the social services industry. You get thrown into the wolves, and learn as you go. If you have a degree or degrees as it were, then you are expected to know everything. Well, Universities do not teach you about minutia such as paperwork, politics of the industry, hierarchies that exist in healthcare industries and the fact that even with a master's degree and a clinical license, sometimes and in some companies you may be looked at as a "caseworker" and talked down to as if you had little education at all.

There was no psychotherapy of cancer and other critically ill people here. Every time I walked by the room I had been ill in, I became nauseated myself. After I would get home in the evening, I ate. I might have had one hot plate, but I sure could cook up a fattening storm on that thing. I know that I ate to fill up that hole emotionally I felt—it was a very uncomfortable feeling being in that place every day. In fact, I ended up gaining 60 pounds from the time I started in January, until I left in July. I started at a size 12, and left a size 22. I also ate every donut, cookie and other carbohydrate I saw lying around the hospital, and as my back got worse, I grew more immobile. I then remained over 250 pounds for the next 8 years or so. That was one very big clue to me that I was not well suited to being around critically medically ill people.

I had to be there 4 days a week during the winter and spring months of 1994. Because they ticketed cars outside my apartment ($35 a ticket) I drove. Students of the hospital could park for free at the Civic Arena. So I would rather drive through the Hill District (straight up Centre Avenue where I lived) than to chance taking a bus (which cost money) and leave my car out to be ticketed. It had been ticketed many, many times already, and I had been at traffic court after midnight and treated like scum of the earth by some judge there who felt that because he had a gavel, he could call you a name because you let your meter expire a few times.

I owed my cousin a couple hundred dollars, and paid that off within six months, and that cut into my already small leftover spending expenses. While it was cold, I still had to cover my battery. I had a "club" on my steering wheel. People used to laugh that the club was worth more than my car, but so what? I sure could not afford to have that car stolen.

It was this time that I had begun to take some of the psychoanalytic courses, and at least I was now getting some academic fulfillment. Our Psychoanalytic professor was a gem. He was a former analyst from New York City. He said one statement that was extremely profound, and that has continued to ring true for years: "Remember this, as you will see this, and you will see it as you become more seasoned. The people in your practice who voluntarily seek treatment, even those who come to you involuntarily, are the healthiest members of their family." Well, I thought about it in terms of my own family. I may not be healthy, but I thought, I am trying to figure out what I can change, and what is wrong here. What can I change?

I have, in years of doing therapy seen people who are overachievers, who cannot seem to find acceptance from a family member, or family members. Yet they will tell me about an abusive mother or alcoholic dad. They will have disdain for their family yet will still knock themselves out to impress or be accepted by them. When they look at me with that "help me understand" look, I tell them how that professor explained all those years ago, that the healthiest one seeks the treatment. Often I get the "aha" look.

This first year of graduate school I think, would have been fun had it not been for the extreme poverty and the pain. Those are two big barriers. Those things keep a person isolated. I had no pain pills. I was getting very desperate, and did not like the taste of alcohol. But I knew that alcohol also was a pain killer. The pain was so horrible that finally in February, I bought alcohol. I had a history of alcohol abuse as a teenager, and have to be careful, but this was for medicinal purposes, I thought.

I can only tolerate alcohol if it is camouflaged in sweet drinks or mixed. I went for Amaretto. I was ok with a couple shots at first, because I had not had any alcohol for years. I felt terrible in the mornings, but

I still made it in to the hospital every day. I did this so that I could at least be knocked out for a few hours because the pain was so bad.

My old doctor had told me he was going to refer me to a neurosurgeon. He felt that this bulging disc may be herniated. I had a lot of problems even getting an appointment with the doctor he referred me to. The first problem I encountered occurred when I gave the receptionist my insurance information. The receptionist explained that they only saw "welfare" patients on certain days of the week. I explained that I was on medical assistance, but was also a graduate student and interning at the hospital across the street. She said, "You are a medical assistant?" I said "No I am a graduate student on medical assistance." She cut me off and said "Hold on."

I listened to music for a long time. She came back on and told me that the doctor would not be able to see me until May, "at the Public clinic with the other welfare patients, okay?" I explained that I was referred by Dr McCollom. She said "If the pain gets worse, call back." I asserted myself and explained that I had been self medicating with the pain via a lot of aspirin and drinking schnapps every night just so that I could get a few hours sleep. I explained that I had pain that started in my buttock every day, and then worked its way down to my left leg, and calf, finally ending up into my heel. I am sure now I was being judged as an alcoholic welfare recipient.

She sighed and put me on hold again, this time for about ten minutes. This time the doctor came back on. He introduced himself as Dr. Burns. He said, "I understand that Dr. McCollom has referred you." I said that he had. He said that he would see me. He said that he also understood that I was in a lot of pain, and asked me to describe it in my words. I again described this pain. I explained how it was in the lower back, and felt like a sharp ball that I woke up with in the buttock area, that then broke up and made its way down my legs, then settling in my calf and then parts of the ball ended up in my heel. I explained that I had to lie in twisted posed with legs up, elevated, something under my back, as it literally felt as if my back was broken.

If I sat too long, I had to bend so that my chest was in my lap, so that I could stretch my muscles. Walking seemed to help the back pain, but it made the leg pain worse. I began to be convinced that if I was like this at age 26, by the time I was 30, I would be in a wheelchair.

In my building, Sarah was helpful, as she would check on my periodically, and there was a nurse who lived upstairs. She saw me struggling with a laundry basket going upstairs. She asked how I had injured my back. I explained that I had a herniated disc. I asked her how she knew I had a bad back, and she explained that she was an employee health nurse and had her M.S.N. degree. She told me if I needed anything to come upstairs and knock on her door. It was nice to have that kid of neighborhood feeling.

Another nice neighbor, Bill, lived directly above me. He was very quiet, but if I had a delivery (I certainly was not doing any shopping) from my aforementioned "business" of tapes, or from Apple Computers (I had an early no frills Apple Macintosh which seemed to always need additional software that Apple was sending), he would knock on my door with the delivery. He told me that he did not feel that this was a good neighborhood to leave a package sitting in, so he hoped I did not mind if he picked it up for me. He was, he told me, an engineering student.

One night, I heard a gunshot. This was commonplace. The next day, there were cleaning people in the stairwell talking about how they had to clean "blood and brains" off the walls, and all over the place. It was awful." I asked them, "What are you talking about?" The woman was absolutely shaking. She said, "Bill, who lived upstairs, killed himself last night."

Dr. Burns said that he wanted to order an X-Ray, and that I could have it done at the hospital. The next day, when I went in for my internship, I went for the X-ray at lunch. I never heard from his office. I had to call them for results. I was pretty certain this was not a pulled muscle. When I called, the office staff had "the attitude" again with me.

I was always polite, but I had to be assertive, and explain that Dr McCollom had referred me, and that I had gotten the X-Ray. The receptionist was always frankly mean with me. She said that she would tell the doctor I had called and hung up, and did not make an attempt to be nice.

Later that day, the doctor called and stated that I had herniated discs, L4 and 5, and he then said, "I understand that you are being mean to my staff." I told him that frankly, it was the other way around.

Each time I called, I was treated poorly, and he said, "I have very professional staff." He said that he would send his recommendations to Dr. McCollom, and that he would ask Dr. McCollom what he recommended to prescribe.

Later that day, after I was home, lying on my heating pad in my apartment, my phone rang, and it was Dr. McCollom. He asked if I had a pharmacy that I used. I did use one three blocks away, near the grocery store I walked to. He said that he was going to phone in a muscle relaxer that was very powerful, and that I should only take it at night. He said that if I was using alcohol to try to get sleep, this muscle relaxer would do the same thing, and to cease using alcohol. He asked if the pharmacy delivered, because, he thought that I should not be walking up hills any longer. I asked, "Why?" He explained that the herniation was very severe, and he said, "Frankly, after talking with Dr. Burns and looking at these X-rays, we are thinking that surgery is your only option, Gus."

I felt that wave of fear that I used to feel when I was much younger, in the hospital, that fight or flight adrenalin rush type of fear, and my instinct was to run away from this situation. I explained to him that I needed to complete this graduate school year, I have a lease on my apartment, and that it is just not a good time. He said, "I know. It is never a good time for surgery, Gus. But I cannot do any more. This is out of my hands now."

It was now the beginning of March. The winter was one of the coldest on record, even for Pittsburgh, but in March, the temperature had broken. On the 15th of March we had rain in Pittsburgh, but when you looked outside, you had no reason to presume it had frozen over. Pittsburghers, for some reason, refer to this as "black ice." This refers to ice that looks like rain that people fall on or wreck their cars on.

I wore a pair of boots with flat soles, a skirt, and turtleneck. I walked outside onto the sidewalk, thinking that I was walking onto wet pavement, but it was ice.. I fell, and tried to break my fall, and my right leg crumpled underneath me. I could feel my lower back pop, and all the weight ended up crashing onto my middle right toe, which hurt the most.

I got up, was wet, and brushed myself off. My back actually felt as if I had somehow popped it into place. I felt as if the pain was not there, or that it was numb. It was my toe that hurt the most. When I got to the hospital, I had a bit of a limp. One of the young resident doctors noticed my gait and asked me about it. I told him what happened, and he had me removed my boot and sock, and he said, "You definitely broke your toe." He said that there was nothing that could be done about the toe. "We can't tape up a toe."

I was no longer experiencing back pain. I had a strange numbness. I was glad to no longer have the pain. I had pain in the toe, and focused on that more, and just tried to be careful not to fall any more, as I was not sure what was going on with my back. In my mind, I had visualized that if the discs were herniated, perhaps they had been "knocked back into place."

Chapter 22 - Denial It's Not Just
a River in, Oh Never Mind

Even though I was educated about the power of visualization, being a powerful tool (I recall writing a paper in college about a man who overheard his doctor describing his heart as having the beating of a loud gallop, and he mistook that t mean "strong as a horse" instead of a terrible irregularity, and that visualization gave him many more years) this turned out to be very poorly misinformation about what had indeed happened to me when I hit that ice.

What really did happen in my mind was quite simple: denial. It was the same denial that occurred seven years earlier when I was taking great pains to wear heavy concealing makeup to cover the lesions on my skin; wearing bulky sweaters, even though I was very hot, to disguise that I was losing weight faster than I could sew or safety pin my pants to make them smaller; and just telling myself that I was "getting older" when really no nineteen year old should have to take a handful of aspirin just to move every morning.

For some people, whether it is addiction an illness, (such as diabetes or Wegener's), when we know that death is imminent or disability is inevitable, we go to great pains to conceal it from others, and to lie to ourselves, even when everyone around us can see the truth. This is what addiction counselors refer to as the "pink elephant." It is big and flamboyant, but the addict or sick person just does not want to talk about it.

So this is what was happening. I managed to lie to myself for two weeks, as I walked around, with only a moderate pain in my lower back, but a strange numbness in my left foot. That "tennis ball" that I had woken up with for months had broken up and now was splattered on the bottom of my left foot. This, I could deal with. I had no idea what really had happened. I still went to my required classes and my internship.

I woke up two weeks after the fall, on a Tuesday, and went to get out of bed and could not move much of the lower half of my body, only the right side, and the left side felt as if I was being stabbed if I moved too much. I had left Sarah alone, as I did not want to bother her. I called her and she offered to come up and help me. I had to let her in, and it was only two feet from my bed to the door; I had crawled to the doorknob, door jam, and chain lock to let her in.

She had a look of shock, but it quickly turned to a look of determined action, which is a look that I knew very well about her. She was a definite person of strength and whom I could trust. It s funny, when I was preparing to write this book, about five of my closest friends either emailed or wrote to me about incidents that they remember from times in the past, and she wrote that she remembered how we would get close but that I kept an "aloofness" about me, even to this day. She explained that she never knew much about me, but when I would call, it was something like a surgery or this day, when I was half paralyzed.

She wrote something so flattering that I had to re-read it. Sarah is someone whom I always feel rather, frankly, dumb around. Her intelligence far surpasses mine, verbally, logically, in world events; her husband is the same way. They are just what the common person would refer to as "intellectuals."

She later became a marathon runner and wrote that she thinks of me at Mile 24, and explained, "Mile 24 is why one is out there running and to think about people one knows who have struggled with things that are much, much harder than this run. Candace is always someone I think of at that moment...I don't think Candace and I ever had or will have a tremendous amount in common, but I always had a deep and abiding respect for her wit...perseverance and fortitude. She is the first person in her family to get a college degree, and then put herself through school and got a graduate degree. "

As I said, we had a bond, and I always felt frankly inferior around Sarah, but I was pretty honored to see that she had these thoughts about me. I highly recommend that everyone write a book, and get your friends' perspectives on your life, as it is kind of akin to a eulogy when you are living.

Sarah is a take action; get it done type of person. Her assessment of this situation was, "Holy shit, man. You need to get to a hospital." I was still in a lot of fear and denial. I obviously could not walk. I knew that I may be paralyzed. But I had to hang on to some kind of hope that maybe I just "threw my back out." I had called the hospital where I was doing my internship, and told Kathy that I would not be coming in, and she sounded very shocked, as I always showed up, no matter what. I told her that I was having difficulty walking today. She asked when I would be back, and I explained that surgery had been recommended for me, and that I did not know what was actually going on. She then sounded very impatient, and as if she did not believe me. I now can understand why: I kept everything secret back then.

I was ashamed of my life, and illness. As of course, she was once my social worker, she knew I had been sick. But she now saw me as someone who had experienced a miraculous recovery, and had no other health problems. Coupled with the ongoing car breakdown problems, which sometime made me late sometimes, I am sure, I looked very unreliable.

I did not let Sarah take me a few blocks away to the University Hospital. No, that would have been too easy. (A few weeks earlier I had walked there to get an X-ray and a kindly X-Ray technician actually drove me home, as she said that I should not be walking with the condition of my back)

I remembered that my father had mentioned that he was coming down today with some food for my refrigerator. He was still driving mostly second shift with hi trucking company. I told her I would wait until my father got here and he could take me. She was very anxious and said, "I think I should take you, or call a F___ing ambulance, and I will wait until he gets here and tell him what happened." I was not nearly as anxious, now that I had gotten up and actually moved across the floor on one leg.

I wanted to get in the shower. She sat there in the one room while I went in the hot shower. When I came out of the bathroom, steam was coming out, as I made the water as hot as I could stand it. She waited until my father got there with me, and he knew the instant the key turned, and he came in that something was wrong. This was the same father who had to carry me to the hospital seven years earlier.

Sarah left after she ascertained that we were ok, and my father assured her that I was either getting to a doctor or hospital today. He said, "You need to call that surgeon's office that you have been dealing with." I called Dr. Burn's office. The same receptionist that I always dealt with came on the line. I explained what was going on. She had me repeat it twice, and I said, "I cannot walk at all." She was very sarcastic and said, "Well did you get to the bathroom? That means you are walking. You aren't crippled. Let me get a message to the doctor. He will call you right back."

My father, who had a nickname (so I have heard from multiple sources) of "Blaze" as a young man, and apparently although, only 5 foot 7, but also built like the cartoon spokesperson "Mr. Clean" in his heyday, was beginning to turn red, and I could see where that nickname came from. I had not seen "Blaze" emerge since the 1970's, and I was not sure I wanted to right now under the influence of muscle relaxers, and in this kind of pain. He was not angry at me. He started to rant and rave about "the incompetent, lazy, irresponsible, poor excuses for human beings." and then the phone rang.

I answered, and it was Dr. Burns. I never saw Dr. Burns, and I had an image of him, from his voice, on the other end of my phone. He said, "Candace. My staff tells me you can't walk. Can you describe to me what is going on?" I did, and explained that I could not move my left leg at all, that it was dragging, that there was numbness completely on the left side, that the pain was beyond a 10 on a scale of 1 to 10 in the lumbar area. He listened and said, "Well, I don't have an opening. Technically, as you know, I uh, did you a favor. You were a Dr. Mcollom patient and also a graduate intern. But you are technically not a real employee of the hospital. I think you need a second opinion immediately,"

I asked him what he meant by this. He said, "You need to get to an E.R. any E.R. Today. After you get your opinion, I will be glad to follow you. Good luck. Okay?" I was stunned and said, "Uh, yeah."

I told my father this and he was now a maroon shade. He said, "I am taking you to the hospital on the way to our house." My parents lived South of Pittsburgh for about five years. The hospital we went to was between the city and their house, in the southern part of the city.

I could not drive, so my father moved my car down the street to an even more dangerous part of town, where there were no meters. At this point, he said, "If it gets stolen, it gets stolen. You can't drive anyway. Your health is more important." (One thing about my father: He does not sugar coat)

I had to lean completely on my father and bounce on my butt down the steps. I could see the pain look on his face. I had great difficulty. The ride to the southern suburbs was very painful, but I was half dozing from the muscle relaxant. I was not capable of ambulating on my own, and as soon as we made it to the sliding E.R. doors of this suburban hospital, the security guard got a wheelchair for me.

I had difficulty sitting upright in the wheelchair. I had to sit on my right hip in order to register. My father was being very protective and attempting to answer all of the questions, but even in my extremely impaired state, I told him, "Dad, I am 26. I have to answer these questions myself. The registration clerk was very sympathetic looking. I explained to her that I had been sent for a second opinion, and that I was being seen as what basically amounted as a professional courtesy by a doctor at a nearby facility. She asked for my insurance, and said, "Oh no. We don't take welfare insurance here. I mean, we could not admit you. We can treat you for an emergency, but we will have to discharge you. I will take the card, give it to me, but we will have to bed search you or you can go back to the city."

It may be very difficult to believe this nowadays, because there are now counties in states in the United States that have rates as high as 90% public funded for their healthcare. We now have a more erratic economy, and frankly, most hospitals, unless they are private hospitals, accept medical assistance. But back in the late 1980's and early 1990's, there was a social stigma, about having "welfare insurance" which is the term I heard over and over again.

I was put out in the waiting room, and since I was not a cardiac patient or an accident, I was not at the top of the priority list. We waited for an hour to be seen, and now my leg that had feeling started to involuntarily move.

I was wheeled back to the triage area, finally and required help up on the gurney, and a nurse asked me to tell my story. I explained why I was here. She asked me point blank if I was looking for narcotics.

I said, "Excuse me?" She said, "We get people on medical assistance a lot from the city here who frankly, are looking for a fix. And they use the old bad back story, you know?" My father spoke up. "Listen, I am a teamster. I have been a teamster for 34 years. My daughter is not a drug addict. She has been sick with a disease called Wegener's granulomatosis. She fell, and has had this bad back now for years. Some doctor that was supposed to see her in the city has been jerking her around, the office staff are a bunch of twinkies who treat her like she is some kind of low life. She is working on her master's degree, and she is not here for drugs. She came here because that doctor told her that she needs a second opinion and an operation. Can't you see she is in pain?"

The nurse said, "We get all kinds, and I have heard it all. I don't understand why, if you live right by the University you would come here. You have no records here. You have no X-rays. You are on welfare; I mean this looks fishy to us." I explained that I was not an addict. I was honest and said that the worst I had done recently was having a few shots of schnapps to get to sleep at night because the pain had gotten so bad. The nurse said, "So if we would do a urine drug screen, what would we find?" I asked, "a urine what?" She said, "If we tested you for drugs, what kind of drugs would we find?"

I told her I was on thyroid medication, and a muscle relaxer, and lots of Bayer. My father, who looked like he was so angry, he could lift the gurney, the nurse, the wheelchair, and throw them all through that front sliding glass door said, "The reason we are here is because she lives in a one room apartment, she is in school, and I wanted to take her to our house because that place is not fit for her to be staying with all the steps she has to climb."

The nurse did not make eye contact, started to walk away and said, "Doctor will be with you shortly." My father was so angry; he was pacing and looked at me incredulously. "Can you believe this?" I glanced at him, and said, "Dad. Welcome to my life." He said, "What?" I told him that this is what I go through quite a bit—not to the extent of defending myself against being a narcotics addict, but, against the assumption that because I am a public funded recipient that I am a prostitute, the carrier of several venereal diseases, someone who has had several pregnancies or hundreds of sexual partners, uneducated (amazing how often registration clerks began to almost talk baby talk when I gave them my "card"), lazy (also clerks treated me like shit and even made comments like "it must be nice to get free medical care when the rest of us have to work").

I explained that "This prejudice shit" was what I dealt with nearly every single time I receive health care, and said, "One day, I will be providing care and I will never treat another human being the way some of these people treat me."

I lay on my side as I waited for the doctor to come in to see me. It was another 45 minute wait. He came in the curtained area, and pulled them open abruptly, making the metal loops on the curtains cause a noise akin to nails on chalkboard against the curtain rods.

The doctor was a blonde, handsome man, who did not smile or offer his hand. He had a clipboard and my file in a manila folder. "Candace, I understand you come to us from the city. You live by several University Hospitals. You claim to be in a lot of pain. What is it that you want from us?"

I explained that I could not walk. I had been in pain for many months, and fell two weeks ago, and the doctor that I had been consulting with on the phone could not see me, so he had suggested I see someone in "any E.R." today. I explained that surgery had been suggested. He listened, had a stern look on his face and said, "Mmm hmm." He asked me to stand up, and to try to walk. He watched as I tried to walk.

His final assessment was, "We do not have a history on you. We have no X-Rays. You technically can ambulate, even if it is with assistance. We don't take or admit medical assistance patients. You can do a couple of things: you can go back to the University Medical Center, you can get an MRI at our outpatient center. I will write a prescription for that today, and you can call that doctor and tell him that you got this second opinion and tell him that what he told you is wrong. You can't just go anywhere. Insurances have a lot to do with where you can go. I am giving you a shot of something for your pain."

He asked if I ever had a narcotic, and I told him that I had after surgery, and also took some oral narcotic meds initially after my Wegener's diagnosis and he said that this would be very powerful, and I may sleep a lot. My father told him, "I am taking her home, we live right up the road." The doctor then apologized about the insurance situation. "I am sorry that you were led to believe that you could come here and be admitted. This drug is powerful, and should cut your pain a lot for maybe a day or two, even. Do not drive. I told him I had no intention of driving at all for a while as I could not feel my left side. He shook his head as if were stunned at this, and said, "Again, please get an MRA, call that doctor, and get to the University Medical Center. They actually have the best neurosurgery department."

He then pulled that curtain open again, with the same nails on chalkboard affect, and I lay there, with only the thought of getting the shot and maybe having some of the misery being taken away for even a while.

He came back, and this time, the nurse who had seen me initially was with him. He reiterated with the nurse what he had told me, and then extended his hand for me to shake. He again said, "This shot is going to likely put you out since you are not used to this kind of medication. I am also going to write you a prescription just to last you a few days for the oral version of this. Don't take the pills until 24 hours from now. You don't want an overdose. Call the University. Get records from that doctor who wrote the prescription for your initial X-rays. The nurse is going to give you this shot. Don't worry-all of this is in your discharge instructions. I am sorry we couldn't help you more."

I thanked him, and thought about how on earth I was going to conduct all of this work and call my internship and class instructors from bed. But now, I just waited for this shot. The nurse had a less judgmental attitude now. She said, "Okay, Candace. This shot is going to hurt." I did not think it could hurt much more than the pain I was already in. I was correct. The shot felt like pressure, but did not really hurt.

After I had the shot, I had to lie and see if there would be a reaction for a few more minutes. I was fine, with no ill reaction, and still had a lot of trouble walking. I just wanted to get somewhere, whether it was my own bed, or my parents' home, and lie down.

I could not walk yet, but I felt frankly, high. I was without a care in the world, and I signed. I was so out of it, I would have signed anything. After the ride up the hill to my parents' home, my father nicely offered to let me lie in his bed. My dog, Marcus, was staying there, and he was at first, very excited to see me, but then he was very cautious around me. He then insisted in staying in the bed with me.

That day, when my mother came home from work, I woke briefly, and heard my father explain what had happened. He was still saying, "I can't believe that a hospital can just send a person home that way, a person who can't walk." I drifted back to sleep, and had dreams that felt as if they were half reality and half dream states. The pain would wake me up, but the effects of the shot were so powerful, I was able to go back to sleep easily that day.

Later that evening, my father said that he was going to go back and get my car. In my feel good, drug haze, I had nearly forgotten that I parked in a tow-away zone. He and my mother drove to pick up my car.

I was in so much pain, and so restless whenever I could not drop off to sleep, that all I could do was twist and turn. It was the same way that it was back at my apartment. My muscles were so atrophied. It was late March, and in my mind, in my drug induced state, I realized it was about the same time that I had been critically ill seven years earlier. I started to think, Maybe I am not going to get any better.

I began to believe that some of the things that were predicted years ago, that I would not walk "normally" again, and that I may need to be on dialysis, and so forth, were slowly becoming a reality. Maybe those educational rehab counselors who were fighting me on going to college and telling me that I should not attempt a career in healthcare knew more about the long term outcome of this illness than I did. Maybe I was simply suffering from hubris, and this was my time to fall.

The next day, my mother took me to get the MRI. Technically the technicians are not supposed to say anything to a patient. The technician was very gentle with me, and said, "This is crucial. You are going to need surgery. I have an obligation to tell you this. Please do what the doctor says as he wrote on your discharge instructions. Call the University Medical Center. This is an emergency situation. I don't want to scare you. This is one of the worst situations I have seen in our outpatient MRI. If you can get those medical records, take them to their E.R. You will likely be a direct admission. "

Chapter 23 - The Backbone's Connected To The..

Also, after 24 hours, it was time for me to have the prescription pain killer filled. I could not take it any more, and I called the pharmacy close to my parent's home and asked if it would be okay if one of my parents filled it since it is a controlled substance. I explained why I was prescribed this. The pharmacist was very nice and said that it would be fine.

My father went to the pharmacy, and about 15 minutes later the same pharmacist called with an agitated tone. She refused to fill the prescription. She was also calling me "Christine." I corrected her, and she said "Whatever. We just filled this." I explained I had never been to her pharmacy before. She said that I just had narcotics at her pharmacy last week, and she knew what I was doing. I was completely confused. She said she was going to hold onto my medical card for twenty-four hours while she investigated this. She asked for my social security number, and I assured her again that my name was not "Christine."

My father came back and apologized, and I told him that it was not his fault. My guess was that she had to investigate a fraudulent situation. Unfortunately sometimes these things happen. It was extremely unfortunate that it was happening right now to me as I was unable to walk or do anything. But this pharmacy did not know me. Once they discovered that I was not Christine, or the person who was trying to get narcotics filled "again" from them, hey would fill this prescription. I attempted to go to their bathroom that was two feet from their bed, and it was a huge struggle. I ended up just dragging myself across the floor like a snake. My father was getting ready to go to work and saw this, and said "You can't stay here alone!" I told him forget it, Mom gets home at three. You are leaving at two. It will be ok."

The dog was almost glued to my side, to the point where I was afraid I would crush him or injure him. After the difficulty I had struggling and slithering across the floor to get to the bathroom and hoist myself into the hot shower, again staying in water as hot as I could humanly stand, thinking that the moist heat would benefit me, I went back to bed and began to make some calls, as I had been instructed by the Emergency department doctor the day before.

I first called the neurosurgery department at the University Medical Center, and explained my situation. The person on the other end put me through to an intake medical receptionist who took all of my information. The first thing that I needed to do, she said was obtain my medical records from Dr Burns so that I could be seen there. I asked how I could do this. She explained "You own your records. No one can deny you those records. You must sign a release. Or if you are indeed bedridden, and Candace, it sounds like you are, let me read to you what our facility asks patients to write…." I had to roll across the huge bed, grab a notepad, and I wrote down her words, verbatim.

The request read that I was requesting my medical records so that another facility may review them, as I was going to need transport imminently, as currently I was medically incapacitated. I then signed my name, and I had my father witness this signature.

My father drove this release to Dr Burns office. He actually met the receptionist who had been giving me trouble. Thankfully, I did get the wording from the University medical center, because they were considered the most respected facility in the city. While he was there, she called and if she had an attitude before, it was much worse now. "Uh, Candace. Your father is here with this (and she emphasized the next word with condemnation so that I could visualize her eyes rolling) *handwritten* release. What are we supposed to do with this?" I was professional and maintained my assertive stance. "I am transferring my care to the University Medical Center. They need my medical records as this is considered an emergency at this time, and based on the information the emergency room doctor I saw yesterday. This morning, the MRI technician also told me to do the same thing, and the people at the University Medical Center told me I own my medical record."

I could hear her loudly sigh, and harrumph. She said, "Well, we have patients here in our office. You are not here!" My father was standing apparently at the window, and spoke up, and told her pretty much what I had just told her: "My daughter cannot walk. She was told by a doctor in the E.R. and the University she needs to get these records and then she will be able to go to the hospital and get this taken care of," and then he added his own smart-assed comment on my behalf, "something that you people apparently were not able to do for whatever reason. Now I need to be at work at 3:00. I live in the extreme southern part of this county. I work in another County and I drive all night. It is now 11:00 a.m. How long is this going to take? I don't know exactly what is wrong with my daughter, but they have told her that this is an emergency, and I would actually like to drive these records over to the University Medical Center today."

I thought, "Thank God I have a back bone (even though it feels like it is broken) and I have a family member who does, too." What about the poor schlubs out there who are treated like crap on a daily basis who do not have a family member or advocate?

She told me that she would have them for him but it would take a half hour. He said he would wait. He asked to talk to me. I told him I would call the University's Neurosurgery Center. Time would be tight. I gave him the name of the person whom I had been speaking to at the Neurosurgery. My father took the X-Rays I had from Dr Burns to Neurosurgery at the University, and I called the department of Neurosurgery and told them that he would be doing so.

I waited and felt powerless. I did not like being reliant on other people for things, but I had no idea that it was going to get much worse. Later that day, the pain got so bad, that I was unable to stand it. I had no pain medication. I had aspirin. My mother asked how I stood this and I honestly told her that I had to drink in the months preceding the fall, before I felt that it was "numbed." She brought me in a shot of amaretto. When that was not enough, she brought me some more. My mom never drank, and could not stand people who were drunk, but asked no questions at this time. I drank until I fell asleep.

Later that evening I woke up, to sunset falling across my parents' bedroom. Marcus was lying across the bottom of my legs, like a watchman. I wondered where I was, and what time it was. I then remembered as I got oriented, and also, remembered my headache. Now I had a hangover to contend with. All I wanted was something to help my pain. What a vicious cycle.

I attempted to get up, and my mother saw me struggle from where she was seated, and she put an end to this. She came in, with a bucket lined with a waste paper liner. "You are not even going to try to walk anymore. Just move your butt off the bed, and go in this bucket. You probably already have a broken back. I don't want you paralyzed."

My mother was good at taking charge of a situation when she had to; this is a trait inherent in all of us. She told me to go to sleep, and to just think about tomorrow, as I may be able to get the medication, and get admitted to the hospital.

I wish I could say that the next day the pharmacy called me, and said that they had made a terrible mistake, and they got me confused with someone else, and filled that prescription, and that the University Medical center called me and made me a direct admission, and I was taken care of immediately. This is not how it played out.

The next day, I called the pharmacy. I asked if my prescription was ready. I had to tell my story to the pharmacy all over again. They again were calling me "Christine" in a very impatient and derogatory manner, and were explaining that they could not refill the medication. I explained that I never had this filled at all, it was a new prescription, I had never had a prescription filled at the pharmacy, and that I was told yesterday that this would be ready today. I am not a narcotics addict, and I am awaiting surgery, and likely have a broken back. I asked them to please cut me a break. I was put on hold for several minutes. Another pharmacist came on the line. He said, "I am sorry, Candace. Apparently, we had you confused with another person with a similar name. You have never been at this pharmacy, have you?" I said, "No, I have not." I again explained my story and that I literally could not walk. I explained that my father would be coming in to pick up my medication. I offered to even have my father bring my driver's license in for further proof of my identification. The pharmacist said that this would be fine.

Late that morning, day three since I had been turned away from the hospital, I finally received my prescription. I took one of the pills and fell asleep. I slept for that entire day, and realized that no one called me that day.

Days four and five were a weekend. Day six I called the University Medical Center as it was a Monday. I was determined. I realized that in this pain pill fog, I could easily just sleep the days away, and lose my motivation. I would take a pill, and sleep away four hours, which is half of a business day. So before this occurred, I asked my mother for a cup of coffee, and four aspirin, no substitute for the narcotic, but still enough to dull my caffeine addict headache, and enough to cut some of the indescribable pain.

I called them, again introduced myself, and now after I started talking, the receptionist remembered me. They had my records. They had my X-rays. They had my MRI results. Now I waited for the nurse to come on. She said that I was a candidate for surgery. She stated that I should call and schedule an ambulance as I should not have family drive me as the discs were shattered. She asked if I was losing control of my bowels or bladder. I told her I was not. She asked if I was moving my bowels. I had not in weeks. This was not uncommon, because with my thyroid problem, I had a very sluggish system. Now with pain pills, this problem was magnified.

The nurse told me I needed to move them before I came in to the University hospital. But that they would expect me to arrive this coming Wednesday, March 30, and schedule my arrival that day.

She gave me a list of ambulances to call. But I fretted over not being able to poop. I was not eating much. I was not moving. These two things do not make pooping happen. I had been in this bed for now close to two weeks. Prior to that, I had been in my own bed. My muscles were lacking in tone.

As long as I lay still, things were not so bad. Well they were bad. But I was accustomed to the misery. But I had to lie completely still. But if I turned, it was excruciating, and I would feel what felt like electrical jolts from the lower part of my back all down to my left toes.

My mother got home from work that afternoon. I told her my plight. My mother started to feel me plain lettuce, carrots, magnesium citrate. I did not even feel anything stir in my abdomen. Nothing did for weeks. I had not been concerned about this, as I did not want to even think about what I had gone through two weeks ago when I tried to slither to the bathroom and almost did not make it back to bed.

Finally after two days of lettuce and hot tea, I felt a strong feeling I had not felt in a long time. I called to my mom in the living room. She told me to hold on, and brought a trash liner to the bucket in the bedroom. This next part is actually one of my funniest memories, because if you don't laugh about things in life, you will go mad. I then was able to move my right leg over the bed and just thought, the quicker I poop, the quicker I get this operation, and the quicker I can get on with my life. I did poop. I was so excited, I called, "Mom! I pooped! I pooped!" My dog was lying on the bed with his little head hanging down looking down into the bucket.

My mom came in and this something only a mother could deal with: she took the bag, took my dog, and they went out and dug a hole and buried it. What made this so funny was that in the dark, from the where I was lying, it looked like my mom and the dog were pulling some kind of heist, carrying the bag, the shovel, with her hoodie sweatshirt, and looking around for the perfect spot to bury this. I had to find the comic relief in the situation, and all I could think is, I can schedule my ambulance now tomorrow, because I finally pooped!

For a minute, I thought, God, what has my life actually come to? I was 26, but I felt so much older. When you are in pain like this, you feel old.

I woke up after sleeping soundly (the pain pills were not cutting the pain, but were at least helping me sleep). I took two of them so that I could slither to the shower on my belly. I could not feel my left leg, other than sharp electrical nerve sensations in my calf and heel.

This shower was extremely painful and quite a task. I had my mother just turn on the water for me. I more or less lay on the floor on my right side and off my damaged right side. At that time, I did not think about how much damage I might have, that is, I did not wonder if I would have any permanent nerve damage or paralysis because I was so focused on the pain that I was in.

After my mother threw a robe over me, I put my arms in the armholes, and wrapped it around myself, and slid back to the bed. I had some sweat pants and a shirt which I asked my mom to help me put on. I wanted to be dressed, because I was going to make the call to the ambulance. I had narrowed the list down that the nurse had provided me with to two. I called the first on the list, and asked first of all if they took medical assistance. I already had some skills as a social worker, from the internship I was doing at the hospital, so I used those skills, in scheduling my own trip. The dispatcher on the other end of the phone was great.

I told her I was expected at the University Hospital today, and that I was non emergent transport. I explained the situation, and they asked if I required oxygen, and put me on hold as they verified through Admissions that I was expected. Once this was verified, I was able to continue giving them information. They told me they would be there at around 1:00 p.m. The two attendants arrived, a male and a female. They were very kind, and patient. These folks are the true heroes of medicine.

I do not remember a whole lot about my ride other than when we got into Oakland, where I lived and where all the University hospitals were, the traffic from lunchtime was backed up for blocks. I looked out the window at all the places that I stopped regularly: the Bagel place, the record store that I combed for rare discs and was able to resell for at least twice their value. At the time that I was lost in a daydream about rare record labels, I heard one of the EMT's say something about putting the signal on. I asked, "Are you guys gonna put the siren on? The woman said, "No we are just going to sound the alert and put the lights on, and people will move for us..check this out."

The signal made a "whoop" sound. Some cars stopped and then cars began to pull off the side, clearing a path for our vehicle to get through. The male drove, and the female stayed with me in the back. We turned up the street by the famous hot dog shop in Oakland, a place everyone knows. As often as I passed it, I have to say, I never ate there. I gave up eating meat in 1987, unless it was a meatball my mom threw in my spaghetti or a piece of chicken here and there. After we went up that street, we made a sharp left and turned up the other hill known to natives and workers in Oakland known as "cardiac hill." It is known as this because the hill is on an 80 degree angle.

Many vehicles have a hard time chugging up the hill. An out of shape person, and even athletic people, urban legend has it, could suffer a heart attack if they tried to walk up that hill without stopping. Parking for ambulances was in the back. They brought me to the registration area, and I was wheeled in and lying immobilized on the backboard gurney.

I waited, while one of the attendants stood with me and tried to comfort me, and I thought, as I always do when I dealt with emergency medical personnel (I have had three ambulance rides in my life and worked with many while dealing in my career with emergency mental health situations) how amazing these folks are. I know one personally, and he describes it as a calling. Just do not call him an "ambulance driver." There is so much more to these folks job than driving the vehicle. The other EMT gave the R.N. in triage the history ("Here we have a 26 year old Caucasian female who cannot ambulate on her own. She is complaining of severe lower back pain that radiates all the way down her left leg.")

The R.N. thanked the "ambulance drivers" and I was then hooked up to an I.V. The nurse explained to me that I would be given a lot of blood work and seen shortly by the neurosurgeon. She asked if I had questions. I did not, as I had been through the drill of surgery before. Surgery involves being cleared with an EKG (electrocardiogram) to see if your heart can handle it. Luckily, Wegener's did not damage my heart, and to this day, has not.

I also had a chest X-Ray-this was a portable X-Ray that they brought to me, and slid under my back, as I was unable to be moved; it was reminiscent of the type of X-ray I had performed following thoracic surgery seven years earlier. They also X-rayed my lower back. I While this was going on, there were phlebotomists taking my blood. All the while, I was assuming that I would have this operation that day. I was provided with intravenous pain medication. This took the edge off of the pain, as well as relaxed me.

In the back triage area, a small room, which was in the emergency department, but which did have the privacy of a door, while I waited, a nurse came in, and took a history on me. Every time I gave a medical history, I was almost amazed at how much I had endured as I rattled of the procedures, operations, and diagnoses that I had behind me.

Another R.N. came in and hung another bag, which she said was a steroidal anti-inflammatory, and said, "This stuff is going to cause a very strange sensation. It is going to make your crotch burn intensely, but then it will go away." I just looked at her, and she said, "I am serious!" She was serious, as it did cause this sensation. The nurse taking my history informed me that the surgeon would be in to see me soon.

I lay there closing my eyes, as the I.V. medicine made me very tired. I was at this point ready for any surgery that would put me out of this misery. I was pretty relaxed, and a man entered the room, who appeared to be maybe 40 year old, slightly overweight, and balding. He said, "Candace, so nice to finally meet you. I have heard a lot about you. Jim Goffey. He proceeded to lift help lift my upper body with the help of a nurse and listen to my lungs with a stethoscope. He said, "Good. This sounds clear."

He then asked if I could feel when he touched my feet, and toes on both extremities. I could feel the harp instrument on both feet, but it did not feel as sharp on my left foot. I was not concerned. I was indeed ignorant.

He held a large envelope and turned on the X-Ray reader and put my latest X-rays in and showed me the X-rays that were just taken an hour ago. In plain language, he said, "Here is what is going on and why you cannot walk. You had a herniated disc. That was evident on the first set of X-rays we got from that other hospital. See that? I said that I did. He pulled that out. He then took the other envelope, and put those slides in.

He showed that I had what he called "free fragments" now. I asked what he meant. He said, "You have a broken back." I had said many times over the past week that I felt like I had a broken back. However to have a neurosurgeon standing there in a white coat telling you this somehow puts it into perspective. I asked, "So what will this surgery do? Am I going to be paralyzed like this forever?" He patted my foot. He said, "You are lucky that you are here now. Your L4 and L5 discs shattered. They are floating up your spinal canal. You could have been paralyzed from the waist down. Had the fragments been just a few centimeters further up, they could have affected both legs. He explained that depending on where the back or neck was broken, that is where paralysis occurs. "For example, if your neck is broken, it affects you sometimes from the neck down, including your arms. If you have a break in the middle of the back, you will have paralysis from the waist down." He must have detected the fear on my face.

Dr. Goffey patted my right foot again, and said, "Not to worry now. We are keeping you immobilized and this is going to happen soon. Then we can deal with any thing else that is a result. I asked him what he meant. He explained, again, in basic terms, that he was going to "suck out the fragments, and squirt some jelly in there to cushion where your discs used to be. I think you will be able to walk again because of your age, and your determination. You organized a lot of this admission yourself. Let me book the operating room."

Chapter 24 - Walking Toward That Purpose

I will never forget what occurred for as long as I live. The nurse told him, "Uh.Dr. Goffey. Before you book the operating room, you have to do that call to insurance." He said, "What? She has medical assistance? " I looked at them both, and the nurse said, "They are going the HMO route now, and you need to pre-authorize…"

He looked at me, and said, "These insurances try to tell us how to practice. The nurse had a slip of paper and dialed the number and said, "Yes, this is about Candace R., ID number 555555, yes, I have Dr. Goffey right here. Thank you. He said, "Yeah. Dr Goffey here. Uh huh. Yes she has two free floating fragments, L4 and L5. 26 year old old Caucasian female. She has to have lost control of her bowels and bladder for you to approve the surgery? Hold on, I am just outside her room now. Oh my God, I think she just lost control of her bladder. Nurse!" He then took out his pen from his lab coat pocket and wrote down something, and gave the phone back to the nurse, and she said, "Thank you" to the person on the other end of the phone.

I had also heard Dr. McCollom complaining at the hospital about how he felt insurance companies were telling doctors how to do their job. In 1996 he broke the news to me that he was going to retire because he did not want to participate in managed care. Sometimes, prior to managed care, when I just started out, after graduate school, he charged me $10 cash, and that was all. I was heartbroken when he stopped practicing.

I knew that whatever they were giving me for pain must be pretty powerful, because I was drifting off every time I was not engaged in a conversation with someone. I started to drift off again, and caught a few

Z's when the nurse came back in. "Candace, I have some news about your surgery. You are not having it today. There is no O.R. available. So you will be prepped very early tomorrow morning, and we are getting you in first thing in the morning. You will be put completely to sleep, and just like Dr. Goffey said, he will suck out the broken fragments that are causing the pressure and pain, and making it hard for you to walk."

I was disappointed that it would not be done that day, but relieved that it would be done. Two weeks ago, I was sent home, and made to endure this suffering. That was not going to happen any more. Now there was a light at the end of the tunnel. The nurse told me that I would be transferred to a regular room and admitted to one of the hospitals (there were several in the University health system in the Oakland area) overnight.

Once I was wheeled upstairs to the 12th floor, my vitals were again checked, and soon a nurse came in and said, "We are taking this IV Pain bag away from your pole." I looked at her, and most likely had a look of horror on my face." She said, "Don't worry! You are getting a drip. This will have a very strong narcotic, and it will have a steady drip of pain medication. Now when it comes in, I am going to show you how to use it, okay?" sure enough, it was brought in, and this was an interesting machine. You would press a little button that was controlled, and you could not press it more often than five minutes from your last self administered drip.

The pain was so intense at night, I was lying there, and I was literally counting like it was New Year's Eve, waiting for the ball to drop, going 4....3...2...1...then pressing that button, and saying "yes!" I was asked the same questions at one point in the evening that I was earlier in the day, regarding my history, but cooperated, and answered. I was just so relieved to be here, and being treated with respect and being given what I considered world class care. This was a small, but private room, as well. I slept peacefully, even if it was drug induced. Vitals were checked on me throughout the evening, and I barely stirred. I was catheterized because they did not want me moving any more with the discs being shattered.

Early the next morning, a nursing assistant and nurse came in to wake me. "Rise and shine. Today's the big day!" I asked, "What do

I have to do?" They laughed. "You do nothing! You stay still and we will do the rest. A nursing assistant came in and soon began to clean my lower back. I then had to sign a number of consents, including one for blood products in the event that I would need a transfusion, and a consent for the surgery itself."

Soon, I was wheeled down to the pre-op room, and asked if I understood what the procedure was going to be again, once I got there, which is what is known as "informed consent." I explained this again, and said that from what I understood, I was going to have free fragments of my lower lumbar discs numbers 4 and 5 removed by suction. The nurse anesthetist said , "Excellent." The nurse explained that he would be administering something to relax me. Dr. Goffey came out and said, "Good morning, Candace! Ready to rock and roll today? I told him I did not think I could rock, but they could roll me in that room!

I was wheeled in, and everyone there greeted me. The anesthesiologist came over, and said that he was going to be there throughout, and that he was going to give me some more medication in my IV. He then explained that when he put the mask over my face, I would not remember anything. I just said, "Okay." I had been through this before. So, I knew the drill.

The next thing I remembered was waking up in my room, on the 12th floor. I do not even remember post-op for this one. I believe that for this operation (and at the time I am finishing this book in early 2009, I have had 17 operations, minor and major) I had more narcotics in my body both preoperatively and postoperatively than in any other of the surgeries.

The surgery was March 31st, 1994. The first thing I noticed when I woke up in my room was that I could fully move my left leg. It seemed like a miracle. I then attempted to move from side to side. The only pain I experienced was the stitches in my lumbar area and the deep ache I had in that area. I had been bedridden for several weeks. My mother and father were in the room. "So how do you feel?" They both were looking at me. I said, "Oh my God. I can't believe it! I can move!" My mom said "We are so glad. We were worried you would be paralyzed. That doctor is great." I told them, "I know." They told me he spoke to them at length afterward, and explained what he did, and how he felt that this was a success.

A nurse came in, and checked my vitals. A tray of gelatin, ginger ale, and, and hot tea was wheeled in. The nurse instructed me to consume all of this. I was parched, so I drank the ginger ale first. It took me a while to consume the rest. I had been taken into surgery at 6:00 a.m. I asked what time it was, and it was now 3:00 p.m. How long had I been in surgery, I asked?

My parents told me I was in surgery for a few hours. Dr. Goffey came in, still in surgical scrubs, "Candace! I think we have a success! Listen, we are going to get you up and around tonight. You are atrophied from lying around all these weeks, so you will be accompanied, but let's waste no time. You can keep this narcotic drip for 24 hours, because this incision is a bitch. But after that, I will give you oral pain meds, and we need to wean you off, deal?"

I looked at him, and looked at my parents, and said, "Deal." My father, said, "Wait, you want her to walk? The doctor said, "Absolutely. We will discharge her hopefully sometime this weekend" (The surgery was a Thursday). I was, I admit, a little scared about this. But I was also determined.

I fell back to sleep, and my parents woke my up to tell me that they were leaving. I thanked them for being there. I pushed my button on my pain medicine, and took another nap. At about 7:00 p.m., a staff member that I did not recognize, came in and flipped on the light above my bed. "Hi. My name is Ralph. Time to get up and walk. Dr Goffey's orders." Ralph pressed the button at the bottom of the bed that raised the head, and told me to take it slow, "When is the last time you were able to actually walk?" he asked. I thought about it, and it had been since mid month, but pain free, well, that was another story. I told him how I had not been completely weight bearing for well over two weeks.

Ralph said, "Okay, now take it slow, hold on to my arm, girl. I will get this I.V. pole and this narcotic drip. Slow and steady. You ain't runnin' no marathon, you dig?" I looked at him, and said, "I dig."

I was absolutely amazed at how I could stand up and put weight on both feet and walk, albeit with trepidation. I walked around the unit. It was a pretty quiet unit. I asked about this. I thought back to 1987, when people were screaming and yelling in the unit at the hospital down the street. Ralph said, "Well, this is a neurological unit..things are pretty laid back here." All I could here was a blip..blip from a monitor, or a television.

After our walk down the hall, we came back to my room, and he said, "Ok, bionic woman, that's enough for tonight." My legs hurt from doing that. But now that I knew I could do it, I was on a mission. At 9:00 p.m. I sat up, pushed that button, and gave myself a little dose of that drug, and dragged both of those machines with me, using them for support. I walked up that hall twice.

I came back to bed, feeling accomplished, and like I might be okay. The only real worry on my mind was graduate school. I had contacted my professors those two weeks that I was at my parents' home. But I still worried. I tried to shut off all the worrying. I closed my eyes, and just concentrated on the humming of all the blip..blip..blip noises.

I awoke to the sound of my own screaming and was sitting upright with blood all across my sheets and had tubing in my right hand. The blood was also on the ped-hose that they had put on me to prevent circulation problems. I had ripped out the port and I.V. in my left arm. I do not remember the nightmare. A night time staff came in. "Oh my. Well, we were going to discontinue this one tomorrow morning anyway. You did this for us." She was very calm. My heart was racing, and I was breathing so hard, my chest was heaving. She did not react, but she did not explain what happened. This type of thing happened a lot to me, back in 1987.

I went back to sleep after she gave me a fresh hospital gown and sheet, and the next morning, I was woken up and the narcotic drip was taken away. I remember feeling sad to see that go! They brought me regular doses of oral narcotics, and explained that they had to wean me off as I had been on them regularly for two weeks, and on muscle relaxants for weeks before.

I was unencumbered. So I asked if I could take a shower. I was not permitted, due to the fact that I had a large incision and stitches. I was permitted to have tub of soapy water, large washcloth, towels. This was not the same as a shower, but better than none at all.

There was a dull ache in my back. And definitely a sharp pulling pain where the stitches were, but compared to what I had experienced in the previous two weeks, crawling, sliding on he floor, being literally paralyzed on one side, and living (unbeknownst) with a broken back, this was nothing! I felt like I had (yet another) second lease on life.

I had a couple of friends in graduate school with whom I had kept updated on what was going on. While I had been staying at my parents' home, they would call their house and I was in so much pain, or drugged, I could not speak to them. The called the hospital, and checked on me. My old faithful friends from college also called. I walked throughout the day, to the point where my leg muscles hurt. I did about five trips around the unit. Early in the evening, a nurse came in and said, "You need to walk! There is no excuse for you to be sitting here!" I said, "I have walked at least five times today." She looked at me stunned. She apologized and asked why it was not documented. I told her I had no idea. She asked when I did walk, and I told her, and she then asked me to try to pass the nurses station or to notify the when I did.

I noticed something that had changed a lot since 1991 when I had last been inpatient: there was a lot less staff. When I was first a patient, I used to have a couple staff members in my room, several times an hour. Now I was lucky to have a couple staff in my room per shift. I realized that I was critically ill in 1987 the first time I was inpatient. I now had an acute problem. I still just experienced major surgery, and it amazed me that hour might go by before seeing another human being.

I often took the time to talk to people who worked and see how they felt about their jobs. One young R.N. on my shift asked me what I did and I explained that I was in graduate school and what I was planning to do, to be a therapist, and how I had thought about nursing school at one time. She said that she was regretting her choice. She said that she saw the cuts in staff in the hospitals as getting worse, and she was thinking of going back for her master's in a different non patient care area. I have seen many changes myself since 1994 in health care but that could be a different book.

I was discharged on Sunday, April 3rd, 3 days after the surgery. My parents let me stay with them for a week. The first week, I was having those strange night terrors every night, and bizarre nightmares. The nightmares all involved themes of death. I still was keeping a journal, thankfully, as I would not be able to remember. One dream was so strange. I was in a house, and everyone was made of old newspaper or paper mache. The old house caught fire, and the people were still talking while they were going up in flames.

I also dreamt that I woke up during surgery and that a chainsaw was being used on me. This was similar, again to 1987. I had morbid, gross dreams after surgery in 1987, also after surgery. I did not immediately make this connection. But, when I followed up with Dr. Goffey, he did connect the dots. He reviewed my records, and also looked at my old records from 1987 that I have since obtained for myself to help my doctors. The culprit is thee IV steroids in my case. I also was withdrawing from narcotics, per my surgeon, another complicating factor. The combination of the pain, anesthesia and the narcotics caused a depression that lasted many months.

The week after surgery, news broke on television that Kurt Cobain, a musician, had committed suicide. He was exactly my age. I became obsessed with this, and the nightmares were not helping. My family convinced me to stay with them another 10 days or so. I was supposed to be off for 6 weeks. I was getting stir crazy. I began to walk around their neighborhood. They lived in a mobile home park, and there were some small hills. I had ankle weights that I strapped on, and walked that neighborhood daily as soon I was given the go ahead to walk.

It was finals time and my professors were understanding, and permitted me to do the finals through the mail, and I had my father get my computer from my apartment, a small Macintosh (not a laptop) and I put it in bed, along with the printer, and I pounded out my papers which were all due by mid April. I did not want to have to defer any semester, and explained this to all of them, due to my funding situation. I had confided to a couple of them. Thankfully, they showed mercy. Kathy, was agreeable to allow me to finish out my internship, but into the summer.

I moved back to my apartment in late April and returned to my internship in May, and finished it in July. In May, I also started physical therapy at the hospital, and attended three times a week. I was able to rotate on all the units in the hospital, including inpatient psychiatry. I knew for sure after spending time on this unit that this is the area that I wanted to and was capable of helping, as it was not to "close to home." I had the experience of reactive depression, so I could empathize.

However, being exposed continuously to medical illnesses was too much, and I counted the days until that placement was over.

My second year in graduate school, this personal experience (which continued even after the surgery) guided me to do some research on the correlation between pain and depression. I wrote about myself in the third person in the introduction:

> It became apparent that although the pain after the surgery was no longer excruciating, (but) it was also not non-existent. The subject's surgeon reasoned with her that the surgery remedied the problem, but it should not be viewed as a "cure." The subject had experienced severe nightmares (each having a morbid theme) after the surgery, and was consumed by thoughts of suicide. The subject strongly believed that if the pain ever became as severe as it was prior to the she would end the pain permanently through suicide. The subject's surgeon attributed anesthesia and the withdrawal of the narcotics. The subject was required to undergo a month of physical therapy in May to rebuild some of the strength of the atrophied leg and lower back muscles.

I searched for all the literature on pain and depression and found five other live volunteer subjects in graduate school, and the conclusion of this research project was that cognitive behavioral therapy can help. This is the type of therapy that I was extensively trained in when I did my second year placement at the University Medical Center in the Outpatient Mental Health Center. When I first met with my soon-to be field instructor, Mike, I asked him what books I should read. He gave me several scholarly books as a suggestion, but said, "The Bible on this subject is something called *Feeling Good: The New Mood Therapy*, by David Burns". He explained that although this is not a scholarly work, and is available through the mass market, if I read this, I could then explain to my soon to be clients in a more easy to understand fashion. He then gave me a giant accordion file of other research papers and workbooks to take with me and digest for the next three weeks.

Great, now I could pack up my apartment, move stuff, clean out the old place, and stuff everything into a small room at my parent's new place, and learn a bunch of new stuff in three weeks! Seriously, I did not complain, much, as I was so excited, I just knew that I was going to love this new venture.

Mike did briefly stop his very professional presentation and asked me why I was moving when I lived a few blocks away. I told him it had come down to affording keeping my car on the road, or keeping my apartment, because I was really the poorest one in grad school. He looked at me, and said "O-kay. Well, maybe it is time to let go of the car and get something cheaper. How big is the car payment? What are you driving?" I told him, "a 1985 Renault." He raised his eyebrows and said, "You *are* poor. I thought you were going to tell me you just leased a new car. Well listen. You will not get rich in this field. But if you are good, you will make a living. And you can sell that car, and get yourself something reliable, and there are many things you can do with this degree and your career—if you are good. You were obviously good enough for the University to recommend you here. So go home, read this stuff."

I found *Feeling Good* in a used paperback store and devoured it until I understood it inside and out. After reading it, I found that if I applied it to myself, it helped me. A lot of the fears I had about being disabled the rest of my life were fears that were irrational. Look at what I was accomplishing right now. I was sitting in bed with a full sized computer with a broken back. I finished out a semester when on a leave from graduate school. I was determined. I refused to be held back.

This therapy proposes that our thoughts cause our feelings, and that we can retrain how we feel about people, situations, and our future. Much of what we think is catastrophizing, or fortune telling of events that we have no statistical proof that will never happen. You retrain yourself, if you are emotional, to become ore logical, and calm and cool. This is the type of therapy I mainly use with clients. I also use some of the psychoanalytic theoretical training to give it a nice balance, and look at the whole situation.

*This author believes that cognitive restructuring is very
helpful for those who are suffering from chronic pain, or those
who are chronically ill. That is that cognitive restructuring
does not come with the promise of taking away pain or
illness. This is not a panacea, or miracle cure. It helps deal*

*with his/her problems directly, and aids in developing and/or
coping skills. It is truly "reality therapy."*

When I first met Mike, he explained to me what this type of therapy
was, and why it was so highly regarded. I would have to be a confident
expert on this subject. He also explained that I would be conducting
all of the intakes one day a week, and that I would need to be skilled at
the diagnosing using the DSM-IV (diagnostic and statistical manual,
fourth edition). He taught me simple things that stuck with me. The
first time we met in July, 1994, I placed my purse on his desk. He placed
it on the floor. He said, "This is a barrier between us."

He sat with me in my first individual session with a client, who
began to cry. I handed her a box of tissue. After the session, he suggested
that the box always be in plain sight, but that you never hand the tissue.
"You must let the client emote. Then if they want to stop crying with
using tissue, they will."

We learned some good things in the classroom as well, that have
always stuck with me, such as never to impose our values on clients. I
understand that my clients are not me. I may choose to work out of my
bed when I cannot walk. I chose to keep on going, when I was told to
give up my dream many times. That does not mean my clients can, or
want to. I may not have the same religious beliefs. I may not have the
same food or musical tastes. Que sera, sera! What I had encountered
many times as a patient, as I now understand as a professional was that
many other professionals either did not get that lesson, or were napping
when that lesion was taught. They judged, and they judged harshly, and
sometimes did not know all the facts (assumed I had AIDS, assumed
I was promiscuous, assumed I used drugs, assumed because I utilized
public funding that I was lazy—these are all unfair assumptions for all
people who are in the underclass) .

As with many of my academic pursuits, I threw myself into this
placement at the University's Medical Center. I arrived at 7:00 a.m,
four days a week, for the next nine months. I attended all of the clinical
staffings, all of the discussions held by staff, educated myself on what a
rule out diagnosis is versus a diagnosis, understood what all 5 Axes of
the Psychiatric diagnoses were, and when I first had to present to the
Chief psychiatrist, I was still intimidated. I gave the client's full history,
and what I believed the client's diagnosis may be.

I then brought the client in. The psychiatrist did the evaluation, and called me back in, when the client left, and yelled about the differences between Acute Stress Disorder and Post Traumatic stress disorder. I then operated out of fear, and did not want to be an embarrassment to myself or the institution again, nor to present a client incorrectly again. Of course, I also did not want to be yelled at., either!

I made sure I knew the criteria inside and out before I presented to this psychiatrist again. The next time I presented to him, he sat silently, listened. When he called me back, he raised his voice and questioned why I thought a client had OCD. I explained why. He told me "Good job." I did not get a diagnosis wrong again, but was " a little obsessive" about getting all the facts and information straight from then on.

As I said earlier, I only got close with a couple of people in graduate school, and one of them happened to work two floors down from me, also very impressed with the excellent education we were receiving here. We would take our lunch break and remark at how glad we were chosen to do our internships here. We would talk about some of the cases we had and try to make sense of the methods we were using. She took her education as seriously as I did. She went to a community mental health center right out of graduate school and has remained there ever since, and has gone on to become a certified hypnotherapist with a private practice, as well. We only catch up now via Christmas cards or occasionally if we have referred clients to each other.

Even though, this placement was only three blocks away from my apartment, I had to look at whether or not I wanted to renew the lease on this place. The rent was going up at the beginning of August, and I was being ticketed more regularly parking there. So I made the decision not to renew. My second year of graduate school, my legal address was my parents, with whom I would stay a few nights a week, but I stayed at a friend's apartment in the city, and sometimes stayed with my cousin. I did not have a place of my own again for another year.

Candy University 1994

Chapter 25 - Miss Mary Sunshine

Even months after surgery, I still had pain in my low back, but it felt like arthritis, and like all surgery sites, it was definitely worse when it was cold and damp. I could not sit for long periods of time. I had to get up and move often, or I would get stiff. This is still the case. After back surgery, you must take care, and it takes a long time to feel better.

I moved the majority of my things back to their house. But mostly, I lived out of a tote bag. I was unsettled for the next year. But, now I had my eye on the prize again, and now it was this master's degree, and with this placement at the University, I felt for the first time, like I did not have to be ashamed of anything. I was excelling at my calling, I was indeed helping people, and soon, all that I had suffered for and worked toward might actually become a reality.

Wednesdays were the longest day for me, as I arrived at 7:00 a.m. and often did not leave until 8:00 p.m. That was the day when I would see the new intakes. At that time, intakes were an hour and a half long. Because it was a research facility, a number of different questionnaires were used in the intake. I also had a regular caseload of individual clients and did group therapy. This was definitely what I wanted to do, and I loved it.

I had taken all of my required courses by this time, and my last semester I took a cross registered course at the School of Law. I took a Psychiatry and Law Course. This was pertinent to the mental health that I was working with. I learned about a very important law known as "Duty to Warn", and learned about its origins and when I later was employed could authoritatively discuss it.

I also did what was called a "self directed research" project that I was very proud of, and took a lot of interest in. The University was in an urban area. When I would drive to see my parents, who resided in the same county (Allegheny) maybe twenty miles south of Pittsburgh, at the time, I noticed that there were neglected pockets in that county. In the county where I grew up, Westmoreland, there were greater rural territories. Then when you got further south, west, east, and north, of Pittsburgh you got even sparser in terms of service availability.

I did not only search the literature, but decided to go out and interview some of the more rural community service providers. I wanted to see what barriers were out there that this Urban University may not be aware of. Many of the MSW grads would be employed at some of these agencies.

Just to take the bus from my parents home when I stayed there, twenty miles from the city to get to the University was an ordeal, as I wrote:

A mobile home "park" is located less than twenty miles outside of Pittsburgh, a major metropolitan area which has one of the best University Medical enters in the country, and countless social service agencies. There is one bus stop for the Port Authority of Allegheny County in the area. If one lacks access to an automobile to get to the bus stop, the walk can exceed five miles. The bus trip (which this author has taken) is a long one--it takes one and one-half hours to get to Downtown Pittsburgh.

As an undergrad, one of my social policies professors was the director of a social service agency in Fayette County (this is in Southwestern Pennsylvania and one of the poorest counties in the Commonwealth). I looked up the agency and called him and asked if I could spend some time with some of the people that go out on the road. He was thrilled to hear from me, and offered for me to spend a day with one of his best Meals On Wheels drivers. He said, "You will see some true poverty. You won't believe how people live, but they are so grateful."

Randi, the driver explained to me that they accepted a donation from those who were able to pay. She explained that the meals were for elderly folks who were homebound or any senior, 60 and over, at any income level, usually living on their own, but unable to prepare meals. Disabled homebound adults ages 18 to 59 could be eligible if approved by the county, too. She explained that the poorest people often were the ones who handed her a dollar every day. I wrote this:

> *The route I took with Randi encompassed the county and city limits of Connellsville. Other drivers go into the rural areas of Westmoreland County. Fayette County seems to get more rural the farther south you travel. On the Connellsville route, it was a study in extremes. There was one house that looked very expensive, replete with a new Lincoln parked out front; but most were old apartment buildings and mobile homes which were not inadequate, but certainly lacking in modernity. There was an unbelievably fragile looking mobile home which could definitely be considered inadequate. It was so old it looked as though a strong wind might blow it over. It was situated on cement blocks. Outside in equally shabby "houses" were five dogs. Randi explained that the woman who lives in the trailer considers the dogs her "children" since she has never married. Randi told me that the camper next to the trailer housed the woman's father. The camper was not a big Winnebago type, but the type that is hitched to the back of an automobile for camping trips. Randi reported that they were extremely thankful when they saw her, and gave her a donation every single day.*

I cited many statistics of how underserved many rural communities were in this research project, and found that in 1995, medically, there were even some counties that did not have one MRI machine or one physician. Of course, in my field, we had a shortage in rural counties, too.

I did work in one of the rural counties later in my career, and found it to be very behind what was going on in Pittsburgh, and frustrating. I wanted so much to help and to change existing policies (I was hired as a program manager), but I felt so frustrated by some of the resistance I felt at times. I would have stayed employed there, had another opportunity not come along, but I know I could not have lived there.

I finally, in my last semester, started to open up, just a little but about some of the daily struggles I encountered. Some of the people had noted, one year earlier, that I was out for six weeks due to the back surgery. They asked why? Was I ok?I was asked by my class mates how I broke my back. It was hard to get into all of this. I explained in very simple terms that I had an illness, and it made my bones brittle, but I was frankly still very withdrawn and in the classroom, I felt "different" from the others. How do you explain this all in one sentence? Since that time, I do not feel quite as cut off. I was extremely serious back in those days. I was not a fun loving kind of student.

Was the back issue directly related to the Wegener's? Yes, it was correlated, per Dr. Goffey. He had explained that I had bones and cartilage that likely were compromised due to three factors: years of being on synthetic thyroid hormones since age four, the fact that I was so severely ill before I was finally treated back in 1987 (that takes a huge toll on one's body), and also due to high doses of corticosteroids and chemotherapy that I was treated with. When I fall, I break. I broke my toe that day I fell and broke the discs in my back. Since then, I have also broken a finger in a car door and that was not a slam but an accidental close of the door, lightly on the finger. I am extremely careful in ice now when I walk. I do not ever wear heels or shoes that may skid.

I attended my last class on a warm evening in April, 1995. I felt kind of numb emotionally by the time classes were over. I was not sad, nor exuberant. I was just really ready to move on. It was a rough couple of years, and time for a new chapter.

Doing that self directed research that I mentioned earlier on the rural social work and mental health needs stalled the receipt of my degree. The rest of my classmates received their master's degree in late April, when classes ended. My degree reads that I graduated in June, 1995. However, commencement was in late April, 1995, and since I did complete all of my requirements, was considered in completion of all of the required coursework and fieldwork. I was therefore, invited to the spring commencement.

I asked my mother and father if they would be going. My mother told me they could not because they were going to a wedding. I decided not to go. My friends asked me to go, but I decided not to and asked the university to mail me my diploma in the mail. I was disappointed, because no one seemed to celebrate my first degree in my family, and now this degree was not too important, either. I also did not have a party or a celebration when I graduated high school. I realized you have to celebrate your own victories and keep on going for one person only: yourself.

I looked at this situation and realized a few things. It was at the time, typical. My education, at the time was not very impressive to my parents. They did not "get it." I was suffering years of numerous, back to back health problems, and they most likely wondered why I would put myself $40,000 in debt for two degrees that they did not understand. I often heard, "You get a check every month. You had a place to live. Why do you want to do this?"

I often had to explain to them, "I just want to help people." It was not until I did my internship at the Mental Health Center that I felt like I was doing what I was meant to do. I was certain I could find work after obtaining my degree. I did not need anyone else's approval, including my parents. I also saved money by not having to get a cap and gown. I still had one from college collecting moth balls.

I started to update my resume and also began studying for my licensing examination immediately. I took my examination in the summer of 1995, and passed. It was pretty uneventful; other than the actual certificate didn't arrive for months, and I had to take the "mug shot" like photo that was taken of me at the exam center to my interviews. The picture was very amusing.

I thought that I would have absolutely no problem in getting a job immediately after I got out of graduate school. The delay of the receipt of my degree slowed things down for me, even though I had my transcripts, and the competition in the job market from my cohorts made it very difficult.

I had sent about 25 cover letters out, along with a copy of my degree the minute I finally received it in June. Along with my degree, I also received something else that I was unaware of. The night of the commencement, which I did not attend, I was presented with an Award of Merit from the University as one of their outstanding scholars. I assumed that everyone that graduated received this, until I spoke to one of my friends who had moved out of state after graduation. She informed me that I was one of less than five who had received that award, and she had informed them that I was unable to attend.

I sent another round of letters, along with a copy of my degree, and a copy of my newly obtained "mug shot" proof of passing my licensure exam after I passed the exam. This I when I started to get callbacks for interviews.

The Renault I had been driving for years finally began to give out that summer. It was a 1985 luxury (I am kidding) edition. Out of ten starts, it turned over maybe three. I wanted to try to keep it at least for a few months into my first professional job, but I did not think it would happen.

It had been towed many times when I lived in the city, and one service station in Oakland refused to service it any longer, because AAA always towed it to them. I was often behind in getting them their money, and they were sick of it. I had two sets of keys, and sometimes I would lock it up, take my spare keys with me, and leave it running because, I was afraid once it was turned off, it would not start back up.

The times that this car would start, I would think, well okay, maybe I can make it last a few more months. I ended up having to borrow my father's pick-up truck to interview at one of those rural community mental health center's that I was so gung-ho about in July of 1995. Well, I may have been passionate about writing about these places when I was doing my self-directed research, and after spending one day with a Meals On Wheels driver. But I took the pickup truck for my 70 mile one way drive from the Southern part of Allegheny County, and was almost at the West Virginia Border.

I had a two part interview that day. I honestly was referred to as "city slicker," and was informed that I may be responsible for passing meds out to children. I was asked if I had any objection to that. I explained that I was not licensed to do that. I then went to another site, and was asked if I would have a problem with some of the problems inherent in the community there, problems that I felt could not possibly be found in "all" rural clients as this interviewer explained.

I came prepared fresh from my training with Cognitive Behavioral Therapy. I was offered the position, but I told them I had to think about this and look over the information. I then hoped I would get another call.

Thankfully I did get another call from another community mental health center that was north of Pittsburgh. It was a warm August morning when I went in for the interview. The Renault luckily decided to cooperate for me that day. The receptionist who greeted me at the desk at 8:00 a.m. was eating from a carton of malted milk balls and asked me if I wanted some. I told her, "Uh..thanks, but I do not partake at this hour." I was about 250 pounds at the time. I had very long, thick, red hair. I was wearing a two piece black pant suit, and my car did not have air conditioning.

A male therapist, also with an MSW degree, interviewed me, and was impressed with my experience at the University, and asked me many questions about the Cognitive Behavioral Therapy. Our interview consisted of talking about this topic, for the most part. I felt that I did well, even though I was nervous. He gave me an application to take home with me, and I became very nervous when there was a question about explaining more than two years of unemployment. I did not want to have to explain disability. I crossed my fingers, and simply put "Full Time school" and prayed that my secret would never be found out.

However I knew if I did get this job I would have to report it to Social Security. I had an appointment with Dr. McCollom that week, and I told him about all of this, and he said, "Good luck to you, kid. I know you will do well. " He asked me how I was doing, and noted that I had some joint stiffness, but nothing out of the ordinary.

Dr. Mcollom filled out a required form that certified that I was physically able to do the work (I was applying to become a mental health therapist) and he ordered some blood work. A couple of days later, he contacted me and in his usually calm voice, he told me, "I don't want you to be upset, because this could mean a number of things, but your ANCA is positive." For those of us with Wegener's granulomatosis, there is a blood test called ANCA (anti-neutrophyl cytoplasmic antibody). This test can show up as positive if our disease is active.

When I was initially diagnosed in 1987, this blood test was not used. As you recall, it was the thoracotomy, or "open lung biopsy" that determined the Vasculitis/Wegener's. In 1989, Dr. McCollom was excited as he reported to me about the ANCA, as a new test. At that time it had to be shipped to California for processing. When I had it done anywhere but University of Pittsburgh, he would instruct me to instruct the lab techs to "use the purple cap for immunology."

In 1995, it was not so uncommon. I used to have it done every two months, and finally in 1990, it was negative. We repeated it, and it was negative. It remained negative thereafter. That was my "official remission" date. This was the first time of a positive. Dr. McCollom said that we needed to repeat it in a week.

I went back to the Mental Health Center for a second interview and was offered the job. I was happy, but scared. I spoke to some of my classmates, who had rules about the salaries that they would or would not accept, and some of them still did not have jobs. The way I looked at it, my salary would increase four times from what I was living on, that is before taxes.

Dr. McCollom called me after the second blood test and told me that the ANCA was negative. I asked him what could have caused this to read positive. He explained that it could have been anything from a lab error, to stress, but he stated that the ANCA test alone is not enough to diagnose the Wegener's and reminded me that back in the old days, they had to go by old fashioned detective work, and did not have that test. He advised that it should be an adjunct when symptoms are occurring, and the bottom line is that symptoms were not occurring for me. He wished me well and told me not to worry about it now.

I did not worry any longer as I once did about getting sick again. The only time I did was when I would have a lower respiratory infection that lasted more than two weeks, or something like that. Then I may get concerned.

I called social security when I knew what my salary would be. The social security disability counselor on the other end accessed my record and said, "Candace, we have you as totally disabled." I told him that I was going to be working. He told me that he felt that I should have started back to the work force slowly. I explained that I had gone to college and graduate school so I could get to this day. I also explained to him that I had a debt of $40,000 in student loans. He informed me that I could make no more than $64 if I wanted to keep my SSI. This was not something that I could do. He stated that after I received my first paycheck, I needed to send back this month's disability check. Now there are safety nets in place for folks who cannot sustain employment within 90 days. They are called "unsuccessful work attempts."

I worked hard to get to this point, and intended to move forward. In fact, for years, I lived in fear of losing my job, because I lived in fear of going back on disability. Again, this was just my goal, and my way of thinking. Others may not be able to get there. The social security counselor stated that I should rethink taking this job, as once I become a full time worker, it would be harder to "get back on disability." He asked several times if I was "sure" if this is what I wanted to do.

I felt that as long as I was not doing the type of work that involved me lifting heavy objects, or doing labor, I would be fine. My family members, father, grandfathers who worked in factories would have a difficult time. I would be the first so called "white collar worker" in the family, but I had, I guess, what you might call blue collar sensibility. I have never been afraid to work. I have been grateful for my ability to work ever since I went back to work.

When I knew I was going to start my job, I took my Renault to a car lot in the South Hills of Pittsburgh. I looked at some new cars, but settled on a 1989 Honda Civic Hatchback. It was the newest car I ever had. I had a payment now, and that was scary. Soon, I would also have another apartment lease, and I have not looked back since then. That car served me well, for years, and I paid it off in three years. I drove it to my first day on the new job. I remembered what led me to my current career path to begin with and what I had told myself all those years of struggling: Keep your eye on the prize—because one day you will be helping people.

So, some of you may wonder, what was that first day of work like? Pittsburgh August days are hot, humid. I decided to tackle a group therapy and was so eager to use my wonderful Cognitive Behavioral Therapy that I got at the University on the clients at this community mental health center.

The difference between these clients and the clients I saw in the city were vast. The city clients were often voluntary, and brief or acute cases. Some of them had "simple phobias" like fears of spiders. The clients at this mental health center were chronic cases and back then, a lot of them were on long standing commitments—they did not want to be there. They had serious disorders like schizophrenia.

So here I was, all excited to come in and give them something new. There were twenty five clients in my group. Some of them were actively hallucinating. Some were under the influence of a substance. I gave a nice big speech about how I was going to help them by helping them to change their thoughts, and in turn, that would change their mood.

One middle aged woman, with long, salt and pepper hair, glasses and a smoky voice, sitting directly across from me said, "Good luck, Miss Mary F*^ing Sunshine. You aint gonna change shit. You come in here. You probably never had one hard day in your life. Miss privileged, I had everything handed to me on a silver spoon. Shit!"

I thought, this is the challenge I have been waiting for. What's that mantra again? Keep my eye on the prize. I want to help people!

Afterward

I stayed at that mental health center for almost two years. I then got a "moonlighting" job, working at an inpatient unit, and discovered while going through some pre-employment medical testing that I was no longer inoculated against the childhood diseases (chicken pox, measles, mumps, and rubella). I had to go through all these again, and was very sick after that for several days. My doctor explained that the illness and chemotherapy may have knocked my immunization out. I had to call my mother who dug out proof of all these shots, but I still needed to be immunized again. I have worked two jobs (and at one point, was working three) since 1995. I may slow down one day.

I left the mental health center, lured away by more money. But I returned to that very same place, and that is my favorite place to work. I think they were wonderful to take me back.

I have worked in every level of care in the mental health field: outpatient, inpatient, and a level in between, called "partial" I had thought about going to law school after completing my master's degree. I actually sat for the LSATs (the law school admissions test) two years after graduate school but was not accepted to the law school that had a part time, evening program, and to return to school full time was not an option. I also entertained the idea of finally going for that nursing degree, four years after grad school, after acceptance into a community college's nursing program. By that time, I was working in an inpatient unit, and not happy (because on an inpatient level—you don't get to spend a lot of time with people).

The hospital would not offer any tuition reimbursement unless it was toward one's current career level. I withdrew from consideration of nursing school. I was unable to afford anymore school on my own while working. I am happiest helping people work out their problems, whether it is through therapy or managing a program or programs (I now do both). I then vowed to be the best I could be, and always stay sharp in my own field. Our field is prone to burnout, and I have experienced periods of it myself. The key is balance and learning to care for oneself. Wegener's patients know that, as well.

I think that we all can learn from mistakes and can turn our lives around, if that is truly what you want to do.

I had my personal story published in the Wegener's Foundation newsletter in 1999 and at that time, I began to think that maybe I needed to tell the whole story after the reaction I got from it. I realized that it could possibly help others. At that time, I shared it with my boss, at the hospital. She said she would have never had any idea I was ill. I began to reach out on internet support groups to other Wegener's patients about that time, as well, and became the Pittsburgh area contact in 2003.

The doctor who diagnosed me, and never gave up on me, has retired. He was winding down about the time I got out of graduate school, and the last time I saw him was 1996. Pretty much everything that he predicted in my health occurred, including the fact that I would be able to live a "normal" work life.

My health has not been "one thing after another," as it was back in the 1980's and 1990's. I credit this to having a purpose, and staying busy, although I may be delusional. I have often said that if I completely relax or slow down, I will die.

The year that I got out of graduate school, I entered early menopause, at age 28. Much later, I would have severe problems, and went for a whole year, in 1997 with very poor health insurance, as a result of working for a contract company, and hemorrhaged due to a ruptured benign tumor, and ended up $9,000 in debt and in a collection agency. I did not miss any work, though. One night, I spent the night in an emergency room, and the next day, I was at work. I ended up having a complete hysterectomy in early 2000, after three months of hemorrhaging again. I have been asked if I "hate" kids. Sometimes it is easy to be flippant and say, "yes." Of course, I do not. The decision was made for me.

I did not want children when I was 18. Have I met any men in my life since that time that I would have changed my mind about that with? Yes. I had that very discussion with another Wegener's survivor on the phone before finishing this book. She also was diagnosed early (age 18). We had two choices: to feel sorry for ourselves, or to carry on, and sometimes with senses of humor that maybe seem sick or sarcastic.

That friend and I also discussed how others seemed to have more difficulty with how our appearances changed as a result of Wegener's (her saddle nose, my scars, and steroid weight gain). This is also an issue that many of us have had to deal with that keeps many of us isolated, maybe angry, or lacking in trust. In my case, I was young, and had one dear friend who stuck by me throughout.

When my looks disappeared, a lot of friends, male and female disappeared. Looks are fleeting. I am now very distrusting of anyone who is shallow and bases their judgment of a person on appearances alone. I am told now that I look "great" for someone who had Wegener's. I never take anything like that for granted, and still see that very overweight person in the mirror, and also, after three reconstructive facial surgeries, was told that no more could be done back in 1992. I know I could possibly have more, as a lot may have changed in plastic/reconstructive surgery in 17 years.

But, with Wegener's as in all grief and loss, you tend to go through stages: shock, depression, anger, bargaining, and acceptance. I think I may have accepted that I have the scars now. I have had scars longer than not. I earned them.

Other issues that I have had are a cholecystectomy (gallbladder removed), and a cerebral aneurysm which may be hereditary, or may be Wegener's related. In any case, it is too small to be operated on. The knowledge of this led me to lose weight, as I met with a neurosurgeon who looked at me, when I probably weighed 280 pounds and told me that I was obese. I knew this, and did not need to be told.

He explained that high blood pressure would be the worst thing that could happen, as it could cause this balloon to burst. He explained that I would be very incapacitated if this occurred, and I needed to be proactive; and getting to a reasonable weight was the first step since surgery was out of the question. This scared me so much that I went on a one meal a day diet for the next year and lost about 120 pounds.

Give or take ten to fifteen pounds, I have kept that weight off. I would not recommend that extreme dieting to anyone with health issues, and I was monitored by my doctor as I did this.

I also had the bladder scare that I and many Wegner's patients are warned about. Again, as I am often in denial and ignorance, my first thought was not bladder cancer. The surgeon told me after the surgery that he was fearful of this. It had been an enlarged, inflamed blood vessel. As our disease is a vascular one, my fear was Vasculitis.

My beloved Marcus, the dachshund, passed away in 1993. He endured a lot of jobs, apartments, and boyfriends with me. Since he left me, there have been more (jobs and boyfriends; not apartments, as I settled into a place in 2001). He was loyal to the end, and waited for me until I got home from vacation with a boyfriend to die. I did have an autopsy done, and he had pancreatic cancer. You would never have known he was that sick.

I feel that more doctors and people in general have heard about Vasculitis and Wegener's granulomatosis. The popular television show, *House*, alone, has made Vasculitis a (pardon the pun) household name.

Some people might look at me from the outside, maybe even relatives, and think, oh how sad, never married, no kids. I have thought about marriage and may get married eventually. I have been lucky to have some happy relationships, and some not so happy. I have been lucky to see the country, and travel with some of my ex'es and wish all of them well.

It is difficult to find someone who understands that we go through a lot. To be able to live a life, giving back to others, is all I ever wanted. Some of the boyfriends I have tried to make it work with were not able to reconcile with the dedication I have for work, and accused, "You work too much." I may, but I can remember when I could not work at all, and for me, it is never just a job.

If you have any questions for me or want to share your story with me, or thoughts about reading this book, feel free to email me at cannella67@yahoo.com .

I also have a number of fellow Wegener's friends on myspace and you can add me there at http://www.myspace.com/car1967.

Kay Candy 2004

Appendix 1

How To Stay Informed and be Proactive In Your Healthcare

Early on, I realized that it was going to be necessary, to keep a log of all the medications, procedures, and hospitalizations that I had experienced, and present them to all doctors that I see. It helped me to be a very educated patient, even well before I was someone with a formal education, and it helped me to feel more in control of a situation that was often out of control.

I eventually obtained the hospital records from 1987 (at least the discharge summary) which showed the course of my illness and how the rheumatologist arrived at his diagnosis. *That discharge summary also explains the thoracotomy, bronchoscopy, etc.*

I also found, that sometimes, especially as my health improved and I looked "normal, it was difficult for some providers to believe that what I was saying was true. When it is a true medical record, then it cannot be disputed.

Here is an excerpt of what all doctors get from me when I go to see them for the first time:

Candace UPDATED Medical History April 2008
DOB :
Blood Type :
Primary Care physician is: Joe Blow, MD 123 Centre Ave Pittsburgh PA 15213 *
Drug Allergies: Tetracycline=Hepatoxemia
Bactrim=anaphylaxis-lips swollen, hives on trunk and thighs, 2007.

Also allergy to Cafergot=Emesis

Past Surgical/Invasive Procedures (most recent listed first):
1. Cystoscopy, January, 2007, John Doe, D.O Outpatient surgical
2. Cholecystectomy, August, 2000, by Jack Doe, MD, University Medical Center
3. Total hysterectomy, left oopherectomy, January, 2000, by L. Doe, MD, University Medical Center
4. Laminectomy of L4 and L5 free fragments, by neurosurgeon, Dr Goffey, MD, University Medical Center , March, 1994......
etcetera

CURRENT Regular Medications -update June 2008
1. Synthroid 150mcg QD (I have been on synthroid since 1972)
2. Topomax, 150 mg. BID Migraines

CURRENT PRN Medications
3. Imitrex 100 mg prn up to 9 p.r.n.

.

VITAMINS—**Multivitamin, Vitamin C, Calcium Citrate, b-complex**

Here is the list of what will help you, especially if you have a lot of appointments, or different doctors:

1. Try to obtain actual medical records, if at all possible. Never give your only copy away.
2. Get a living will and /or Durable Power of Attorney. This is your declaration of how you would like your medical decisions made if you cannot speak for yourself. In my case, one of my best friends (a registered nurse) is the person whom I have named my health care proxy. Another friend is my financial power of attorney. The laws may vary by state. Again, take a copy to each inpatient stay, and doctor.

3. Take an updated list of medications, and allergies with you to your appointments
4. List all hospitalizations.
5. List all past surgeries.
6. List Blood Type (I needed to have a blood transfusion once and did not know this answer—that will never happen again; it slows down the process)
7. Get a Medic Alert Bracelet if you have allergies or other conditions in addition to your Wegener's.

Being an informed patient will help you, and will also help you to increase the communication with your doctor. If you do not feel that you can communicate with your doctor, then you have a couple of choices: you can try to assert yourself by expressing that you feel unheard, or you can try to find another doctor. I had a great doctor, as I detailed in this book, who went above and beyond in 1987, in finding the answer to what was wrong. I was not very assertive before I had Wegener's. Another positive that came out of getting sick, was that I had to become assertive.

When that doctor retired, I found a doctor who did not respect me. He also did not know much about Wegener's. He patronized me. I then found another doctor, who I have stuck with to this day. He is a primary care physician, not a specialist, but is able to handle a wide variety of problems; he is in Pittsburgh, and he has that same dedicated manner that I recognized in the doctor from when I was ill. My "new" doctor had solved a few medical mysteries I have presented him with over the past decade, and he also has a good sense of humor.

The key here is communication. If you are not communicating well with your doctor, or provider (therapist, nurse practitioner, whoever) then it is not going to be helpful. Take your list with you, and write down concerns, and questions. Doctors are under pressure and time limited today, and we often go there fearful and forget that they cannot read minds.

Appendix II

This is the survey that I wanted to send out in 1992 to the
Wegener's support group. It was thwarted at that time,
and I later found it, and posted it on myspace in 2008
and got responses. The results are posted in the following
chapter.

Dear Wegener's questionnaire participant,

The following questionnaire is not a scientific study, as I am not a researcher. I am, like yourself, a Wegener's Granulomatosis patient. I am an undergraduate student and I have enough knowledge to compile and compute this informal questionnaire.

My reason for doing this is because I understand very well the wide range of emotions a Wegener's patient experiences. The feelings can range from horror to rage, and can ultimately lead to feelings of defeat. My experience has taught me that when you are armed with knowledge about this disease, your attitude changes. It is very beneficial for a patient to become an active participant in his/her own recovery, for it takes away some of that sense of being a "victim" and therefore causes one to feel as if he/she is a "survivor."

The Wegener's Granulomatosis Support Group is what really helped me to learn all that I could about the disease. Before I found the Support Group, I knew that I was ready to learn all that I could, but I could not find the information. I think that the knowledge is one of the many beneficial things about this support group. The others are knowing that you are not alone in the world, and that there are people who do understand you perfectly.

One of the main things I hope to achieve by this questionnaire is to allow Wegener's patients a chance to speak out. I encourage comments to be voiced. When I tally up the results of the questionnaire, I will also devote a section to comments. It is your choice as to whether you wish to remain anonymous or be identified in the outcome.

I look forward to getting the results as I am sure that you do. Thank you,

Candace Ross

Wegener's Granulomatosis questionnaire

PART I:

Please answer the following questions by circling the appropriate answer or filling in the blank space provided. Feel free to add comments on any of the questions in the margins or on the reverse side. Thank you.

1. What is your gender?   Male   Female
2. What is your age?
3. What year were you diagnosed with Wegener's Granulomatosis?

4. Under what specialty was the physician(s) who diagnosed you? (e.g., rheumatology, nephrology, etc.)

5. To the best of your knowledge, how much time passed between onset of your initial symptomsand the actual diagnosis of Wegener's Granulomatosis?

6. Were you ever diagnosed with other conditions/diseases before the diagnosis of Wegener's?
    Yes   No

7. If you answered "yes" to Question 6, what were you diagnosed with prior to your diagnosis of Wegener's?

8. Please indicate (by circling) here whether or not you experienced the following complications from Wegener's Granulomatosis. Feel free to elaborate.

    a.   upper respiratory system disturbance (e.g., sinusitis)

    b.   lower respiratory system disturbance
            (eg., heavy coughing, pleurisy)

    c.   eye disturbances (e.g., red and or painful eyes)

    d. inner ear disturbances (hearing loss)

    e. kidney disturbances

    f. arthritis or other joint problems

    g. Raynaud's phenomenon (sensitivity in fingers/toes to cold temperatures)

    h. skin (lesions, rashes)

    i. nasal cartilage (saddle nose syndrome)

    j. other (please specify)

9. Please indicate (by circling) which forms of drug therapy were used in your treatment?
    a. corticosteroids (Prednisone, etc.)
    b. Cylophosphamide (Cytoxan)
    c. other (please specify)

10. What medications are you on currently for the treatment of Wegener's granulomatosis?
    a. steroids
    b. Cytoxan
    c. other _____
    d. not on any treatment for Wegener's at this time

11.   What is your health status now? For example, are you in remission (complete or partial)?
    a. I am still very ill and require daily medication for Wegener's
    b. I am still ill, but I feel as though I am improving steadily
    c. I am in partial remission (I still have active Wegener's in some parts of my body, but other syterns are fine now)
    d. I am in complete remission

12. If you are in **complete remission,** how long has it been since you were declared so?

13. Are you familiar with the blood test ANCA (anti neutrophyl cytoplasmic antibodies)?
   a. yes
   b. no

14. Are you tested at least once every six months for your ANCA levels?
   a. yes
   b. no

15. Please indicate (by circling) if you were exposed to the following agents before your diagnosis of Wegener's Granulomatosis?
   a.Tobacco smoke: first-hand (you smoked tobacco products)
   b Tobacco smoke: second-hand (you were in regular contact with smoker)
   c. chemical lawn treatments ("Chemi-lawn," "Spray-A-Lawn," etc.)
   d. none of the above

16. If you circled any of the above answers, please indicate to the best of your knowledge, how long you were exposed to the agents.
   a. first-hand tobacco smoke _____
   b. second hand tobacco smoke _____
   c. chemical lawn treatments
   d. not applicable

17. If you answered yes to Question # 15, please indicate which agent(s) you are currently exposed to.
   a. first-hand tobacco smoke
   b. second-hand tobacco smoke
   c. chemical lawn treatments

18. If you smoke now, how would you describe your smoking habits? (please circle)
   a. light (an occasional cigarette, but certainly not a habit)

    b.   moderate (one half pack or less a day)

    c.   heavy (a pack or more a day)

    d.   I do not smoke

19. If you breathe second-hand tobacco smoke, how often do you come in contact with it?

    a.   infrequently, such as when I eat in a restaurant or see an old friend who smokes

    b.   frequently; I live with and/or work with a smoker

    c.   I am not around a smoker or smokers regularly

20. If you are in contact with chemical lawn treatment under what circumstances are you exposed to it?

    a.   I have chemical lawn treatments on my own lawn.

    b.   My neighbors' lawn(s) are treated with chemical lawn treatments.

    c.   I am not around chemical lawn treatments

21. If you are exposed to chemical lawn treatment, how often are you exposed to it in a given year?

    a. infrequently (one to two times per year)

    b. moderately (three to five times per year)

    c. frequently (six or more times per year)

    d .not applicable

Wegener's Granulomatosis questionnaire

PART II: Please circle the appropriate answer and/or fill in blank space. Again, as in Part I, feel free to make comments in the margins or the back of the page.

1. Before you became ill with Wegener's Granulomatosis, how would you characterize your **physical** health in general? Were you: (circle one)
   a. very healthy
   b. healthy
   c. not really unhealthy, but not completely healthy either
   d. unhealthy
   e. very unhealthy

2. Before you became ill with Wegener's, how would you characterize your emotions in general? Were you: (circle one)
   a. very happy
   b. happy
   c. neither extremely happy nor extremely depressed
   d. depressed
   e. depressed, not satisfied with my life

3. When you were aware that you were ill, but were not yet diagnosed, what are some of the emotions that you were feeling? (circle all that apply)
   I felt:
   a. confident that it was not serious and that it would pass
   b. fearful of the rapid progression of symptoms
   c. self-blaming (I did something to cause the symptoms)
   d. anger at others, such as doctors for not finding what the exact problem was
   e. depressed (perhaps thinking that the cause of pain would not be found
   f. resignation (thinking that the exact cause of the symptoms would not be found)

e. other{s}(please specify)

4. After your diagnosis of Wegener's Granulomatosis, what were some of your feelings about it then? (circle all that apply)
    a.   relief (over the fact that there was finally a name for it)
    b.   confusion over what the future would now bring (Am I still going to die? Did too much time lapse?)
    c.   fear over the still possible complications
    d.   determination (I don't care what the possibilities are; I will beat it!)
    e.   self blame in thinking that past behavior may have caused the illness or at least specific features
    f.   anger over the fact that the treatment also had some very undesirable features (such as weight gain from the Prednisone, etc.)
    g.   other{s} _____

5. After the beginning of your treatment, how would you characterize the amount of lethargy and weakness that you felt? (circle one)
    a.   little to no tiredness
    b.   some tiredness but I was not bedridden
    c.   a moderate amount; I had to rest sometimes during the day
    d.   extreme tiredness; nearly incapacitating

6. If you have had some facial disfigurement, what experiences have you had with (or do you expect to have with) reconstructive and plastic surgery? (circle one)
    a.   I cannot be operated on yet due to my condition at this moment
    b.   I expect to have plastic surgery soon for the first time for this problem
    c.   I have had some plastic surgery, but I have more to be performed in the future
    d.   I have had all of the necessary procedures performed
    e.   not applicable

7. Regarding your feelings now about your facial appearance, please indicate how you feel right now (whether or not you have had any reconstructive surgery), as opposed to how you felt initially, (circle one)
   a. it was not a huge issue with me before, and it still is not
   b. I feel more at ease with it now
   c. I feel less at ease now
   d. I am very upset about it, but I feel that I will feel better in time
   e. I feel devastated about it, and honestly don't think I will ever accept it
   f. not applicable

8. In general, how would you characterize the effect that your experience with Wegener's has had on your personality? (circle one)
   a. it has made me a more grateful and generous person
   b. it has made me a more depressed and unhappy person
   c. it has made me a very bitter person
   d. it has made me a more rounded person; I have my moments of bitterness, but I also have more compassion and understanding now than I did before.
   e. I am the same person as before—I feel the same as I did before I became ill.

Thank you for completing this questionnaire.

Appendix III

I initially composed a survey for Wegener's patients way back in 1992, as I was in college, taking statistics and research. I had a hypothesis about what may have caused my Wegener's, since all that was available in the early 1990's was that it was possibly linked to an inhaled antigen.

Even though I had been told by the one doctor long ago, in that small town hospital, that I was responsible for my Wegener's, by my lifestyle and not taking my thyroid pill, I did not want to hear it. Now, I do believe that at least, not taking a thyroid pill when you have a severe thyroid condition is very harmful. I saw my own sister become extremely ill prior to her diagnosis of hypothyroidism.

This survey was stopped in 1992 prior to the merging of the support group and the Wegener's foundation, but I have always been very curious to see about my hypothesis that chemical lawn spray was correlated to my illness and to see if indeed thyroid illness was also correlated in Wegener's patients.

I want to point out here, that I am not a researcher, nor am I a physician. I have done research on reporting on statistics in my employment, in the most basic form, and have had undergraduate , and graduate level, behavioral health statistics and research.

I am just someone with Wegener's who was very curious about other patients with Wegener's. Therefore, I am going to simply report, in a manner that hopefully, is easy to understand, on this very small sample of respondents I would like to add the disclaimer that if you would sample a small group of other Wegener's patients, you may or may not get different results. I have never seen another survey like this in the 17 years since I first put this one together, so if anyone at the Vasculitis Foundation would like to work with me on perfecting this, I would be glad to work with you, particularly on the mental health/emotional effects, since this is something I know a little more about.

This is an extremely small sample of people who responded to the survey in the summer and fall of 2008. Seven people responded, and I am also part of this sample. This may not be considered the most reliable scientific sample, based on the small number, and the fact that only females answered. If the results do not always add up to 100%, it is because sometimes the respondents checked more than one answer.

All of the respondents who answered had the diagnosis of Wegener's (I had this posted on my myspace page) and I also had one of my long time cohorts answer this whom I had known from the Pittsburgh area support group.

These were the results:

Seven females answered the survey, so therefore 100% of the respondents were female. The average age of the respondents was 34, with the oldest being 49, and the youngest being 21. The earliest year that a respondent was diagnosed was 1978, and the most recent that a participant was diagnosed was in 2008. The average time that passed from initial presentation of symptoms and diagnosis of Wegener's was 4.5 years, with the longest period of time being reported by one respondents as "11 years" and the shortest amount of time being reported as "6 months."

Specialists diagnosed the Wegener's in all of those polled. Forty-three percent were diagnosed by Ear Nose Throat Specialists; 29% were diagnosed by rheumatologists; 14% were diagnosed by infectious disease specialists; and 14% were diagnosed by nephrologists.

When asked if another diagnosis was made prior to the Wegener's diagnosis, 85 % of the respondents affirmed that they had been diagnosed with other conditions. Here is a breakdown of those conditions. Fifty-seven percent had been diagnosed prior to Wegener's with hypothyroidism. Twenty-nine percent were diagnosed with pneumonia. Fourteen percent were diagnosed with the following conditions: Rheumatoid arthritis, sinusitis, asthma, fibromyalgia, GERD, asthma.

When asked about symptom manifestation prior to their diagnosis, here is how the disease presented: 100% had joint/arthritic symptoms; 86% had upper respiratory symptoms; 86% had lower respiratory symptoms; 57% had Raynaud's or circulation problems; 43% had skin involvement; 43% had inner ear involvement; 29% had Saddle Nose; 14% had kidney involvement; and 14% had "other" (heart) involvement.

After diagnosis of Wegener's granulomatosis, 100% of subjects were treated with prednisone (corticosteroids) at some point, and 100% were also treated with Cytoxan (cyclophosphamide). Forty-three percent of subjects were treated with methotrexate. Fourteen percent reported to have been treated with the following agents at some point in their treatment: imuran, chlorambucil, sulfamethoxazole, or dexamethasone.

The respondents polled are still taking the following medications: 86% are taking prednisone, 86% are taking Cytoxan, 14% are taking imuran, and 14% are taking bactrim. Fourteen percent polled are on no medications at all for their Wegener's granulomatosis.

When asked about their health status currently, 43% responded that they were in complete remission; 29% reported "I am still very ill and require daily medication for Wegener's;" 29% reported "I am still ill, but I feel as though I am improving steadily;" and 14% reported "I am in partial remission (I still have active Wegener's in some parts of my body, but other systems are fine now").

Those who reported that they were in remission were asked to define how long they were in remission. The shortest amount of time reported was "3 weeks," and the longest amount of time reported was 18 years. The average amount of remission based on these numbers was 11.5 years.

All of the respondents were familiar with the ANCA blood test, and when asked if they had this blood test at least once every six months, 71 % answered yes, and 29% answered no.

Seventy-one percent of the subjects had been exposed to second hand smoke prior to their diagnosis of Wegener's. Twenty nine percent of the respondents themselves had smoked prior to diagnosis.

Twenty nine percent had been exposed to chemical lawn treatments or pesticides. Fourteen percent of the respondents had no prior exposure to cigarette/cigar smoke (first or second hand) nor chemical lawn spray or pesticides.

For those who were exposed to the above agents, they were asked how long they had been exposed to them. The two smokers both smoked six years prior to the diagnosis of Wegener's. Of those who were exposed to second hand smoke, the average amount of time that those respondents were exposed to the smoke was 11.25 years. Of those who were exposed to chemical lawn treatments, the average amount of time that they were exposed was 10 years.

Fourteen percent of the subjects polled still occasionally smoke, while 86 % do not smoke at all. Seventy-two percent of the respondents are not around smokers, while 14% either live with or are around a smoker regularly. Another 14% answered that they are around smokers infrequently, such as at a bar/restaurant.

Seventy-two percent of the respondents are not around chemical lawn spray at this time o a regular basis, while 28% still is exposed to it. Of those 28%, one half states that they are exposed to the pesticides "infrequently," (once or twice a year) while the other half are exposed to it "frequently" (6 or ore times per year).

When asked to describe their overall health status, 43% checked status as "neither extremely happy nor extremely depressed," 29% checked their status as "happy," 14% checked their status as "very happy," and another 14% described their status as "depressed."

When asked to check what feelings they were experiencing while ill, but not yet diagnosed, respondents answered in this manner (these answers will not ad up to 100% as multiple answers were able to be chosen): 57% felt anger at others, such as doctors for not finding what the exact problem was; 29% were confident that it was not serious and that it would pass; 29% were fearful of the rapid progression of symptoms; 14% were depressed (perhaps thinking that the cause of pain would not be found; 14% felt resignation (thinking that the exact cause of the symptoms would not be found); and 14% wrote in "suicidal".

After the diagnosis of Wegener's here are some of the emotions that respondents indicated (also, these answers will not ad up to 100% as multiple answers were able to be chosen): 71% expressed relief over the fact that there was finally a name for it; 43% checked that they felt determination (I don't care what the possibilities are; I will beat it!); 29% expressed confusion over what their future would bring; another 29% were fearful over complications that still lay ahead of them; 29% were angry about the fact that treatment had undesirable side effects such as weight gain and other unpleasant side effects; and interestingly 49% of those polled wrote in the same exact thing for "other" ("frustration over side effects and lack of understanding")

After the beginning of treatment, in describing the amount of lethargy and weakness felt, respondents answered this way: 71.5% checked that they felt extreme tiredness which was nearly incapacitating, and 28.5% checked that they felt a moderate amount; to the point that had to rest sometimes during the day.

Fifty seven percent of those surveyed had some facial disfigurement from the Wegener's. Seventy-five percent of those polled are unable to be operated on at this time because of their illness. The other 25% reported to having all of the necessary procedures performed.

When asked about their feelings regarding the facial disfigurement (this could be scarring or saddle nose deformity) of the Wegener's, those 57% checked: "I am very upset about it, but I feel that I will feel better in time" (40%); "I feel more at ease with it now" (40%); and "it was not a huge issue with me before, and it still is not" (10%).

Lastly, when asked to check off how this illness has overall affected their mood and personality, here was how those polled answered: Forty-three percent checked " it has made me a more rounded person; I have my moments of bitterness, but I also have more compassion and understanding now than I did before, " 29% checked that "it has made me a more grateful and generous person," and 29% checked " I am the same person as before—I feel the same as I did before I became ill."

About the author

Candace Ross, is a psychotherapist with over fourteen years experience helping adults, families, groups, and couples. She obtained a Master's Degree from the University of Pittsburgh in 1995. Her experience is in Outpatient, inpatient, and she also had years of experience working in, and managing programs in community mental health.

Lightning Source UK Ltd.
Milton Keynes UK
UKOW03f2022270317

297633UK00001B/187/P